THE BEDFORD SERIES IN HISTORY AND CULTURE

Southern Horrors and Other Writings

The Anti-Lynching Campaign of Ida B. Wells, 1892–1900

Related Titles in
THE BEDFORD SERIES IN HISTORY AND CULTURE
Advisory Editors: Lynn Hunt, *University of California, Los Angeles*
David W. Blight, *Yale University*
Bonnie G. Smith, *Rutgers University*
Natalie Zemon Davis, *Princeton University*
Ernest R. May, *Harvard University*

THE BEDFORD SERIES IN HISTORY AND CULTURE

Southern Horrors and Other Writings

The Anti-Lynching Campaign of Ida B. Wells, 1892–1900

Edited with an Introduction by

Jacqueline Jones Royster

Ohio State University

BEDFORD/ST. MARTIN'S   Boston ♦ New York

For Bedford/St. Martin's

President and Publisher: Charles H. Christensen
General Manager and Associate Publisher: Joan E. Feinberg
History Editor: Katherine E. Kurzman
Developmental Editor: Louise D. Townsend
Editorial Assistant: Charisse M. Kiino
Managing Editor: Elizabeth M. Schaaf
Production Editor: Karen S. Baart
Production Assistant: Ellen C. Thibault
Copyeditor: Barbara Sutton
Indexer: Steve Csipke
Text Design: Claire Seng-Niemoeller
Cover Design: Richard Emery Design
Cover Art: Photograph of Ida B. Wells, The Joseph Regenstein Library, University of Chicago. Photograph of a lynch mob, 1893, Library of Congress.

Library of Congress Catalog Card Number: 95–83519
Copyright © 1997 by Bedford Books

Manufactured in the United States of America.

6

q p o n m l

For information, write: Bedford/St. Martin's, 75 Arlington Street, Boston, MA 02116
(617-399-4000)

ISBN: 0–312–11695–0   (paperback)
ISBN: 0–312–12812–6   (hardcover)

Acknowledgments

Pages xii, 42–45: Courtesy of the Schomburg Center for Research in Black Culture, The New York Public Library.

Pages 49, 73, 104, 118, 119, 158, 159: Courtesy of the Moorland-Spingarn Research Center, Howard University.

Foreword

The Bedford Series in History and Culture is designed so that readers can study the past as historians do.

The historian's first task is finding the evidence. Documents, letters, memoirs, interviews, pictures, movies, novels, or poems can provide facts and clues. Then the historian questions and compares the sources. There is more to do than in a courtroom, for hearsay evidence is welcome, and the historian is usually looking for answers beyond act and motive. Different views of an event may be as important as a single verdict. How a story is told may yield as much information as what it says.

Along the way the historian seeks help from other historians and perhaps from specialists in other disciplines. Finally, it is time to write, to decide on an interpretation and how to arrange the evidence for readers.

Each book in this series contains an important historical document or group of documents, each document a witness from the past and open to interpretation in different ways. The documents are combined with some element of historical narrative—an introduction or a biographical essay, for example—that provides students with an analysis of the primary source material and important background information about the world in which it was produced.

Each book in the series focuses on a specific topic within a specific historical period. Each provides a basis for lively thought and discussion about several aspects of the topic and the historian's role. Each is short enough (and inexpensive enough) to be a reasonable one-week assignment in a college course. Whether as classroom or personal reading, each book in the series provides firsthand experience of the challenge—and fun—of discovering, recreating, and interpreting the past.

Lynn Hunt
David W. Blight
Bonnie G. Smith
Natalie Zemon Davis
Ernest R. May

Preface

Ida B. Wells was an African American who achieved national and international fame as a journalist, public speaker, and community activist. This volume collects the three pamphlets that constitute her major works during the anti-lynching movement: *Southern Horrors: Lynch Law in All Its Phases, A Red Record,* and *Mob Rule in New Orleans.*

In introducing these documents, I have sought to contextualize mob violence in general and lynching in particular as a "strange" though not really mysterious "fruit"[1] of American culture. I look closely at Wells's campaign in light of what Wahneema Lubiano[2] calls "cover" stories—in this case master narratives of mob violence that have embedded within them myths and realities. Lubiano reminds us that there are things that we say, things that we do not say, things that we subvert, and things that our subversions conceal.

My task has been to define lynching, in the company of other acts of mob violence, as a multilayered aspect of American history, with dimensions related to political and economic power as well as to race and gender control. Wells disassembled and targeted separately the many contradictions and hypocrisies built into the broad myths that white southerners had used to justify lynching, making a case for justice at a particular moment in time. Through the pamphlets we can recognize lynchings as more than isolated incidents arbitrarily happening to African Americans and occasionally to Americans of other ethnic groups. We see instead lynching's complex relationships to systems of power and domination, to public discourse, and

---

[1] *Strange fruit* as an image of the lynched bodies of African Americans hanging from southern trees was popularized in both literature and music. Two examples bearing this title are a song made famous by Billie Holiday (with words by Lewis Allen) and a 1944 novel by Lillian E. Smith.

[2] Wahneema Lubiano, "Black Ladies, Welfare Queens, and State Minstrels: Ideological War by Narrative Means," in *Race-ing Justice, En-gendering Power,"* ed. Toni Morrison (New York: Pantheon, 1992), 323–63.

to social activism, including the activism of African American women.

As complements to each other, *Southern Horrors: Lynch Law in All Its Phases* and *A Red Record* clearly state Wells's position on lynching, revealing the insight and perception with which she was able to launch the most successful of the early anti-lynching campaigns. Wells's courageous analysis helps us to understand the told and untold story of this sinister thread in the fabric of American life. The third pamphlet, *Mob Rule in New Orleans,* is a case study that dramatically details an individual incident as it escalates in the absence of law, order, and the application of justice to become yet another striking example of "southern horror."

I have also sought to establish an appropriate framework for understanding the personal achievements of Ida B. Wells. Born into slavery, Wells went on to garner a place of respect as a nationally and internationally prominent journalist and as a leader in the black clubwomen's movement. Wells was one among a relatively small but growing number of "public" women in an era when public arenas were not considered the place for women. Going against this grain, Wells earned a reputation as an outspoken and steadfast crusader for justice, and the three pamphlets presented here are testimony to her achievement.

Fundamentally, therefore, this collection is an occasion to look at Wells, her work, and her accomplishments so that we might more carefully consider the complex of issues and actions that converge in making lynching such a disquieting phenomenon. *Southern Horrors and Other Writings: The Anti-Lynching Campaign of Ida B. Wells, 1892–1900* is a gateway to a much needed dialogue on lynching as an American experience.

A NOTE ON THE PAMPHLETS

Please note that this volume preserves the spelling and punctuation of the original documents, including errors. When an error makes meaning unclear, I have explained it in my annotations, noting for example when words and phrases are out of order. Rather than correct obvious mistakes or impose contemporary writing conventions, in the interest of preserving historical accuracy we have reprinted the documents in this collection as they originally appeared.

ACKNOWLEDGMENTS

My acknowledgments begin with an expression of gratitude to Charles Christensen and Joan Feinberg, who first suggested this project to me. I am grateful that they saw connections between my research and the possibility of this volume and that their encouragement continued to be so gracious and forthcoming throughout the project. I also owe a special debt of gratitude to Louise Townsend, the Bedford development editor, who was so thoughtful in helping me to work through how this volume might be; to the Bedford advertising staff for providing a visual image of Wells and her campaign that haunts me still; to the copyeditor, Barbara Sutton; and to a remarkable collective of other Bedford staff members, including managing editor Elizabeth Schaaf, assistant production editor Karen Baart, and assistants Charisse Kiino and Ellen Thibault, for the support and assistance that they provided in bringing this book to its completion.

In addition, I want to thank Dolores Straker and Andrea Lunsford, whose comments on the earliest draft of Part One were very useful; Darlene Clark Hine, Clarence E. Walker, and Paula Giddings, for their insights, advice, and counsel on lynching and on the era during which the pamphlets were written; Diana Lachatanere and Anthony M. Toussaint at the Schomburg Research Center, for their assistance in locating documents and photographs that helped to bring Ida B. Wells and her time to life; and James Cameron, founder and director of the Black Holocaust Museum in Milwaukee, Wisconsin, whose story of survival and whose dedication to the historical documentation of this injustice have been so inspirational.

As always, I am grateful to my family: Pat, Rebecca, and Giles, without whose love and support nothing seems possible or worthwhile.

Jacqueline Jones Royster

Contents

Ida B. Wells, ca. 1887
At the time of this photograph, Wells was teaching in the Memphis, Tennessee, public schools and writing a weekly column for the *Living Way*.

PART ONE

Introduction:
Equity and Justice
for All

LYNCHING AND RECONSTRUCTION

Eight Negroes lynched since last issue of the *Free Speech* one at Little
Rock, Ark., last Saturday morning where the citizens broke (?) into the
penitentiary and got their man; three near Anniston, Ala., one near New
Orleans; and three at Clarksville, Ga., the last three for killing a white
man, and five on the same old racket—the new alarm about raping
white women. The same programme of hanging, then shooting bullets
into the lifeless bodies was carried out to the letter. Nobody in this section believes the old threadbare lie that Negro men assault white
women. If Southern white men are not careful, they will over-reach
themselves and public sentiment will have a reaction; a conclusion will
then be reached which will be very damaging to the moral reputation
of their women.[1]

Ida B. Wells wrote this editorial on May 21, 1892. An African American
woman who was co-owner, editor, reporter, and publisher of the *Free
Speech,* a weekly newspaper in Memphis, Tennessee, Wells was what we

---

[1]See in this volume *A Red Record,* p. 79. All further references to the Wells pam-
phlets will be included parenthetically in the text using the abbreviations *SH (Southern
Horrors: Lynch Law in All Its Phases), RR (A Red Record),* and *MR (Mob Rule in New
Orleans).*

might today call an investigative journalist. Typically, she would identify a problem or issue, collect data that served to instruct and enlighten, and report the findings to her readers. She was known for stating her case simply and directly, without mincing words. This editorial, however, which describes eight incidents of lynching, was incredibly bold, even for an outspoken journalist, because of what it suggested about the "truth" of lynching.

Inspired by the data that she had been collecting for more than two months, Wells raised several very uncomfortable specters between the lines of this editorial. The unstated question was, "If assaulting white women is a threadbare lie, then what might the truth be?" In suggesting such a question, Wells permitted all sorts of codes of etiquette to be broken by alluding to relationships between black men and white women that in 1892 would have been unspeakable, and certainly not spoken about in the newspaper by an African American woman. She hinted that the truth might be more obvious than the crafters of the threadbare lie were willing to acknowledge—more obvious, that is, if readers actually paid attention to the facts. The editorial invited the readers to do just that—to pay attention to the facts.

As documented by *Crusade for Justice: The Autobiography of Ida B. Wells,*[2] Wells campaigned energetically for truth and justice throughout her life, with anti-lynching activities figuring prominently among the causes to which she gave her attention. The activities between May 21, 1892 (when she wrote her provocative editorial), and September 1, 1900 (when she signed the introduction to *Mob Rule in New Orleans,* her third pamphlet on lynching), however, mark the most intense portion of her contributions to the anti-lynching movement.[3]

Wells chronicled a change in her understanding of lynching that began with the lynching of three friends (*SH* pp. 64–65; *RR* pp. 133–34). On the morning of March 9, 1892, the bodies of Thomas Moss, Calvin McDowell, and Wil Stewart[4] were found shot to pieces in a field a mile north of Memphis, Tennessee, "by hands unknown." The men had owned and operated the People's Grocery Store, a store in competition with a grocery owned and operated by a white man. The stores were located across the street from each other in an area

---

[2]Published posthumously in 1970 by her daughter, Alfreda M. Duster, who served as editor.

[3]See A Wells Chronology (1862–1931) in this volume for an account of her life and work.

[4]Stewart is listed variously by Wells and others as Wil, William, Henry, and Lee.

known in Memphis as the Curve, an area that was beyond the Memphis city limits and beyond police protection. A few days before, an altercation instigated by the white store owner had resulted in a late-night shoot-out at the People's Grocery and the wounding of three white men. In the wake of the shoot-out, numbers of African American men were randomly arrested, guns were confiscated throughout the African American community, and the three business partners were jailed and charged with wounding white men, despite their doing so in what they had thought was the defense of their property. By law the wounding of a white person, as compared with the killing of a white person, was not punishable by death. Nonetheless, on March 9, lynch law prevailed, and between two and three o'clock in the morning the three men, who were not yet convicted by law, were removed from their jail cells, put in a railroad car, carried north of the city, and shot to death.

Word came to Wells about the lynching while she was in Natchez, Mississippi, on one of her many trips as co-owner, editor, and reporter for the *Free Speech*.[5] Thomas Moss and his family were Wells's closest friends. She was devastated by the news but also incensed that such a thing could happen. Before this incident, Wells had abhored lynching but had accepted the idea that it was the horror of rape and other crimes that incited such violence. With this lynching, however—the lynching of men whom she knew to be leading citizens of Memphis— her eyes were opened to the truth. Lynching was not simply a spontaneous punishment for crimes but an act of terror perpetrated against a race of people in order to maintain power and control. She began to see that these ritualized murders were acts of violence and intimidation designed to retard the progress of African Americans in their efforts to participate more fully in social, political, and economic life. As she explained in her autobiography,

> Thomas Moss, Calvin McDowell, and Lee Stewart had been lynched in Memphis, one of the leading cities of the South, in which no lynching had taken place before, with just as much brutality as other victims of the mob; and they had committed no crime against white women.

[5]Details about Wells's life and work are based on information presented in Alfreda M. Duster, ed., *Crusade for Justice: The Autobiography of Ida B. Wells* (Chicago: University of Chicago Press, 1970), and Mildred I. Thompson, *Ida B. Wells-Barnett: An Exploratory Study of an American Black Woman, 1893–1930* (New York: Carlson Publishing, 1990).

This is what opened my eyes to what lynching really was. An excuse to get rid of Negroes who were acquiring wealth and property and thus keep the race terrorized and "keep the nigger down."[6]

Wells's immediate response to the lynchings was to write editorials that encouraged African Americans in Memphis to leave a city that offered no protection of their rights of citizenship and to go west to Kansas and Oklahoma. Her editorials were successful, affecting in a significant way the migration of thousands of African Americans to the West.[7] Wells also began collecting data on other lynchings, and on May 21, 1892, she wrote the editorial quoted at the start of this introduction.

Wells's actions were extraordinary for her time. To appreciate fully just how bold and courageous she was, we need to examine two sets of factors relative to the period in which she lived: the rise and fall of Reconstruction and the backdrop that it provided for mob violence against African Americans, and the emergence of a "woman's era," a time during which women were questioning, redefining, and reshaping the "woman's sphere."

The Rise and Fall of Reconstruction

The era in which Wells was writing is known as the post-Reconstruction era. It is defined largely by the ways that social and political practices began to shift and settle after Reconstruction, when federal troops were withdrawn from the South and local governments began to institute, or in many cases reinstitute, laws and practices that took away liberties that had been achieved for African Americans by means of the Thirteenth, Fourteenth, and Fifteenth Amendments.

The victory of the North over the South in the Civil War signalled both the end of slavery and the beginning of disagreement and tension over how the eleven defeated southern states would be restored to the Union. "Reconstruction" activities actually began as early as 1862, before the end of the Civil War, when President Abraham Lincoln appointed provisional military governors for Louisiana, Tennessee, and North Car-

---

[6]Duster, 64.

[7]More information about her campaign to get African Americans to migrate west is available in the following sources: William Greaves, producer, *Ida B. Wells: A Passion for Justice*, installment of the PBS series *The American Experience* (New York: Video Dub, 1990); Mary M. B. Hutton, "The Rhetoric of Ida B. Wells: The Genesis of the Anti-Lynch Movement," Ph.D. diss., University of Indiana, 1990; David M. Tucker, "Miss Ida B. Wells and Memphis Lynching," *Black Women in American History: From Colonial Times through the Nineteenth Century*, ed. Darlene Clark Hine (New York: Carlson Publishing, 1990), 1085–95.

olina. Also, on December 8, 1863, President Lincoln issued a Proclamation of Amnesty and Reconstruction. The policy it outlined was lenient. It permitted the recognition of southern state governments based simply on a swearing of allegiance to the Union and to the Constitution of the United States by one-tenth of the voting population in a given state. Tennessee was the first of the eleven states to be readmitted in 1866.

In legislating the reentry of the southern states into the Union, the Proclamation for Amnesty and Reconstruction made no specific provision for the social, political, or economic entry of the four million slaves (including approximately one hundred eight-five thousand veterans of the Union Army) that were released on January 1, 1863, by the Emancipation Proclamation. Neither Lincoln nor his successor, Andrew Johnson, insisted that the freed slaves should have the right to vote. Instead, Lincoln suggested that black soldiers who had fought gallantly during the Civil War, or perhaps those few black men[8] who showed particular "intelligence," might be awarded voting privileges. In addition, neither Lincoln nor Johnson was an advocate for the redistribution to blacks of plantation lands that had been confiscated for abandonment and nonpayment of taxes.

On March 3, 1865, Congress charged the Bureau of Refugees, Freedmen, and Abandoned Lands, better known as the Freedmen's Bureau, with the task of facilitating the transition of African Americans into a life of freedom. The bureau functioned in all of the southern states, providing assistance with the negotiation of land purchase contracts and thus serving as the primary mechanism enabling freed men and women to acquire land. The bureau also provided other services. For example, it took over the administration of justice for freed men and women by establishing court systems responsible for the protection of civil rights. It provided food and medical care, and perhaps most significantly of all, it established day, night, industrial, and Sunday schools, and supported newly established institutions of higher education (for example, Atlanta, Howard, and Fisk Universities). The bureau functioned successfully until about 1870 and with limited activity until about 1874, much to the benefit of millions of African Americans across the South.

By the time that its activities ended, the bureau had established well over four thousand schools and offered educational opportunities to tens of thousands of African Americans.[9] Without advocacy, how-

[8]At this point women had not gained the right to vote.

[9]For a detailed chronicling of schooling in the South for African Americans, see James D. Anderson, *The Education of Blacks in the South, 1860–1935* (Chapel Hill: University of North Carolina Press, 1988), and Jacqueline Jones, *Soldiers of Light, Soldiers of*

ever, the bureau was not able to make much headway in the redistribution of confiscated plantation lands. In fact, in May of 1865 President Johnson issued a proclamation granting amnesty to Confederate leaders and restoring their property rights in exchange for their oaths of allegiance. Much of the confiscated land that might have been made available to the freed men and women to begin making their own lives was ultimately either sold to northern speculators or restored to the former owners. President Johnson's lack of support for the plan, therefore, made this part of the original charge to the bureau impossible.

Further, the presidential pardons of the old leadership made it possible for the Confederates to participate once again in the "new" governments and in the political decision-making processes of the post–Civil War South. With this restoration of power, southern states began enacting legislation that placed the freed men and women in a state of virtual bondage. These laws, known as the Black Codes, reinscribed systems of control that were reminiscent of the old Slave Codes. Slave Codes developed from a general philosophy that the enslaved Africans were property and not human beings. The laws were designed to protect the property owner and to secure the labor supply. While these codes varied from state to state and changed periodically in order to adapt to new needs for economic power or social control, they firmly established the color line and legally restricted the personal, social, political, and economic lives of all of the enslaved people.

The Black Codes enacted at the end of the Civil War resembled these Slave Codes. Although there were a few changes, this legislation was still designed to secure a cheap labor force; to carry out a philosophy that openly stated a belief in the inferiority of people of African descent; and to control the participation of African Americans socially, politically, and economically in society. The freed men and women were permitted to marry and to have legal offspring, but interracial marriages were prohibited. They could sue, be sued, and testify in court but only in cases involving other African Americans, and still they were not allowed to vote or to serve on juries. They were allowed to own property, but typically the areas where they could purchase or rent property were restricted. Newly established vagrancy laws compelled African Americans to work by the dictates of whites, no matter what the conditions for working might be. If found to be unemployed and without permanent residence, they could be arrested and fined. If

Love: Northern Teachers and Georgia Blacks, 1865–1873 (Chapel Hill: University of North Carolina Press, 1980).

they were unable to pay the fines, they could be required to provide unpaid labor for whites in order to "work off" their debts. Also, apprentice laws made it possible for orphans and other children to be "hired out" as well, often to their former masters. Further, African Americans were not permitted to handle firearms or other weapons or to possess alcoholic beverages. They were excluded from certain businesses and some skilled trades, and they could not "insult" white people. Obviously, very little federal attention was being paid at this time to the quality of life of freed African American men and women.

From 1862 to 1865 Reconstruction was conducted with moderation primarily through presidential proclamations. More radical members of Congress, northerners who thought presidential policies too lenient, and a great many African Americans were dissatisfied. The freed men and women were falling easy victims to economic exploitation, political intimidation, and violence (as evidenced by anti-black riots in 1866 in New Orleans and Memphis), and many felt that the cause of justice was clearly not being served. After the national elections of 1866, however, Republicans who wanted to take a more aggressive stance toward Reconstruction were well-represented in Congress. These Radical Republicans, as they came to be known, assumed a more active role and shifted the focus of change from presidential orders to acts of Congress. This era of congressional Reconstruction is usually called Radical Reconstruction, a period that lasted about ten years.

Radical Reconstruction is usually marked by the rescinding of the Black Codes and the passing of the Reconstruction Acts of 1867. Under this legislation the ten remaining southern states (Tennessee having already been admitted to the Union) were divided into five military districts that were supervised by federal troops. Between 1868 and 1870 all ten states were readmitted to the Union, but the conditions for reentry differed from those in the era of the Proclamation for Amnesty and Reconstruction. Each state requesting to be recognized had to accept the Constitution of the United States. With the more aggressive actions of the Radical Republicans, though, accepting the Constitution at that point meant more than accepting the Thirteenth Amendment, which abolished slavery and established citizenship for African Americans. It meant also accepting the Fourteenth Amendment, ratified in 1868 (which was designed to assure basic rights and equality under the law for every citizen, regardless of color), and the Fifteenth Amendment, ratified in 1870 (which guaranteed that no state could discriminate in voting rights based on race). Nevertheless, as demonstrated by strategies employed in southern states by the 1890s, the Fifteenth Amendment did not close the door to discrimination based on literacy, poll taxation, property requirements, or "grandfather" clauses that demanded proof that a grandfather had voted in the 1860 national elections.

The state governments established during Radical Reconstruction were usually Republican, formed from a coalition of African Americans, who were entering political arenas for the first time; northerners who had gone South (traditionally known as carpetbaggers); and southerners who were cooperating with these two groups (traditionally known as scalawags). These governments were not accepted as legitimate by most southern whites (the Democrats), who considered these legislatures imposed upon them by outsiders—northerners and Republicans. Southern resentment of this situation was high, and the general environment very hostile.

By the 1870s secret terrorist organizations such as the Ku Klux Klan (first organized in 1866), the Knights of the White Camelia, the Red Shirts, and the White Line gained momentum. These groups specialized in mutilating, humiliating, intimidating, and even murdering African Americans and anyone else whom the terrorist groups viewed as African American sympathizers or whom they perceived to be in opposition in any way to their beliefs and desires. During this period, lynching and other acts of mob violence began to escalate.

A History of Lynching

A look at the history of lynching in the United States offers evidence of a shady and questionable past. Uses of lynching in the nineteenth century (and continuing into the twentieth century) against African Americans, however, offer provocative evidence that these practices were particularly malevolent and barbarous. According to *The Oxford English Dictionary (OED),* the origins of the word *lynching* are rather obscure. Its earliest discovered use in any form in literature was in 1817. The historian W. Fitzhugh Brundage,[10] on the other hand, posits two earlier origins—one in seventeenth-century Ireland and a second in the eighteenth-century United States. Whatever the case, lynching was an established custom in the United States by the end of the colonial period, as evidenced by the sources in the *OED* for the term *lynch law.*

The *OED* attributes *lynch law* to Judge Charles Lynch, a justice of the peace in Virginia who in 1780 illegally fined and imprisoned

[10]W. Fitzhugh Brundage, *Lynching in the New South: Georgia and Virginia, 1880–1930* (Urbana: University of Illinois Press, 1993).

British loyalists. The entry states that Judge Lynch's name (or perhaps that of another perpetrator of illegal punishment named Lynch) came to be associated with any acts of punishment not sanctioned by law, including whipping, tarring and feathering, and other acts of humiliation and degradation. As time passed, though, *lynch law* came to refer mainly to unlawful sentences of death.

A second explanation in the *OED* for *lynch law* indicates that it might also be attributed to a place, Lynche's Creek in South Carolina. By 1768 this place was known as a meeting site for the Regulators, a group of men who committed many acts of violence throughout the Carolinas against people who were suspected of being loyalists and thus enemies of local efforts to establish and maintain power structures. The Regulators circumvented the law by attacking people who could be perceived as vying with them for economic and political power and control.

A conception of lynching that has helped to make its lawlessness more palatable has been its relation to the notion of "frontier justice,"[11] whereby punishments outside the law are deemed a necessary, even an appropriate, response to two situations. The first situation is when law and order does not exist, as in the early western frontier. In such cases people are compelled to take justice into their own hands in paving the way for the establishment of legal systems. When legal systems are in place, "frontier justice" is expected to end. The second situation is when law and order does not satisfy the needs of justice and can therefore be "rightly" ignored or circumvented. Such was the position taken by late-nineteenth-century lynchers of African Americans. This group justified lynching with the basic argument that "law" was out of order. By the post-Reconstruction era, southerners coded all that was wrong in the South by asserting the urgent need to defend their women and stop "black brutes." They believed that virtuous white women should see their evil attackers punished quickly and with finality. Nonetheless, such justifications were inadequate to account for actual lynching practices.

The formal public record of lynchings in the United States reveals that during the post–Civil War era, lynching and other acts of mob violence against African Americans (for instance, the destruction of farms, businesses, and other property owned or operated by African Americans) steadily increased, with the first peak occurring in 1892. In the antebellum period, lynching was not typically used against

[11]See Donald L. Grant, *The Anti-Lynching Movement: 1883–1932* (San Francisco: R & E Research Associates, 1975).

blacks but against whites who deviated in some way from the local norm—for example, as batterers of wives and children or as people who held unorthodox beliefs or unpopular political positions (as in the case of British loyalists in the eighteenth century). The lynching of slaves was rare, first and foremost because it would result in a loss of "property" and profit. Obviously, it was more profitable to sell slaves than to kill them. Second, there was more advantage to planters when slaves were executed within the law, as planters were compensated for their lost "property." Third, the lynching of slaves served to undermine the power base of the South's wealthy, white, landowning aristocracy. In effect, mob violence against slaves would have transferred the power of life and death from the hands of planters to the hands of the mob, whose numbers were quite likely to include non-elite whites as well. Such a transfer of power would have loosened the systems of control, the general stronghold of the landed aristocracy over both economic and political life. The lynching of African Americans before the Civil War, therefore, was exceptional indeed.

After the Civil War, however, a distinctive shift occurred. While the victims of lynching across the country still included whites, Native Americans, Chicanos, and Asians, by 1892, as reported by Wells in *A Red Record,* the majority of the victims were African American and the majority of the lynchings were in the South. Wells reported that during a single year, 1892, 241 men, women, and children across twenty-six states were lynched. Of the 241, 160 were identified as African Americans, which represented an increase of 200 percent over the ten-year period since 1882, when the number of African Americans lynched was fifty-two. This change cemented a connection between lynching and both race and region that continued to gain strength until 1953, the first year when there was not a recorded lynching. Between 1882 and 1968, 4,743 lynchings were recorded, including fifty African American women between 1889 and 1918. These data indicate the dramatic increase of African Americans in the total number of lynchings from 46 percent in 1882 to an average of 89 percent between 1900 and 1910, with seven of the eleven years showing rates above 90 percent.[12]

The increased lynchings of the post–Civil War era targeted not only African Americans but African American sympathizers as well. This group included, among others, anyone who worked for the Freed-

[12]The sources of these data include Thompson, Brundage, Grant, and Robert L. Zangrando, *The NAACP Crusade against Lynching, 1909–1950* (Philadelphia: Temple University Press, 1980).

men's Bureau. The response to the bureau's activities by southerners ranged from tolerance with resentment to open and bitter opposition. Some southerners rebelled through the violent and intimidating practices of their secret organizations and other acts of resistance directed against African Americans and their white allies. These actions offered evidence of the passionate desire of southern leadership to regain control of their governments and to secure white supremacy. Despite acts of violence and intimidation, however, the bureau functioned successfully until about 1870 and with limited activity until about 1874, much to the benefit of millions of African Americans across the South.

The Response of the African American Community

Reconstruction as a positive force in the lives of freed men and women is marked roughly from the end of the Civil War in 1865 until President Rutherford B. Hayes issued orders in 1877 removing the last of the federal troops from the South. By 1876 most of the Reconstruction coalitions had already lost control of local legislatures. In Virginia, North Carolina, Tennessee, and Georgia, Confederates had been quickly reenfranchised. The process took much longer in Mississippi, Louisiana, and South Carolina, where shifts in political power were sometimes violently wrought through coercion, intimidation, and other acts of force. By removing federal oversight in 1877, President Hayes returned home rule to the South and full power to ex-Confederates and Southern Democrats. By the 1878 national elections, Democrats, rather than Republicans, controlled the U.S. Senate and the House of Representatives. The erosion of gains for African American people was well on its way.

Chief among the reasons for the failure of Reconstruction was that without the redistribution of land in the South, African Americans were unable to develop an economic base for their newly acquired political rights. In addition, after years of turmoil the attention of northerners was focusing more on reconciliation and economic opportunities in the South and less on the terrorist methods by which power and control were being reestablished and maintained. Further, with the return of home rule, southerners were free to construct white supremacy as they chose. Unmistakably, by the 1880s the era of post-Reconstruction had begun. While African Americans continued to struggle for voting rights and civil liberties, hindering their progress was yet another reenactment of many of the provisions of the Black

Codes in the newly established Jim Crow laws. These laws firmly reinscribed boundaries between whites and African Americans; controlled their social, political, and economic lives; and became the way of southern life until such practices were finally ended with the passage of the Civil Rights Act of 1964.[13]

During this time of increased mob activity, African American leaders recognized the precarious position of their people and spoke out passionately to reduce the rising tide of violence. They saw that it was open season on them—for intimidation, wanton destruction of their crops and property, and open "punishment" outside of the law without fear of retaliation or formal prosecution. African Americans found themselves disfranchised, economically at risk, and powerless to protect themselves, and they recognized that these patterns of domination needed to be vehemently resisted. Leaders called for various forms of community action. Conservative positions envisioned change as slow and incremental: This stance would later be epitomized by Booker T. Washington, president of Tuskegee Institute and national spokesperson for African American concerns. More radical positions (such as those assumed by T. Thomas Fortune, editor of the *New York Age,* and Monroe Trotter, editor of the Boston *Guardian*) saw change emerging from a more direct confrontation with the issues.

One early form of community action was mass meetings to raise support funds and to develop responses to specific outrages in a given community. National and statewide political conventions constituted another strategy. Community leaders such as Frederick Douglass (noted abolitionist, writer, orator, diplomat), Blanche K. Bruce (senator from Mississippi), John Mercer Langston (U.S. representative from Virginia), Bishop James Alexander Shorter of the African Methodist Episcopal Church, and others called meetings to draw the attention of the African American community to an array of concerns.

The national convention called by Frederick Douglass was typical. On September 24, 1883, three hundred delegates from twenty-seven states met in Louisville, Kentucky. At this meeting Douglass denounced lynching, setting a pattern for future conventions in placing lynching prominently on the agenda. The need for solidarity and for cooperation with white allies was also discussed. These meetings demonstrated the active commitment of African Americans to causes

---

[13]The Civil Rights Act of 1964 forbids discrimination in the use of public facilities.

of justice, equality, and empowerment, but despite their dedication to reform, the political conventions were largely unsuccessful in stemming the tide of mob violence.[14]

In addition to political conventions, other organizational efforts signaled that African Americans were far from passive in response to mob violence. While leaders like Douglass sought to forge alliances with white activists, more radical leaders such as T. Thomas Fortune had come to prefer independent action that did not seek alliances with whites.[15] In May of 1887 Fortune established the Afro-American League, envisioned as an all-black, self-help organization. At the beginning the league established lynching as a central issue, but after the first convention, attention shifted to antidiscrimination activities, agitating for social equality as well as political and economic opportunity. Fortune was endorsed in this effort by African American newspaper editors across the country, including Ida B. Wells, and he was successful in organizing local branches of the organization and in holding two national conventions.

By 1893, however, the national organization no longer functioned. A central problem was that Fortune and the other editors were unable to garner a base of support among the masses of African Americans in critical sectors of community activity; for example, within the black church and among black Republicans. The majority of these leaders were southern and were not inclined to defy southern attitudes about social behavior or to forego white patronage in agitating for social equality. In essence, the league did not develop effective lines of communication with the majority of African Americans, and their attention to antidiscrimination action and social equality rather than to protection from lynching as the common problem across socioeconomic strata set them apart as elitist.

A second organization established to address the problem of lynching was the Equal Rights Council. Bishop Henry McNeal Turner of the African Methodist Episcopal Church issued a call for a convention to be held in Cincinnati, Ohio, from November 28 through December 1, 1893. George L. Knox, editor of the Indianapolis *Freeman,* was instrumental in publishing the ideas of prominent leaders about the convention and in establishing a national organization. After a short

---

[14]For a more detailed discussion of this type of community activism, see Grant (1975).
[15]It is worth noting that after Booker T. Washington rose in prominence as the central facilitator of support for black people, Fortune became an ally.

while the council merged with the Afro-American League, but in neither configuration did these organizations garner strength as an antilynching movement.

WELLS AND THE AMERICAN AGENDA

Ida B. Wells came of age during Radical Reconstruction. She was born a slave in Holly Springs, Mississippi, on July 16, 1862, the eldest daughter of James Wells, a carpenter, and Elizabeth Warrenton Wells, a cook. After the Civil War, Wells's parents were politically active in Holly Springs. Her father became locally known as a "race" man, a term assigned to African American men, and women, who were intimately involved in the leadership of African American communities, the securing of civil rights and the betterment of political, economic, and social conditions. James Wells was a local businessman, a Mason, and a member of the Board of Trustees of Shaw University (supported by the Freedmen's Bureau), which later became Rust College.

Both of Wells's parents provided Wells with strong role models. They worked hard and held places of respect in the community as forward-looking people. They educated their children in Freedmen's Bureau schools and were committed to helping to forge a brighter world around them. Despite the considerable odds against African Americans in making the transition from slavery to freedom, the Wells family shared with others a sense of great expectations for a future in freedom. Released from the legal restrictions of slavery, James and Elizabeth Wells and their children expected justice under the law for all.

In her autobiography Wells discusses the spirit of activism and achievement that enriched her family's lives during the early years:

> My earliest recollections are of reading the newspaper to my father and an admiring group of his friends. He was interested in politics and I heard the words Ku Klux Klan long before I knew what they meant. I knew dimly that it meant something fearful, by the anxious way my mother walked the floor at night when my father was out to a political meeting. . . . Our job was to go to school and learn all we could. . . . My mother went along to school with us until she learned to read the Bible. After that she visited the school regularly to see how we were getting along. . . . She was not forty when she died, but she had borne eight children and brought us up with a strict discipline that many mothers who have had educational advantages have not exceeded.[16]

[16]Duster, 9.

By such attitudes and actions, James and Elizabeth Wells instilled in their daughter a keen sense of duty to God, family, and community. When Wells was sixteen, her parents and her youngest brother died suddenly in a yellow fever epidemic. In keeping with the deeply felt sense of obligation inherited from her parents, Wells assumed responsibility for herself and for her remaining five siblings (another brother had died some years earlier of spinal meningitis). Her childhood ended abruptly, and a life of independence and service to others began. Wells left school, made herself look older, passed the teaching examination in her county, and obtained a teaching position six miles outside of town. During the week, Wells fulfilled her teaching responsibilities while an old friend of her mother's took care of the children. On the weekends, Wells came home to become head of the family and take on the full burden of household chores before returning to her country school on Sunday evening.

After a year of this grueling schedule, Wells's aunt (her mother's sister) invited her to move to Memphis, Tennessee, to better her circumstances. Recognizing opportunity, Wells agreed to relocate. She arranged for her two brothers to be apprenticed with local tradesmen and for a physically handicapped sister to be taken care of by relatives in Holly Springs; she took her two youngest sisters with her to Memphis. Wells also carried with her habits and preferences that would constitute a foundation for her new life. She had acquired a strong sense of self, confident in her ability to work hard and to provide for her own needs and for those of her family. In having assumed adult responsibilities so successfully, she had an uncommon sense of independence as a young professional woman. Given the background of activism in which she had been nurtured, Wells had internalized a sense of social responsibility and a desire to participate actively in community development.

When Wells reached Memphis, she was eventually able to secure a position in the Shelby County school system and began studying for an examination that would make her eligible for employment in the Memphis city schools. As in Holly Springs, the African American community of Memphis took pride in being forward-looking and culturally and intellectually vibrant. They worked aggressively to take advantage of opportunities and to operate as productive and responsible citizens. Wells's years in the richly endowed African American community of Memphis were excellent training for the public life that she seemed destined to lead.[17]

[17]For more information on the Memphis years, see Miriam DeCosta-Willis, *Ida B. Wells: The Memphis Diaries* (Boston: Beacon Press, 1994).

Wells continued to be active in her own church, the African Methodist Episcopal (AME) Church, as well as in others. She came into contact with AME bishops, such as Henry McNeal Turner, who were learned men, excellent orators, and politically active. By 1891 she had met and heard nationally renowned, politically astute figures, including Frederick Douglass, Blanche K. Bruce, and Frances Ellen Watkins Harper (one of the most highly respected creative writers, public speakers, and community activists of her day). Wells also came to know and respect local African American leaders, such as Robert Church,[18] one of the first African Americans in the Memphis area to acquire wealth and property.

Wells joined a lyceum, composed primarily of public school teachers, whose members enjoyed music, read together, gave recitations, wrote and presented essays, and debated issues of the day. Associated with the lyceum was a periodical, the *Evening Star.* By 1886 Wells had been asked to assume its editorship. With her success as editor and because of a lawsuit that she filed against the Chesapeake, Ohio, and Southwestern railroad company, she was also asked to write a regular column, in the form of letters to the readers, for the *Living Way,* a religious weekly paper. She signed the letters "Iola"[19] and wrote about conditions and problems that were of critical concern to her people. As she stated in her autobiography,

> I had an instinctive feeling that the people who had little or no school training should have something coming into their homes weekly which dealt with their problems in a simple, helpful way. So in weekly letters to the *Living Way,* I wrote in a plain, common-sense way on the things which concerned our people. Knowing that their education was limited, I never used a word of two syllables where one would serve the purpose.[20]

Success with her "Iola" column led to Wells's syndication across the country in the African American periodical press.

During this period Wells became a leading community activist through a sequence of pivotal events. First, in 1884 on a trip from Memphis back to her Shelby County school, Wells was forcibly

---

[18]Robert Church was also the father of Mary Church Terrell, first president of the National Association of Colored Women (the national organization for a nationwide network of black women's clubs that engaged actively in community development work). Terrell also became a rival for Wells in many of Wells's attempts as a national leader in the black clubwomen's movement. Terrell usually won in these contests.

[19]The name Iola may actually have resulted from a misreading of letters as they appeared in print. "Ida" may have been perceived as "Iola," and it stuck.

[20]Duster, 24.

removed from a train for taking a seat in the ladies' coach rather than the smoking car, a privilege to which the conductor asserted verbally and physically that she had no right. Wells was not inclined to accept this treatment, believing it to be an infringement of her rights and an insult to her person. She sued the Chesapeake, Ohio, and Southwestern railroad company and won. The railroad company appealed to the Tennessee Supreme Court, and the decision was overturned. This ruling was one among many incidents during this period that confirmed the regaining of political and social control by the white southern power elite and the mending of the North/South rift in the interest of participating in a global economy. The Wells case became a minor pawn within a display of resurgent power.[21]

The retrenchments of the post-Reconstruction era were a blow for Wells. She was incensed when Jim Crow laws were instituted (they dictated, for example, that African Americans could not ride in the first-class car on the train even with the purchase of a first-class ticket). When she witnessed the inequities in the educational system with the removal of the advocacy of the Freedmen's Bureau (controlled by northerners) and the establishment of public schools (controlled by white southerners), she was appalled. And she was infuriated when she saw that African American citizens had little or no protection against violence. Wells recognized that such encroachments on the rights of American citizens were unlawful. She was inspired to speak out, and speak she did.

After the disappointment with her lawsuit, Wells was asked to write her first article for the *Living Way* about her ordeal. With the success of this first editorial in 1884, she was invited to write the "Iola" column for the *Living Way,* and by 1889 she had become co-owner of a newspaper, the *Free Speech and Headlight,* with Rev. F. Nightingale and J. L. Fleming. During 1889 Wells represented the paper at the convention of the National Press Association, where she was elected secretary of that organization. By 1891 she and Fleming had bought out Nightingale's interest in the paper and shortened its name to the *Free Speech,* and she had also secured an income competitive with her teaching salary, which was an important achievement since her editorials against the school board led to her being fired from her teaching post.

Wells had firmly established herself as a bold woman who spoke the truth and as a respected journalist of considerable renown. Within

---

[21] For more information about the intersection of post-Reconstruction and imperialistic agenda, see John Hope Franklin and Alfred A. Moss, Jr., *From Slavery to Freedom: A History of Negro Americans,* 6th ed. (New York: McGraw-Hill, 1988).

the decade since her parents' death, she had become a business-woman, an active journalist in her own community, a syndicated columnist in African American periodicals throughout the country, and an officeholder in her professional organization during a time when very few women, and even fewer African American women, could make any such claims.

By March 9, 1892, when her three friends were murdered, Wells had a reputation as a sharp-tongued political observer. With these lynchings, however, she was touched much more deeply than she had ever expected to be by such events, for these had occurred in Memphis, a civilized city, and the victims were people that she knew very well. She began asking herself basic questions—"How can this be? What's really going on here?"—and collecting data on lynchings more systematically. Her findings were eye-opening, and she was energized to launch an anti-lynching campaign in order to counter misconceptions and to encourage the application of justice.

When Wells published her May 21 editorial, she did so hurriedly. She was on her way to Philadelphia for the annual meeting of the African Methodist Episcopal Church. After the conference Wells was to visit New York as the guest of T. Thomas Fortune, editor of the *New York Age,* a paper in which her "Iola" column was syndicated. When Wells reached New York, she learned from Fortune that the offices of her paper had been ransacked and the equipment destroyed; that her partner, J. L. Fleming, had barely escaped Memphis with his life; and that some white men in Memphis had promised to torture and kill her on sight if she ever set foot in Tennessee again. In effect, Wells was forced into exile. She would not go south again for another thirty years. Wells became a reporter for the *New York Age,* where she told her story of exile in a feature article on June 25, 1892. As she stated in her autobiography, "Having lost my paper, had a price put on my life, and been made an exile from home for hinting at the truth, I felt that I owed it to myself and to my race to tell the whole truth now that I was where I could do so freely."[22] Wells's anti-lynching campaign gained momentum.

Having become a victim of terrorism herself, Wells was transformed from a regional figure with readers in several cities to a national figure and ultimately to an international one. Her public status, however, was atypical of women's experience during this era. In the 1890s women who discussed social and political issues (rather

[22]Duster, 69.

than concerns of the home) in public arenas were pioneers in territory that was fundamentally gender-restricted—that is, for males only. Wells, operating as an African American woman in such gender-defined space and writing about issues that were both race- and gender-sensitive, was remarkable indeed.

Woman's Sphere

At the same time that lines of power and authority were being drawn around issues of race, gender restrictions were being seriously questioned. Beginning as early as 1848 with the Seneca Falls Convention on Women's Rights, the organized struggle for female equality and autonomy was gaining momentum. Nineteenth-century women activists had learned two important lessons from the abolitionist movement. On the one hand, they discovered striking similarities between chattel slavery and women's oppression. On the other, they accrued valuable strategies for organization, political activity, and especially public speaking. After the Civil War, these women established a matrix of organizations in the interest of women's causes (the Equal Rights Association in 1866, the Women's Christian Temperance Union in 1874, and the National American Woman Suffrage Association in 1890, to name a few).

At the dawn of the nineteenth century, women's lives were significantly shaped by male-held economic and legal authority. By custom and by their invisibility in the law, women had no authority. For example, their property, whether inherited or acquired, was controlled legally by fathers, husbands, or even brothers. If a woman worked outside of the home or had a business of some sort, any earnings legally belonged to the head of her household: her father or her husband. Further, married women were defined in law essentially as their husbands' property. Only husbands could sue for divorce, and in the event of a separation all family property, including the guardianship of the children, went to the husband. With very few exceptions, women could not vote or engage in political activity of any kind. Women also were not sanctioned—except, for example, in Quaker communities—even to speak in public. Their fathers and husbands spoke for them, and, of course, the doors to institutions of higher education and to the professions were closed to them. The lives of women were thoroughly dominated by the power and privilege of men.

This context defined womanhood and specified the home as the "appropriate" sphere for women's activity, regardless of the extent to which particular women's lives did not fit the model. Two examples of a bad fit stand out. One was poor immigrant women and other working-class women who needed to work outside the home, often in mill town factories and urban sweatshops, to help provide for their families. Another was women of African descent. For more than half of the century, enslaved women had absolutely no control over their lives, and for the remaining part of the century they were compelled to work more often than not as fieldworkers or as caretakers of other women's homes, not their own. Despite such discontinuities, however, and the fact that this standard assumed middle- and upper-class privilege, it remained the ideal toward which all women, regardless of race or social class, were to aspire.

True womanhood was defined within the sphere of "domestic" or private rather than "public" interests. Women were supposed to be the moral, stabilizing, civilizing influence in the home. They were "responsible" for the heart and the spirit. "Good" women were supposed to be pure, pious, modest, above the weaknesses of the physical body (that is, uninterested in sexual pleasure), and focused on the care of children, husband, and household. Their space was not the street, not the workplace, not the podium, not the written page—nothing that would draw attention to them in a "public" way. "Public" women were not "good" women.

While the cult of true womanhood operated well into the twentieth century, particular forces and events from the early 1800s served to undermine this model of domesticity. Technological innovation in transportation, encouraged by the rise of industrialism in the United States, permitted women to travel in unsupervised ways much more frequently and without automatically being labeled "public" women. The increase in stagecoach lines, train travel, and steamboat and canal boat travel made it possible for women to go from place to place and appear in public spaces, with their safety in those spaces significantly tied to their deportment as "good" women, as "ladies," rather than as bad women who invited the attention of men. Changes also resulted from the era's remarkable number of inventions, such as the vaccuum cleaner and washing machine, that redefined work in the home and provided women who were able to own them the privilege of more leisure time. Inventions also reshaped "office" work, as with the typewriter. To accommodate the view that women were well-suited for typing because of their finger dexterity, the position of "secretary" was redefined. In 1870 there were 9,982 women employed as secretaries;

in 1900 there were 238,982.[23] The job of secretary was no longer an apprenticeship to management but instead had become basically a dead-end, low-paying job for women. Nevertheless, the entry of women into the world of office work was part of a general increase of women in the public work force.

The struggle of women for higher education also expanded woman's sphere. Oberlin College was the first institution of higher education to open its doors to women and to people of color. The first women were admitted in 1837. Educational opportunities generally remained scarce, however, until after the Civil War, when the emergence of women's colleges and public universities offered many more choices. Vassar, one of the earliest women's colleges, was founded in 1865. Smith and Wellesley began in 1875. The Atlanta Baptist Female Seminary (later Spelman College), one of the first institutions for women of African descent, began in 1881. By 1870, 30 percent of colleges and universities were open to women, and by 1900, 70 percent were open.[24] By post-Reconstruction women were college-educated and entering the professions for the first time in significant numbers. Most became teachers (with the rise in the 1870s of public education), but women were also entering the work force as physicians, nurses, and other health care providers; as lawyers, businesswomen, and social services agents; and as writers, public speakers, and political activists.

During this era African American women could be counted in steadily increasing numbers among these professional groups. In 1864 Rebecca Lee was the first African American woman to become a physician. In 1872 Charlotte E. Ray was awarded a law degree and became the first African American woman to practice law in the United States and among the first women of any race to be admitted to the bar in Washington, D.C. In 1921 Sadie T. M. Alexander was the first African American woman to be awarded a Ph.D. from an American university (in economics from the University of Pennsylvania). These African Americans constituted the first wave of college-educated women. They

---

[23]Glenna Matthews, *The Rise of Public Woman: Woman's Power and Woman's Place in the United States, 1630–1970* (New York: Oxford University Press, 1992), 149.

[24]For more details on the entry of women into colleges and universities, see Mariam K. Chamberlain, ed., *Women in Academe: Progress and Prospects* (New York: Russell Sage Foundation, 1988); Carol S. Pearson, Donna L. Shavlik, and Judith G. Touchton, eds., *Educating the Majority: Women Challenge Tradition in Higher Education* (New York: American Council on Education/Macmillan Publishing, 1989).

were women who not only had the general desire and the determination to participate actively in "public" arenas but also had the wherewithal to do so in both formal and informal training.

These changes in women's aspirations and activities were inspired and facilitated by the movement among women for social equality and legal reform. Even though the nineteenth-century women's movement has been perceived as essentially the domain of white middle-class women, working-class white women, African American women, and other women of color were actively involved in women's reform activities. They cooperated with elite white women (sometimes smoothly, sometimes not) in mutually beneficial activities, and they were also active in various groups of their own. Typically, though, the more publicized record of political activity for women is defined by the interests of middle- and upper-class white women. While this elite group learned and sometimes benefited from various alliances with other women, its members were more interested in furthering their own causes—women's suffrage, temperance, and educational opportunity, for example—than in addressing issues like workers' rights or anti-lynching reform.

The nineteenth century was indeed an era of tremendous change in the lives of women, even though the role of African American women in bringing about this change has only recently been acknowledged. By the post-Reconstruction era new possibilities for women's autonomy were very much in evidence. It was a "woman's era," as the women of that time described it. Women across all classes and races had opportunities to belong to clubs and other organized groups working collectively toward social change. These remarkable women questioned provocatively the distinctions between women's sphere and men's sphere, and by their very existence they reshaped these domains and created new options for women's lives.

During this period, Ida B. Wells emerged as one of the most well known of these "new" women among African American women. Like other professional women, she was challenged to adhere to nineteenth-century standards of "ladyhood," modesty, decorum, and propriety, even as she ventured ever more boldly as an African American woman into male-dominated "public" space. For African American women, the need to maintain feminine decorum was especially troublesome. The lash of slavery cut deeply. A primary task was to define oneself not just as a "true woman" but as "human," as capable and deserving of human regard. Privileged African American women (the group to which Wells belonged because of her access to education, her status as a professional woman, and the elite circles in which she was able to travel) felt obligated to defend both their race and their gender in order to carve out a space for participation and achievement. The story of African American women in public arenas, then, is a story of passion—a passion for the acquisition of literacy and for the opportunity to develop one's talents and abilities fully, to demonstrate one's potential and to commit oneself to the betterment both of self and of the race. Personal potential was inextricably tied to collective possibility in the ways race, gender, and class privilege were determined in the society and access to opportunity was allowed or denied.

The Black Clubwomen's Movement

When Wells's feature story was published in the *New York Age* on June 25, 1892, two African American women, Victoria Earle Matthews of New York and Maritcha Lyons of Brooklyn, decided to host a testimonial dinner for Wells. Matthews, a fellow journalist for the *New York Age* and several other newspapers around the country, is perhaps best known as the founding director of the White Rose Mission, a shelter for African American women and girls who had recently migrated from the South. It also functioned as a community center for women and children, teaching self-improvement and Christian living. Maritcha Lyons, an educator and writer, was one of the first African American women to be named assistant principal in a Brooklyn public school. Both women were active in social reform and experienced in ministering to the needs of their communities. Two months after the testimonial dinner they founded a club, the Women's Loyal Union of New York and Brooklyn, with Matthews serving as the first president.[25]

In hosting the dinner for Wells, Matthews and Lyons wanted to pay tribute to Wells's admirable and courageous work and to raise funds to help her continue that work. On October 5, 1892, at Lyric Hall in New York, they brought together 250 African American women from New York, Philadelphia, and Boston, including some of the most rec-

---

[25]For more information on African American women and organized social reform, see Dorothy Salem, *To Better Our World: Black Women in Organized Reform, 1890–1920* (New York: Carlson Publishing, 1990); Darlene Clark Hine, ed., *Black Women in America: An Historical Encyclopedia*, 2 vols. (New York: Carlson Publishing, 1993); Beverly Washington Jones, *Quest for Equality: The Life and Writings of Mary Eliza Church Terrell, 1863–1954* (New York: Carlson Publishing, 1990); Charles Harris Wesley, *The History of the National Association of Colored Women's Clubs: A Legacy of Service* (Washington: National Association of Colored Women's Clubs, 1984).

ognized and notable women of the day. There was Josephine St. Pierre Ruffin, known for working across racial lines as a leader in the charitable work of women's clubs in Boston and throughout Massachusetts. She was also a journalist and a member of the New England Women's Press Association, composed largely of white women. Gertrude Bustill Mossell, a member of one of Philadelphia's most politically active African American families, was a nationally prominent journalist and creative writer. Susan McKinney Smith Steward and Sarah Smith Garnet were sisters who lived in New York. Both broke new ground for African American women, Steward as the first to practice medicine in New York State, and Garnet as the first to be named a principal of an integrated public school in Manhattan. Most, if not all, of the others in attendance were community leaders active in charities and social reform. After hearing Wells's story the women awarded her five hundred dollars and a gold, pen-shaped brooch.

In drawing together groups from three states, the Wells testimonial made clear that the seeds of organized reform at the national level were firmly rooted. Josephine St. Pierre Ruffin and her daughter Florence Ridley played central roles in establishing the Boston Woman's Era Club a few months later. They also founded the first monthly magazine to be published by African American women, *Woman's Era,* which drew correspondents from clubs across the nation and whose department heads included Victoria Earle Matthews (New York), Fannie Barrier Williams (Chicago), Josephine Silone-Yates (Kansas City, Missouri), Mary Church Terrell (Washington, D.C.), Elizabeth Ensley (Denver), and Alice Ruth Moore (New Orleans). Read primarily by elite African American women, *Woman's Era* became a primary vehicle for messages of political and social reform. The magazine was a vital source of information about family life and fashion as well as a place to discuss critical issues such as health care, educational opportunities, the participation of women in community development, and, of course, lynching. Just as influential as the Woman's Era Club was the Colored Woman's League of Washington, D.C., led by Helen A. Cook, Mary Church Terrell, Anna Julia Cooper, Charlotte Forten Grimké, Josephine B. Bruce, Mary Jane Patterson, and others.[26]

[26]Helen A. Cook was a member of a well-established African American family in Washington, D.C. Mary Church Terrell was the daughter of Robert Church, a man of wealth in Memphis, Tennessee; the wife of Robert Terrell, a municipal judge in Washington, D.C.; a well-respected writer and orator; and the first president of the National Association of Club Women. A member of a very politically active family in Philadelphia, Charlotte Forten Grimké was the first African American member of the Port Royal Commission, a group of volunteers who went south during the Civil War to set up schools for slaves; a nationally recognized creative writer; and the wife of Francis Grimké, a

African American women had long valued volunteerism, cooperative endeavor, and community service. The first women's clubs were established as early as the 1790s as auxiliaries to churches—for example, the Daughters of Allen of the African Methodist Episcopal Church. These groups primarily sought to care for the weak and infirm, feed the hungry, clothe and shelter the needy, and provide education and cultural enrichment. By the 1830s the organizational efforts in the North shifted away from the church and focused more directly on educational, political, and cultural activities, as would later be the case with the lyceum to which Wells belonged during her years in Memphis. The northern groups included the Afric-American Female Intelligence Society (formed in Boston in 1832), before which spoke Maria Stewart, long assumed to be the first African American woman to have publicly addressed an audience of both men and women.

By the post-Reconstruction era African American women had a long history of community activism and operated several different networks of literary, benevolent, and other community organizations. Before and during the Civil War, they had participated in both black and white abolitionist societies, and after the Civil War they joined in the woman suffrage movement and the temperance movement, which also concerned itself with issues related to home, family, and community development. On July 21, 1896, two national organizations—the Washington, D.C.–based National Colored Women's League and the Boston-based National Federation of Afro-American Women—joined to form the National Association of Colored Women (NACW).

In August 1896 the NACW's newly elected president, Mary Church Terrell, announced in *Woman's Era:*

> We, the Colored Women of America, stand before the country today a united sisterhood, pledged to promote the welfare of our race, along all the lines that tend to its development and advancement. . . . We hope to run the whole gamut of human progress and reform. . . . In myself I am nothing, but with the loyal support of conscientious, capable women, all things are possible to us. . . . The magnitude of the work to which we seem divinely called and are solemnly pledged, far from affrighting and depressing us, inspires to greater effort.[27]

---

renowned minister and national leader. Josephine Bruce was the wife of Blanche K. Bruce, the second African American man to be elected to the U.S. Senate. Educator Mary Jane Patterson held the distinction of being the first African American woman to be awarded a bachelor of arts degree from an established American college, Oberlin College in Ohio.

[27] Salem, 131–32.

With the motto "Lifting as We Climb," they called for the careful and conscientious study of questions that deeply and directly affected African
American people in general and African American women in particular.
They sought to improve housing, education, health care, and other conditions, to better the lives of children, to improve conditions for working
women, and to maintain a healthy public opinion about the race and its
women. The agenda also included attention to issues such as Jim Crow
laws, prison reform, and lynching.

African American clubwomen played a vital role in the anti-
lynching movement from its beginning. Anti-lynching committees
were formed at the NACW's local and national levels, and these
groups made a special point of publicizing the lynching of African
American women. Supported by this nationwide network of committees, NACW leaders were active on many anti-lynching fronts, including the National Association for the Advancement of Colored People
(NAACP): Mary Church Terrell and Ida B. Wells participated in its
formation and in establishing protection against mob violence as one
of its priorities. NACW leaders spoke often in public against lynching
and addressed the issue in various periodicals. In 1922 Mary Burnett
Talbert, NACW president from 1916 to 1920, formed the Anti-
Lynching Crusaders, a group whose membership went from sixteen
women to more than nine hundred in just three months. The group
included women who worked with settlement houses, black women's
clubs, the Young Women's Christian Association, the woman's committee of the Council of National Defense, and the NAACP. Like
Wells, the Crusaders advocated federal anti-lynching legislation and
actively sought the support of white women, particularly southern
white women.

The Crusaders and the other lobbyists were not successful in pushing forth federal legislation, but they were able to increase the awareness of lynching as a national problem. They managed to gain the support of some white women leaders on the Women's Committee of the
Commission on Interracial Cooperation (CIC) and the National Council of Women, though not at the level they desired. In fact, among
white women, substantial support for the anti-lynching cause did not
occur until the 1930s with the formation of the Association of Southern
Women for the Prevention of Lynching (ASWPL). Although the success of the Crusaders and others was modest, one point stands clear:
the diverse national network of African American women leaders,
Wells included, was significant in placing lynching on the national
agenda.

THE CASE ACCORDING TO WELLS

Ida B. Wells wanted lynching to stop, and she understood that increasing public awareness and being persistent in calling for action were necessary to attain this goal. In *A Red Record* she states that the first step was to tell the world the facts: "When the Christian world knows the alarming growth and extent of outlawry in our land, some means will be found to stop it" (*RR*, p. 157). She sought to recast lynching in the public eye so that it was no longer perceived as an understandable though unpleasant response to heinous acts but as itself a crime against American values.

Wells's pamphlets define "lynching" by example, painting a vivid picture of incredibly brutal acts at the hands of a lawless mob. She begins *Southern Horrors* with a recounting of her May 21 editorial about eight men lynched, pointing out that the first victim was removed unlawfully from the penitentiary (implying that it surely must have been purposely unguarded); that he, like all of the eight, was killed without being convicted of his alleged crime in a court of law; and that in all eight cases the killings followed a "programme," a ritual—a hanging and then the shooting of bullets into a lifeless body (*SH*, p. 52). She continues this account by referring to an editorial published on the same day as her own in the Memphis *Evening Scimitar,* a white newspaper. This editorial stated the consequences for "whoever" wrote the *Free Speech* editorial:

> If the negroes themselves do not apply the remedy without delay it will be the duty of those whom he has attacked to tie the wretch who utters these calumnies to a stake [typically for burning] at the intersection of Main and Madison Sts., brand him in the forehead with a hot iron and perform upon him a surgical operation [i.e., the removal of the male genitals] with a pair of tailor's shears. (*SH*, p. 52)

For condemning the lynchings, the *Free Speech* editorial writer was to be brutalized several times over by an unlawful, unnamed group of southern white men whose patience "he" had tried.

Wells continues to define lynching as unlawful acts of mob violence throughout all three pamphlets. She chronicles and catalogs specific examples, documenting in *A Red Record* (pp. 82–87) four hundred cases that had been recorded in 1892 and 1893, not just through her own research as an African American woman journalist whose credibility might be questioned, but also by the *Chicago Tribune,* a well-respected white newspaper. She points out racial and regional patterns in the numbers, highlighting, for example, that 160 of the 241 lynchings reported in 1892 were of African Americans and that 180 of the 241 occurred in southern states.[28] She also shows discontinuities between the public perception of lynching—as being in defense of white women's virtue—and the details of actual lynchings. She notes that the alleged crimes ranged from murder to barn burning to no offense; that the victims included five African American women; and that at least one group of victims was a fourteen-year-old girl and her sixteen-year-old brother, who were hanged alongside their father, the alleged criminal.

In *Mob Rule in New Orleans* Wells presents the case of Robert Charles, showing how a single act of discrimination can lead to barbaric consequences when law and order are not equitably applied. Wells closes Charles's story with another listing of incidents of brutality by unlawful mobs and a summary list of lynchings from 1882 to 1900, the year that this last pamphlet was published. In bringing forward these accounts of lynching, as told through the white press, and in listing the statistics with minimum modification, Wells makes a compelling point. She underscores the fact that lynching as practiced against African American people was an act of terrorism waged against not just African American men but also women and children. She demonstrates that the public assumptions about the reasons for lynching were not the truth. The rationale of lynching as a necessary act to stop black male brutes was designed to conceal a racist agenda and to keep power in the hands of southern white men. Wells emphasizes also that the law had been violated and that the United States, as a land of freedom and opportunity, needed to take immediate action.

Wells's campaign was essentially a one-woman enterprise, the primary weapons being her pen and voice. She unraveled the social and political complexities of lynching and identified four basic inconsistencies between the rationale for lynching and its actual execution. First, African Americans were being lynched in parts of the country where legal systems were in place and very much operational. Wells notes in *A Red Record* (p. 87) that a great majority of the lynchings recorded for 1892 took place in the South, an area under lawful jurisdiction; in the Far West, where one might expect to find greater lawlessness, there were comparatively few lynchings. Second, the charges being leveled against African American lynching victims were not limited to rape, indicating again that there was no urgent, unmet need for pun-

---

[28]The remaining eighty-one lynchings in the South include, among others, whites who were African American sympathizers. In the Southwest and Far West, they include Native Americans, Chicanos, Asians, African Americans, and some whites.

ishment outside the law. Third, Wells's investigations often revealed that the "crimes" were actually "achievements": Sometimes the victim was a successful merchant whose business (like the People's Grocery) would be ransacked during the lynching, or a prosperous farmer whose house and crops would be burned; sometimes the victim was simply exercising the right to vote, speaking out publicly for the rights and freedoms of African Americans, or not being "appropriately" deferential to whites. Fourth, the alleged rapists were often in consensual liaisons with white women.

Wells crafted her argument by examining these inconsistencies, concluding that the rape of white women was not the "cause" of lynching at all, often not even the charge. Blacks were being lynched for allegations of murder, burglary, arson, poisoning water and livestock, insulting whites, being insolent, and other perceived "offenses," and sometimes they were lynched on no charges at all. Wells also documented that several lynching victims were not men, the assumed perpetrators of rape, but women and children. With this evidence, she reasoned that if most lynchings could be shown not to be caused by the horror of rape, then the barbarity with which lynching was applied to African Americans was even more unjust, especially since all of the offenses—including rape—were only alleged. They could and should have been handled in a court of law and not before an unlawful mob.

Wells also argued that even when rape was the charge, the charge was not always the truth. Wells cited evidence that some of the liaisons between African American men and white women were long-term, not incidental. She found also that many of the relationships, incidental and otherwise, were with the consent and quite often at the instigation and encouragement of white women. Wells suggested that white women were not being violated at all but were instead very willing partners, belying the fallacy that white women were uninterested in sexual pleasure and uninterested in African American men. She reasoned that because we know from centuries of historical fact that white men desire African American women, why wouldn't white women be comparably interested in African American men? Wells quotes J. C. Duke, editor of the Montgomery, Alabama *Herald,* who suggested that there was a "growing appreciation of white Juliets for colored Romeos" (*SH,* p. 53).

In raising such a question, Wells conceded that culpability in sexual liaisons between white women and African American men might indeed be placed on the men for succumbing to the ill-considered advances of white women, but she also reasoned that such culpability did not make them guilty as a group of being uncontrollably lustful. Her proof was that there were no such concerns before and during the Civil War and no evidence to suggest that African American men had at any time demonstrated character flaws that would support the opinion that women were unsafe in their presence.

Wells further asserted that African American women could not be held responsible for these "crimes" either. She pointed out that although black women were themselves long-standing victims of rape, they were also accused in these lynching scenarios of being amoral and "naturally licentious" and thereby incapable of providing a stabilizing and moral influence for their men. Wells stressed that African American women should not be blamed for their own victimization.

Wells's case suggested that lynching encoded several race and gender stereotypes regarding pleasure and desire: White women were pure, virginal, and uninterested in sexual pleasure. They needed and deserved protection. African American women were wanton, licentious, promiscuous. White men (who had obviously engaged in sexual acts with African American women over the decades, given the range of skin colors among African Americans) could not be accused of raping "bad" women. "Bad," amoral women did not need or deserve protection. African American women, as amoral women, were not capable of providing a moral influence on African American men or anyone else. African American men were lustful beasts who could not be trusted in the company of "good" women, white women. White men were champions of justice in defense of their women and in the preservation of "civilization." Wells understood that white womanhood was portrayed as "respectable," chaste, and vulnerable; that African American womanhood was constructed as wanton, unredeemable, and irrelevant; and that African American men were made out to be ignorant, evil brutes. It was also clear to Wells that white manhood was positioned outside of this schema as rightfully in control.

Wells's argument declared all of this to be false: cover stories designed to perpetuate an evil mythology. As a writer, Wells faced a multilayered challenge. To defend African American people from mob violence, she had to dismantle stereotypes that were based on both gender and race. She was required to identify each of the players, their roles, and their culpability—white women, African American men, African American women, and white men. In her May 21 editorial, therefore, she was not simply casting aspersions on white womanhood, as the *Evening Scimitar* editorial would have its readers believe; she was debunking myths, trying to preserve the lives of her people as well as law and order and justice.

Wells's third argument drew from knowledge deeply imbedded in her second argument: She stated that the term *rapist* more logically applied to white men than to black men. Race mixing between white men and black women was indisputable, and Wells, like other opponents of lynching, reasoned that "mulattoes" existed in large part because white men were free, before the Civil War and after, to assault African American women without fear of retaliation. After Reconstruction, even if African American women or their families were courageous enough to bring charges of rape against white men and, by some remarkable twist, the men were actually found guilty, the obvious inequity between African American and white rapists was that the white rapists were never in danger of being lynched.

Wells brought to light the reality that violations of African American womanhood by white men—much more frequent than that of white womanhood by African American men—went unacknowledged and unavenged. She states,

> A leading journal in South Carolina openly said some months ago that "it is not the same thing for a white man to assault a colored woman as for a colored man to assault a white woman, because the colored woman had no finer feelings nor virtue to be outraged!" Yet colored women have always had far more reason to complain of white men in this respect than ever white women have had of Negroes. (p. 127)

Wells goes on to make a poignant case for the fact that rape as a justification for lynching only applied to some women, not all, and most certainly not African American women. Wells presents evidence to demonstrate that the African American community did not have the license to lynch and thus intensified her argument that lynching and mob violence were unjust on several counts.

In *Southern Horrors* Wells says that

> to palliate this record (which grows worse as the Afro-American becomes intelligent) and excuse some of the most heinous crimes that ever stained the history of a country, the South is shielding itself behind the plausible screen of defending the honor of its women. (p. 61)

She seemed to intuit here what we have gone on to think about much more deeply since her day.[29] She recognized that white men did many

---

[29]See, for example, Ellen Carol Du Bois and Linda Gordon, "Seeking Ecstasy on the Battlefield: Danger and Pleasure in Nineteenth-Century Feminist Sexual Thought," *Pleasure and Danger: Exploring Female Sexuality,* ed. Carole S. Vance (Boston: Routledge &

things behind a screen, a code of "honor" and "manners." The rape of white women became a symbol for all that southerners believed was out of order in the post–Civil War world, and they attributed many of their feelings of disorder to the newly freed slaves and the "liberties" that African Americans were granted during Radical Reconstruction. The historian Jacquelyn Dowd Hall observes that rape was not viewed so much as an act of violence against women as it was an assault on male honor:

> The "false chivalry" of lynching cast [white] women as Christ-like symbols of racial purity and regional identity and translated every sign of black self-assertion into a metaphor for rape—black over white, a world turned upside down.[30]

After the Civil War, African Americans were acquiring political and economic power and had the potential to achieve social equality. Their manners were no longer controlled by the total domination of their lives and bodies by white landowners. Neither African American men nor white women were compelled by law, as they had been in the past, to be deferential in the presence of whiteness in the case of African Americans and white maleness in the case of white women. They were constrained at this point mainly by social conditioning and, where there was mob violence, by intimidation. In both gender and race control, however, southern white men in the post-Reconstruction era reclaimed power, honor, pride, and their version of southern manners with the rope, the gun, and a cultural ideology that allowed them to define lynching and mob violence not as terrorism and race and gender control but as "right" action to avenge their honor, their manhood, their women.

Wells's fourth and most comprehensive argument was that the charge of the rape of white women was used to justify lynching and other mob violence in order to terrorize, oppress, and control African Americans. Crediting the arguments of Frederick Douglass, Wells pointed out that such rationales had evolved over the years until the post-Reconstruction era, when the rape narrative had finally placed African Americans "beyond the pale of human sympathy" (*RR,* p. 78). Using Douglass's analysis, she explained that immediately after the Civil War, lynching was said to be needed to repress alleged race riots. During Reconstruction lynching was supposed to prevent an

---

Kegan Paul, 1984), 31–49; Martha Banta, "The Razor, the Pistol, and the Ideology of Race Etiquette." Public lecture given at the Ohio State University, Columbus, Ohio, April 20, 1994.

[30] Jacquelyn Dowd Hall, *Revolt against Chivalry* (New York: Columbia University Press, 1993), xxi.

"unlawful" domination of whites by African Americans. After African Americans were disfranchised in the post-Reconstruction era, the excuse that won the day was the rape of white women. Stripping away these mythological trappings, Wells called this problem by what she felt was its "true name."[31] She demonstrated how a well-entrenched patriarchal system was able to control the behavior of African American men and women as well as white women. In stories of lynching, white women were the instruments by which the signal was sounded for life or death, for rending apart African American families, and for controlling their social, economic, and political lives. In accepting "protection," the central place of "honor" in this tale of white male chivalry, white women, in general, did not systematically question (until the rise of the ASWPL in 1930) the extent to which their own lives were controlled through myths and stereotypes.

Wells's analysis raised provocative questions about the "truths" imbedded and unacknowledged in mob violence. During the intense period of her anti-lynching campaign, the shaping of her arguments remained constant—from her first editorial on May 21, 1892, throughout the publication of the three pamphlets. Her pamphlets openly proclaimed that lynching was not punishment for the heinous crime of rape but an act of terrorism and oppression. She based her case on reason, logic, and ethics and established that knowing the truth of injustice requires acting against it, not just in the interest of African Americans but in the interest of the nation. She established a line of thought that struck deeply into the core values and beliefs in both the South and the United States as a whole—values and beliefs that in complicated ways embodied a history of race and gender oppression and political and economic domination. As a strident and discordant voice in exile from the South, Wells became a champion of truth and justice and a highly visible international leader against mob violence, disorder, and lawlessness.

The Wells Campaign as a National and International Cause

At the time Ida B. Wells was writing, the United States was seeking economic expansion beyond its national boundaries in an age of global imperialism. Earlier in the nineteenth century expansion had been

---

[31]See Jacqueline Jones Royster, "To Call a Thing by Its True Name: The Rhetoric of Ida B. Wells," in *Reclaiming Rhetorica: Women in the Rhetorical Tradition,* ed. Andrea A. Lunsford (Pittsburgh: University of Pittsburgh Press, 1995), 167–84.

confined to the continent, extending territorial boundaries westward in keeping with the notion of manifest destiny, the idea that the United States was destined to conquer the continent (prime examples are incursions into Indian Territory, the war with Mexico to acquire Texas, and the purchase of Alaska). Accompanying these imperialistic tendencies was the idea that Christian values made the United States duty-bound to create an "empire of liberty," to be exemplars of democracy. Moreover, manifest destiny was tied to the social Darwinist belief in the survival of the fittest. Those who made and influenced national policy believed that the United States needed to seize all the world resources it could to ensure its economic survival. The interests of business, industry, and finance thus became the interests of governments, and the competition from nation to nation for new territory and new markets was intense.

By the post-Reconstruction era, national leaders began to see the United States as part of a larger Atlantic community wherein the respect of other industrial nations was essential to secure economic power. These leaders sought foreign markets for manufacturing and investment. They did not want the nation's reputation tarnished by accounts of lynching and other barbaric forms of violence.

In the interest of the United States as a world power, silence on such issues as lynching and mob violence became literally golden. The sociopolitical environment in the South and the nation as a whole supported two "master narratives" of what lynching was all about: One said that lynching and mob violence were isolated incidents of passion and not evidence of a systemic "race" problem; the other maintained that the United States championed truth, justice, and equality in the world and protected all of its citizens at home.

Wells's messages about lynching did not fit well with these narratives. She linked imperialism abroad to racism at home, and her analyses questioned the equation between whiteness and civilization. In making these discontinuities public, Wells was able to turn imperialist attitudes on their heads and position whites in the United States as "savages" in a "civilized" world. In *A Red Record* she states,

> Surely the humanitarian spirit of this country which reaches out to denounce the treatment of the Russian Jews, the Armenian Christians, the laboring poor of Europe, the Siberian exiles and the native women of India—will not longer refuse to lift its voice on this subject. If it were known that the cannibals or the savage Indians had burned three human beings alive in the past two years, the whole of Christendom

would be roused, to devise ways and means to put a stop to it. Can you remain silent and inactive when such things are done in our own community and country? (p. 154)

To Wells the problem was straightforward: While the United States presented itself as a securer of freedom and democracy abroad, it had a very serious race problem at home. From the government's perspective, there was great incentive to pursue policies that would maintain delicate economic and political balances within and preserve face without, and its position was one of neglect and inaction. Calls from the African American community for an end to mob violence were ignored.[32]

Nevertheless, Wells continued to attack the problem on a number of fronts. The 1892 testimonial dinner for Wells opened the way for her career as a public speaker and a national and international representative of her cause. Rather than reestablish the *Free Speech,* she used the five hundred dollars generated by the dinner to publish her first pamphlet, *Southern Horrors.*

On a speaking tour in Washington, D.C., as the guest of Frederick Douglass, Wells received an invitation from Isabelle Fyvie Mayo, a Scottish writer who was very active in reform movements in Great Britain. Mayo and her friend and colleague in reform, Catherine Impey,[33] were appalled by an account of a human burning in Texas.[34] After requesting initially that Douglass come to Great Britain to speak about lynching practices, they followed Douglass's recommendation and asked Wells to come instead.

This invitation gave Wells the opportunity to bring British influence to bear on this problem, as Douglass and other abolitionists had done earlier by using British money and influence to internationalize the antislavery cause. That movement sought to end the illegal slave trade by ending the need for slaves—that is, by ending slavery in the United States. Both the United States and Great Britain had already made the trading in humans illegal, and Great Britain, whose trade partnership and whose good opinion the United States greatly desired, was well-positioned to press for abolition. The importance of British influence had not changed by the time of the Wells campaign. Again,

---

[32]See John Hope Franklin and Alfred A. Moss, Jr., *From Slavery to Freedom: History of Negro Americans,* 6th ed. (New York: McGraw-Hill, 1988).

[33]Catherine Impey was the editor of *Anti-Caste,* an anti-imperialist Scottish journal that defended the rights of the people of India against British colonial rule.

[34]In *A Red Record* (p. 100) Wells describes the savage murder of Henry Smith from Paris, Texas, and his stepson, William Butler.

the political and economic leadership of the United States wanted the country to be perceived as respectable, as major players on the world scene, not as barbaric "cousins" across the sea who demonstrated all the evils of imperialism.

Having the high regard of British elites in her anti-lynching campaign was indeed leverage for Wells at home. She left for Great Britain on April 5, 1893, on the first of two British tours. As a strategy designed to embarrass the United States and its "civilized" people, Wells and others sent back to Memphis clippings about her activities from British papers. Memphis was one of the largest exporters of cotton, and leaders in the white community did not want to be looked upon unfavorably in the international marketplace. The Memphis Chamber of Commerce, which included owners of the local newspapers, felt compelled to print what Wells was saying and to respond. For the first time the Memphis newspapers spoke out against lynching and apparently affected both public opinion and action in a positive way. After Wells's British campaign, no lynchings occurred in Memphis for more than twenty years.

The response to Wells in the reform community in England was strong. In London the Anti-Lynching Committee was established, with a long, very distinguished membership list. Speaking engagements brought in funds to support Wells's stateside campaign and also connections, especially from the clergy, who used their influence to secure prestigious domestic speaking engagements to which Wells would not otherwise have had access.

Another international forum for Wells's campaign came upon her return from her first tour. The year 1892 marked the four hundredth anniversary of Columbus's landing in North America, and the United States was planning the Columbian Exposition in Chicago, the city that had become Wells's home, to celebrate and showcase four centuries of progress, achievement, and civilization. Unfortunately, African Americans were being systematically excluded from exhibiting or participating in the exposition, and leaders of the African American community were waging battles from several quarters to remedy the situation.

One effort was spearheaded by Frederick Douglass, who was allowed to participate not as a U.S. citizen but as the U.S. ambassador to Haiti. Douglass collaborated with Wells; her future husband, Ferdinand L. Barnett (a Chicago lawyer and the editor of that city's first African American newspaper, *The Conservator*); and I. Garland Penn (secretary of the Freedmen's Aid Society of the Methodist Episcopal

Church and a highly respected journalist) to produce an eighty-one-page booklet, *The Reason Why the Colored American Is Not in the World's Columbian Exposition.* The production of the booklet was supposed to have been under way while Wells was touring Great Britain. When she returned to Chicago, however, she found that plans for publication were failing. She brought the issue to the attention of Chicago's African American clubwomen, who assisted her in raising five hundred dollars to help in the printing of twenty thousand copies of the booklet in English, with prefaces in French and German. Included in the collection was an account by Wells of lynching. Wells distributed all of the copies, free of charge, from the Haitian Pavilion.

In February 1894 Wells left for her second tour of Great Britain. This was the more successful tour in its impact in the United States. It was longer—six months—and Wells had been hired by the Chicago *Inter Ocean* (a white newspaper edited by William Penn Nixon) to send back accounts of her experiences for publication. As a white publication, the *Inter Ocean* provided Wells a vehicle for reaching a much larger audience.

During the second tour, however, Wells suffered retaliatory blows against her character and veracity. In her speeches, she told stories about the horrors of lynching, presented statistics and other evidence, and stated the need for action. When word of what she was saying came back to the southern white community, counterattacks were made. The most pernicious was attempted by John W. Jacks, president of the Missouri Press Association, who wrote an incendiary letter to Florence Balgarnie, secretary of the Anti-Lynching Society of England, in which he attacked Wells's character and blatantly stated that African American women in general were without morals. Jacks had sought to damage Wells's credibility, to remove her British support, and to stop the tour, but Balgarnie was duly outraged by the letter and sent it to a colleague in reform, Josephine St. Pierre Ruffin, who very astutely used its unsavory message as a call to arms of African American women in the First National Conference of Colored Women of America, held in Boston from July 29 to July 31, 1895. Jacks's letter was set aside and not discussed at all at the conference, and the women proceeded with their efforts to establish a national organization of clubwomen, which ultimately led to the formation of the National Association of Colored Women in 1896.

Another incident during Wells's second tour arose from questioning begun during her first tour. Near the end of the first series of speaking engagements Wells was asked about Frances Willard, national president of the Women's Christian Temperance Union (WCTU) from 1879 until her death in 1898. Willard was internationally recognized as a former abolitionist, a highly respected social reformer, and a leader of great vision. The questioner began by asking Wells to explain what actions had been taken against lynching by churches and reform organizations such as the WCTU. This was a critical rhetorical moment for Wells. She chose to respond truthfully and say that these voices were silent and that they ignored the problem. When the questioner asked more directly about Frances Willard, Wells explained that Willard accepted the southern position that lynchings were caused by the rape of white women by menacing black men and that she condoned lynching as the response. Wells concluded that Willard apparently was "no better or worse than the great bulk of white Americans on the Negro questions" (*RR*, p. 144), and she offered Willard's own words as evidence of this assertion.

When Wells returned to England on her second tour, the questions about Willard were increasingly problematic, as Willard was in England on an extended visit. Willard responded in an interview to reports of what Wells was saying. She denounced Wells as being wrong about white women and overly zealous. In effect, Willard defended white women. She did not condemn lynching, although she did join the Anti-Lynching Committee. The controversy caused a rift between Willard and Wells and added to Wells's reputation for being too radical and outspoken. Wells devotes chapter 8 of *A Red Record* to an explanation of the turmoil that her response created, defending her character and the accuracy of her words about Willard (see *RR*, pp. 138–48).

With *Southern Horrors,* two British tours, and the Columbian Exposition behind her, Wells redirected her campaign to speaking out against lynching at engagements throughout the United States. With the 1895 publication of *A Red Record* she made her most comprehensive argument. In this pamphlet she acknowledges her use of a pamphlet prepared by Douglass, *Why Is the Negro Lynched?,* as a starting place. She goes on from his analysis to reconstruct the basic argument in *Southern Horrors* and to synthesize data on lynching that she had been collecting over the years. Wells ends the document with a five-point plan of action and a call for readers to support the Blair Bill,[35] which was offered as a resolution in the House of Representatives in August 1894. The resolution began,

---

[35]Proposed by Senator Henry W. Blair, Republican from New Hampshire.

> Resolved, By the House of Representatives and Senate in congress assembled, That the committee on labor be instructed to investigate and report the number, location, and date of all alleged assaults by males upon females throughout the country during the ten years last preceding the passing of this joint resolution. (*RR,* p. 155)

The resolution did not pass.

Neither Victory nor Defeat

With the publication of *A Red Record* in 1895, much about the anti-lynching movement was changing: Frederick Douglass had died on February 20, 1895, and on the rise were the black clubwomen's movement, a cadre of African American male intellectual and political leaders, and an ideology of accommodation (that is, an agreement to change as a slow and incremental process and an agreement not to push for social equality) espoused by Booker T. Washington. A specific change amid this environment for Wells was that on June 27, 1895, she married Ferdinand L. Barnett and proceeded immediately to raise a family. While her activism never ended, she limited its scope and entered what she called a "semi-retirement." After the turn of the century she was more identifiable as a community leader in Chicago and throughout Illinois than as a national figure.

Wells periodically assumed a role against lynching on a national level, however. She continued to investigate incidents of lynching, to write newspaper articles and editorials, and to speak occasionally about mob violence. In 1900 she published her third and last pamphlet, *Mob Rule in New Orleans.* With the dawning of a new century and the revival of the Afro-American Council, she was named chairperson of their Anti-Lynching Bureau, and she was one of the founders, in 1909, of the National Association for the Advancement of Colored People (NAACP). Her commitment to anti-lynching activities remained constant, and at her death on March 25, 1931, W. E. B. Du Bois[36] wrote,

> Ida Wells-Barnett was the pioneer of the anti-lynching crusade in the United States. As a young woman in Memphis, she began her work

[36]William Edward Burghardt Du Bois (1868–1963) was a preeminent African American scholar. As a professor of sociology, he is recognized for several landmark publications, including *The Souls of Black Folk* (1903). As an activist, he is probably best known for his leadership roles in the Niagara and Pan-Africanism movements, for the founding of the NAACP, and for his editing of *Crisis Magazine,* a publication of the NAACP.

and carried it over the United States and even to England. She roused the white South to vigorous and bitter defense and she began the awakening of the conscience of the nation.[37]

In accounting for Wells's impact on lynching, one noteworthy point stands out. From the beginning of her campaign she saw her most central task to be placing the facts before the American people and later before the world. Her primary effort was not really to change the law, though she certainly felt that the protection of all citizens within the law was the ultimate imperative. Her chief purpose was instead to intervene boldly in public discourse and to change public opinion so that the application of justice for all could prevail. In her autobiography she notes that the invitation to tour Great Britain

> seemed like an open door in a stone wall. For nearly a year I had been in the North, hoping to spread the truth and get moral support for my demand that those accused of crimes be given a fair trial and punished by law instead of by mob. Only in one city—Boston—had I been given even a meager hearing, and the press was dumb. I refer, of course, to the white press, since it was the medium through which I hoped to reach the white people of the country, who alone could mold public sentiment.[38]

Wells believed that the public influence of good and righteous citizens should be brought to bear on the unspeakable horror of mob violence and that white citizens had the power, authority, and resources for change, and, thereby, the obligation to bring it about. She believed that African Americans also had obligations, central among which was the responsibility to be well-informed about atrocities and not to remain silent in the face of injustice. Wells was never silent.

Sadly, the legal history of anti-lynching activities shows no success. Congress was unable to pass the Blair Bill, the Dyer Bill,[39] or any other legislation that would stem the tide of violence. Much more successful were the ways in which collective resistance forced national debate of the issues and produced changes in public sentiment. In the twentieth century, the black clubwomen remained consistent in their support of anti-lynching activities. After 1909 the NAACP assumed a lead position and continued to do so relentlessly until this century's civil rights movement. White southern liberal organizations emerged

[37]Thompson, 126.

[38]Duster, 86.

[39]Leonidas Dyer, Republican from Missouri, introduced the first version of his anti-lynching bill in the House of Representatives in April 1918. This bill became the prototype for subsequent anti-lynching legislation supported by the NAACP and NACW.

in the 1920s: The CIC, for example, was involved in anti-lynching activities by 1919, and the ASWPL by 1930. This collective agitation did not change laws, but it did change the cultural ethos that permitted mob violence without retribution.

With the evidence of a revolutionized cultural ethos, one can easily conclude, as Du Bois did, that the anti-lynching campaign of Ida B. Wells was successful. She spoke out. She was heard in multiple communities. With her leadership, lynching was named a national crime.

While lynchings did not end during her lifetime, their numbers were significantly reduced from 1892 to 1900, during the height of Wells's campaigning, and ultimately people across regional, national, race, and gender boundaries joined in her appeal. Between 1892 and 1900 Wells dropped an anti-lynching pebble into the pond of American public sentiment, and for the first time placed mob violence on the American agenda and established a pathway to change.

On the following pages: This spread from *Harper's Weekly* of March 23, 1867, addresses the lawlessness and disorder that prevailed in the South after the Civil War. The lives and property of African Americans and "northern sympathizers" were at constant risk. Tensions between the North and the South were high, and military rule in the southern states was greatly contested. With the removal of military oversight came escalating violence against African Americans. By the time of Wells's campaign in 1892, lynching, intimidation, and other acts of terrorism were common.

TENNESSEE.

THE MURDER OF SENATOR CASE.

VIRGINIA.

DRIVING THEM OFF THE PLANTATIONS WITHOUT WAGES AND SHOOTING THEM

IF HE IS A SOUTHERN GENTLEMAN,

VERDICT, "A GOOD JOKE ON A NIGGER".

SOUTHER

And the President's Veto

SOUTH CAROLINA.

THREE U.S. SOLDIERS MURDERED.

TWENTY TWO NEGRO PRISONERS BURNED TO DEATH.

......Feb 19—

Journal's special correspondence says that a mob, composed of the remains of Quantrell's guerrillas, broke open Mr. Carey's house at Parkesville, and and hung Mr Carey. He had been tried for stealing a horse to escape from rebel's at the burn of Perryville.

CHARLESTON, SOUTH CAROLINA.—Three soldiers of the army of the United States were murdered in October, 1865, in South Carolina, under circumstances of peculiar cruelty, and several persons were arrested, tried, and condemned by military commission for said murder. Said persons, so condemned, were subsequently reprieved and transferred to Fort Delaware, from which they were released by writ of habeas corpus and set free.

JAN., 1867.—The jail at Kingstree, South Carolina, has been destroyed by fire, and 22 colored prisoners smothered or burned to death, while the only white man ever imprisoned to escape.—MAJOR-GENERAL J. C. ROBINSON.

BELL COUNTY, TEXAS.—On the night of December 3 a mob of about eight entered the jail, murdered old Mr. Lindley, his son, and another inmate of the man who was an entire stranger to the Lindleys....GRAYSON COUNTY.—Two negroes have been most brutally murdered within the last few days.

SAVANNAH, GEORGIA.—The police, however, arrested several negroes, whom they treated in the most brutal and barbarous manner—beating them over the head as severely as to cause the blood to flow profusely. No attempts were made to arrest any of the white men, although they were the parties who began, controlled the strike from beginning to end.

"Driving them off the plantations without wages, or, as has been done in many cases, shooting them; a gentleman who commits a homicide of that kind gets his gentlemen friends together—and they are nearly all magistrates—and they swear him and discharge him."—GENERAL SCHOFIELD, *Department of Virginia.*

"My own opinion is that the trial of a white man for the murder of a freedman in Texas would be a farce, and in making the statement I make it because it answers me, and for no other rea on."—GENERAL SHERIDAN.

"You could not find a jury in South Carolina that would convict a man for killing a Union soldier, no matter what the testimony."—GENERAL SICKLES.

"Homicides of Union men, soldiers, and freedmen, are on the increase."—GENERAL THOMAS J. WOOD.

"If a freedman is murdered by men who had been in the rebellion, it is impossible to get the criminal arrested even; and if he is arrested, he is sure to be released on very low bail."—GENERAL BAIRD.

"I do not believe there is much chance of conviction a resident or citizen of Georgia for the murder of the victim or a Union man or a negro."—GEN. THOMAS

THE POLICE AND THE FREEDMEN.

THE HANGING OF H. CAREY.

IF HE IS A UNION MAN OR A FREEDMAN.

'VERDICT', "HANG THE D— YANKEE AND NIGGER."

TEXAS.

THE LINDLEY MURDER.

WHOLESALE MURDER OF FREEDMEN.

The Military Government Bill.

It declares that there exists in those States no legal Governments, and no adequate protection for life or property, and asserts the necessity of enforcing peace and good order within their limits......They are organized like the other States of the Union, and like them they make, administer, and execute the laws which concern the domestic affairs.....The provisions which these Governments have made for the preservation of order, the suppression of crime, and the redress of private injuries, are in substance and in mode the same as those which prevail in the Northern States and in other civilized countries.....It is undoubtedly true that these evils have been much increased and exaggerated, North and South, by the demoralizing influences of civil war, and by the ravenous passions which the contest has engendered.....The military rule which it establishes is plainly to be used not for any purpose of order, or for the prevention of crime, but solely as a means of coercing the people into the adoption of principles and measures to which it is known that they are opposed, and upon which they have no undeniable right to exercise their own judgment......The power thus given to the commanding officer over all the people of each district is that of an absolute monarch......Being bound by no State law, and there being no other law to regulate the subject, he may make a criminal code of his own, and he can make it as bloody as any recorded in history, or he can reserve the privilege of acting upon the impulse of his private passions in each case that arises.....Instead of mitigating the harshness of his single rules, such a tribunal would be used much more, probably, to divide the responsibility of making it more cruel and unjust......Can it be expected that military officers will understand or follow a rule expressed in language so purely technical, and not pertaining in the least degree to their profession? If so, then each officer may define cruelty according to his own temper, and if not small, he will make it cruel. Corporal punishment—the gag, the ball and chain, and the other almost insupportable forms of torture invented for military punishment—lie within the range of choice......It is plain that the authority here given to the military offices amounts to absolute despotism.....It reduces the whole population of the ten States, all persons of every color, sex, and condition, and every age-cover within their limits, to the most abject and degrading slavery.....It protects not only the citizen of the United States which are within the Union, but it shields every human being who comes or is brought under our jurisdiction.....Over a very large comprised in the five military districts life, liberty, and property are secured by State laws and Federal laws, and the national Constitution in every place in force and every where obeyed. The Courts, State and Federal, are open and in the full exercise of their proper authority. What, then, is the ground on which this bill proceeds?.....We are providing now for a time of profound peace, where there is not an armed soldier within our borders except those who are in the service of the Government.....The Constitution declares that no person shall be deprived of life, liberty, or property without due process of law.....The evils which spring from the unsettled state of our Government will be acknowledged by

—A. Johnson.

Frederick Douglass

Wells considered Frederick Douglass a role model and mentor. He provided her guidance and counsel, especially in the early days of her campaign; wrote the introduction to her first pamphlet, *Southern Horrors;* and introduced her to the reformers who arranged her two speaking tours of Great Britain.

T. Thomas Fortune

T[imothy] Thomas Fortune, renowned civil rights leader and editor and co-owner (with Jerome B. Peterson) of the *New York Age,* was a colleague and friend of Wells. Wells agreed with Fortune's analyses of race problems in his 1880s editorials, and when he and others founded the Afro-American League, Wells was among its supporters. In 1892, when Wells was forced into exile from the South, Fortune and Peterson employed her as a writer with the *New York Age* and published the first account of her Memphis story.

Victoria Earle Matthews

Victoria Earle Matthews was born a slave in Georgia but went on to create a remarkable record in New York as a journalist, public speaker, social activist, and pioneering settlement worker. With Maritcha Lyons, Matthews organized the testimonial for Wells on October 5, 1892, at Lyric Hall in New York City. This event helped to launch Wells's anti-lynching campaign, and it was also instrumental in the founding of the Woman's Loyal Union of New York City and Brooklyn, of which Matthews was the first president. Matthews is perhaps best known as the founder, in 1897, of the White Rose Mission, a New York community center for women and children and a shelter for the young black women who were migrating in significant numbers from the South during this time.

Maritcha Lyons

An educator, biographer, and social activist, Maritcha Lyons worked with Victoria Earle Matthews to organize the Lyric Hall testimonial for Wells. She was also active in the founding of the Woman's Loyal Union and in the reform activities that became the trademark of the black clubwomen's movement.

45

PART TWO

The Documents

SOUTHERN HORRORS.

LYNCH LAW

IN ALL

ITS PHASES

Miss IDA B. WELLS,

Price, · · · Fifteen Cents.

THE NEW YORK AGE PRINT,

1892.

PREFACE

The greater part of what is contained in these pages was published in the *New York Age* June 25, 1892, in explanation of the editorial which the Memphis whites considered sufficiently infamous to justify the destruction of my paper, *The Free Speech.*

Since the appearance of that statement, requests have come from all parts of the country that "Exiled," (the name under which it then appeared) be issued in pamphlet form. Some donations were made, but not enough for that purpose. The noble effort of the ladies of New York and Brooklyn Oct 5 have enabled me to comply with this request and give the world a true, unvarnished account of the causes of lynch law in the South.

This statement is not a shield for the despoiler of virtue, nor altogether a defense for the poor blind Afro-American Sampsons who suffer themselves to be betrayed by white Delilahs. It is a contribution to truth, an array of facts, the perusal of which it is hoped will stimulate this great American Republic to demand that justice be done though the heavens fall.

It is with no pleasure I have dipped my hands in the corruption here exposed. Somebody must show that the Afro-American race is more sinned against than sinning, and it seems to have fallen upon me to do so. The awful death-roll that Judge Lynch is calling every week is appalling, not only because of the lives it takes, the rank cruelty and outrage to the victims, but because of the prejudice it fosters and the stain it places against the good name of a weak race.

The Afro-American is not a bestial race. If this work can contribute in any way toward proving this, and at the same time arouse the conscience of the American people to a demand for justice to every citizen, and punishment by law for the lawless, I shall feel I have done my race a service. Other considerations are of minor importance.

New York City, Oct. 26, 1892.   IDA B. WELLS.

To the Afro-American women of New York and Brooklyn, whose race love, earnest zeal and unselfish effort at Lyric Hall, in the City of New York, on the night of October 5th, 1892,—made possible its publication, this pamphlet is gratefully dedicated by the author.

HON. FRED. DOUGLASS'S LETTER

Dear Miss Wells:

Let me give you thanks for your faithful paper on the lynch abomination now generally practiced against colored people in the South. There has been no word equal to it in convincing power. I have spoken, but my word is feeble in comparison. You give us what you know and testify from actual knowledge. You have dealt with the facts with cool, painstaking fidelity and left those naked and uncontradicted facts to speak for themselves.

Brave woman! you have done your people and mine a service which can neither be weighed nor measured. If American conscience were only half alive, if the American church and clergy were only half christianized, if American moral sensibility were not hardened by persistent infliction of outrage and crime against colored people, a scream of horror, shame and indignation would rise to Heaven wherever your pamphlet shall be read.

But alas! even crime has power to reproduce itself and create conditions favorable to its own existence. It sometimes seems we are deserted by earth and Heaven—yet we must still think, speak and work, and trust in the power of a merciful God for final deliverance.

Very truly and gratefully yours,

Cedar Hill, Anacostia, D.C., Oct. 25, 1892.   FREDERICK DOUGLASS.

CHAPTER I.   THE OFFENSE

Wednesday evening May 24th, 1892, the city of Memphis was filled with excitement. Editorials in the daily papers of that date caused a meeting to be held in the Cotton Exchange Building; a committee was sent for the editors of the "Free Speech" an Afro-American journal published in that city, and the only reason the open threats of lynching that were made were not carried out was because they could not be found. The cause of all this commotion was the following editorial published in the "Free Speech" May 21st, 1892, the Saturday previous.

"Eight negroes lynched since last issue of the "Free Speech" one at Little Rock, Ark., last Saturday morning where the citizens broke (?)[1] into the penitentiary and got their man; three near Anniston, Ala., one

---

[1] Question marks in parentheses throughout the documents are presumably Wells's. [All footnotes are the editor's.]

near New Orleans; and three at Clarksville, Ga., the last three for killing a white man, and five on the same old racket—the new alarm about raping white women. The same programme of hanging, then shooting bullets into the lifeless bodies was carried out to the letter.

Nobody in this section of the country believes the old thread bare lie that Negro men rape white women. If Southern white men are not careful, they will over-reach themselves and public sentiment will have a reaction; a conclusion will then be reached which will be very damaging to the moral reputation of their women."

"The Daily Commercial" of Wednesday following, May 25th, contained the following leader:

"Those negroes who are attempting to make the lynching of individuals of their race a means for arousing the worst passions of their kind are playing with a dangerous sentiment. The negroes may as well understand that there is no mercy for the negro rapist and little patience with his defenders. A negro organ printed in this city, in a recent issue publishes the following atrocious paragraph: 'Nobody in this section of the country believes the old thread-bare lie that negro men rape white women. If Southern white men are not careful they will over-reach themselves, and public sentiment will have a reaction; and a conclusion will be reached which will be very damaging to the moral reputation of their women.'

The fact that a black scoundrel is allowed to live and utter such loathsome and repulsive calumnies is a volume of evidence as to the wonderful patience of Southern whites. But we have had enough of it.

There are some things that the Southern white man will not tolerate, and the obscene intimations of the foregoing have brought the writer to the very outermost limit of public patience. We hope we have said enough."

The "Evening Scimitar" of same date, copied the "Commercial's" editorial with these words of comment: "Patience under such circumstances is not a virtue. If the negroes themselves do not apply the remedy without delay it will be the duty of those whom he has attacked to tie the wretch who utters these calumnies to a stake at the intersection of Main and Madison Sts., brand him in the forehead with a hot iron and perform upon him a surgical operation with a pair of tailor's shears."

Acting upon this advice, the leading citizens met in the Cotton Exchange Building the same evening, and threats of lynching were freely indulged, not by the lawless element upon which the deviltry of the South is usually saddled—but by the leading business men, in their leading business centre. Mr. Fleming, the business manager and owning a half interest the Free Speech, had to leave town to escape the mob, and was afterwards ordered not to return; letters and telegrams sent me in New York where I was spending my vacation advised me that bodily harm awaited my return. Creditors took possession of the office and sold the outfit, and the "Free Speech" was as if it had never been.

The editorial in question was prompted by the many inhuman and fiendish lynchings of Afro-Americans which have recently taken place and was meant as a warning. Eight lynched in one week and five of them charged with rape! The thinking public will not easily believe freedom and education more brutalizing than slavery, and the world knows that the crime of rape was unknown during four years of civil war, when the white women of the South were at the mercy of the race which is all at once charged with being a bestial one.

Since my business has been destroyed and I am an exile from home because of that editorial, the issue has been forced, and as the writer of it I feel that the race and the public generally should have a statement of the facts as they exist. They will serve at the same time as a defense for the Afro-Americans Sampsons who suffer themselves to be betrayed by white Delilahs.

The whites of Montgomery, Ala., knew J. C. Duke sounded the keynote of the situation—which they would gladly hide from the world, when he said in his paper, "The Herald," five years ago: "Why is it that white women attract negro men now more than in former days? There was a time when such a thing was unheard of. There is a secret to this thing, and we greatly suspect it is the growing appreciation of white Juliets for colored Romeos." Mr. Duke, like the "Free Speech" proprietors, was forced to leave the city for reflecting on the "honah" of white women and his paper suppressed; but the truth remains that Afro-American men do not always rape (?) white women without their consent.

Mr. Duke, before leaving Montgomery, signed a card disclaiming any intention of slandering Southern white women. The editor of the "Free Speech" has no disclaimer to enter, but asserts instead that there are many white women in the South who would marry colored men if such an act would not place them at once beyond the pale of society and within the clutches of the law. The miscegnation laws of the South only operate against the legitimate union of the races; they leave the white man free to seduce all the colored girls he can, but it is death to the colored man who yields to the force and advances of a similar attraction in white women. White men lynch the offending Afro-American, not because he is a despoiler of virtue, but because he succumbs to the smiles of white women.

CHAPTER II. THE BLACK AND WHITE OF IT

The "Cleveland Gazette" of January 16, 1892, publishes a case in point. Mrs. J. S. Underwood, the wife of a minister of Elyria, Ohio, accused an Afro-American of rape. She told her husband that during his absence in 1888, stumping the State for the Prohibition Party, the man came to the kitchen door, forced his way in the house and insulted her. She tried to drive him out with a heavy poker, but he overpowered and chloroformed her, and when she revived her clothing was torn and she was in a horrible condition. She did not know the man but could identify him. She pointed out William Offett, a married man, who was arrested and, being in Ohio, was granted a trial.

The prisoner vehemently denied the charge of rape, but confessed he went to Mrs. Underwood's residence at her invitation and was criminally intimate with her at her request. This availed him nothing against the sworn testimony of a minister's wife, a lady of the highest respectability. He was found guilty, and entered the penitentiary, December 14, 1888, for fifteen years. Some time afterwards the woman's remorse led her to confess to her husband that the man was innocent.

These are her words: "I met Offett at the Post Office. It was raining. He was polite to me, and as I had several bundles in my arms he offered to carry them home for me, which he did. He had a strange fascination for me, and I invited him to call on me. He called, bringing chestnuts and candy for the children. By this means we got them to leave us alone in the room. Then I sat on his lap. He made a proposal to me and I readily consented. Why I did so, I do not know, but that I did is true. He visited me several times after that and each time I was indiscreet. I did not care after the first time. In fact I could not have resisted, and had no desire to resist."

When asked by her husband why she told him she had been outraged, she said: "I had several reasons for telling you. One was the neighbors saw the fellows here, another was, I was afraid I had contracted a loathsome disease, and still another was that I feared I might give birth to a Negro baby. I hoped to save my reputation by telling you a deliberate lie." Her husband horrified by the confession had

Offett, who had already served four years, released and secured a divorce.

There are thousands of such cases throughout the South, with the difference that the Southern white men in insatiate fury wreak their vengeance without intervention of law upon the Afro-Americans who consort with their women. A few instances to substantiate the assertion that some white women love the company of the Afro-American will not be out of place. Most of these cases were reported by the daily papers of the South.

In the winter of 1885–6 the wife of a practicing physician in Memphis, in good social standing whose name has escaped me, left home, husband and children, and ran away with her black coachman. She was with him a month before her husband found and brought her home. The coachman could not be found. The doctor moved his family away from Memphis, and is living in another city under an assumed name.

In the same city last year a white girl in the dusk of evening screamed at the approach of some parties that a Negro had assaulted her on the street. He was captured, tried by a white judge and jury, that acquitted him of the charge. It is needless to add if there had been a scrap of evidence on which to convict him of so grave a charge he would have been convicted.

Sarah Clark of Memphis loved a black man and lived openly with him. When she was indicted last spring for miscegenation, she swore in court that she was *not* a white woman. This she did to escape the the penitentiary and continued her illicit relation undisturbed. That she is of the lower class of whites, does not disturb the fact that she is a white woman. "The leading citizens" of Memphis are defending the "honor" of *all* white women, *demi-monde* included.

Since the manager of the "Free Speech" has been run away from Memphis by the guardians of the honor of Southern white women, a young girl living on Poplar St., who was discovered in intimate relations with a handsome mulatto young colored man, Will Morgan by name, stole her father's money to send the young fellow away from that father's wrath. She has since joined him in Chicago.

The Memphis "Ledger" for June 8th has the following; "If Lillie Bailey, a rather pretty white girl seventeen years of age, who is now at the City Hospital, would be somewhat less reserved about her disgrace there would be some very nauseating details in the story of her life. She is the mother of a little coon. The truth might reveal fearful depravity or it might reveal the evidence of a rank outrage. She will not divulge the name of the man who has left such black evidence of her disgrace, and, in fact, says it is a matter in which there can be no interest to the outside world. She came to Memphis nearly three months ago and was taken in at the Woman's Refuge in the southern part of the city. She remained there until a few weeks ago, when the child was born. The ladies in charge of the Refuge were horified. The girl was at once sent to the City Hospital, where she has been since May 30th. She is a country girl. She came to Memphis from her father's farm, a short distance from Hernando, Miss. Just when she left there she would not say. In fact she says she came to Memphis from Arkansas, and says her home is in that State. She is rather good looking, has blue eyes, a low forehead and dark red hair. The ladies at the Woman's Refuge do not know anything about the girl further than what they learned when she was an inmate of the institution; and she would not tell much. When the child was born an attempt was made to get the girl to reveal the name of the Negro who had disgraced her, she obstinately refused and it was impossible to elicit any information from her on the subject."

Note the wording. "The truth might reveal fearful depravity or rank outrage." If it had been a white child or Lillie Bailey had told a pitiful story of Negro outrage, it would have been a case of woman's weakness or assault and she could have remained at the Woman's Refuge. But a Negro child and to withhold its father's name and thus prevent the killing of another Negro "rapist." A case of "fearful depravity."

The very week the "leading citizens" of Memphis were making a spectacle of themselves in defense of all white women of every kind, an Afro-American, Mr. Stricklin, was found in a white woman's room in that city. Although she made no outcry of rape, he was jailed and would have been lynched, but the woman stated she bought curtains of him (he was a furniture dealer) and his business in her room that night was to put them up. A white woman's word was taken as absolutely in this case as when the cry of rape is made, and he was freed.

What is true of Memphis is true of the entire South. The daily papers last year reported a farmer's wife in Alabama had given birth to a Negro child. When the Negro farm hand who was plowing in the field heard it he took the mule from the plow and fled. The dispatches also told of a woman in South Carolina who gave birth to a Negro child and charged three men with being its father, *every one of whom has since disappeared.* In Tuscumbia, Ala., the colored boy who was lynched there last year for assaulting a white girl told her before his accusers that he had met her there in the woods often before.

Frank Weems of Chattanooga who was not lynched in May only

because the prominent citizens became his body guard until the doors of the penitentiary closed on him, had letters in his pocket from the white woman in the case, making the appointment with him. Edward Coy who was burned alive in Texarkana, January 1, 1892, died protesting his innocence. Investigation since as given by the Bystander in the Chicago Inter-Ocean, October 1, proves:

1. The woman who was paraded as a victim of violence was of bad character; her husband was a drunkard and a gambler.
2. She was publicly reported and generally known to have been criminally intimate with Coy for more than a year previous.
3. She was compelled by threats, if not by violence, to make the charge against the victim[.]
4. When she came to apply the match Coy asked her if she would burn him after they had 'been sweethearting' so long.
5. A large majority of the 'superior' white men prominent in the affair are the reputed fathers of mulatto children.

These are not pleasant facts, but they are illustrative of the vital phase of the so-called 'race question,' which should properly be designated an earnest inquiry as to the best methods by which religion, science, law and political power may be employed to excuse injustice, barbarity and crime done to a people because of race and color. There can be no possible belief that these people were inspired by any consuming zeal to vindicate God's law against miscegnationists of the most practical sort. The woman was a willing partner in the victim's guilt, and being of the 'superior' race must naturally have been more guilty."

In Natchez, Miss., Mrs. Marshall, one of the *creme de la creme* of the city, created a tremendous sensation several years ago. She has a black coachman who was married, and had been in her employ several years. During this time she gave birth to a child whose color was remarked, but traced to some brunette ancestor, and one of the fashionable dames of the city was its godmother. Mrs. Marshall's social position was unquestioned, and wealth showered every dainty on this child which was idolized with its brothers and sisters by its white papa. In course of time another child appeared on the scene, but it was unmistakably dark. All were alarmed, and "rush of blood, strangulation" were the conjectures, but the doctor, when asked the cause, grimly told them it was a Negro child. There was a family conclave, the coachman heard of it and leaving his own family went West, and has never returned. As soon as Mrs. Marshall was able to travel she was sent away in deep disgrace. Her husband died within the year of a broken heart.

Ebenzer Fowler, the wealthiest colored man in Issaquena County, Miss., was shot down on the street in Mayersville, January 30, 1885, just before dark by an armed body of white men who filled his body with bullets. They charged him with writing a note to a white woman of the place, which they intercepted and which proved there was an intimacy existing between them.

Hundreds of such cases might be cited, but enough have been given to prove the assertion that there are white women in the South who love the Afro-American's company even as there are white men notorious for their preference for Afro-American women.

There is hardly a town in the South which has not an instance of the kind which is well-known, and hence the assertion is reiterated that "nobody in the South believes the old thread bare lie that negro men rape white women." Hence there is a growing demand among Afro-Americans that the guilt or innocence of parties accused of rape be fully established. They know the men of the section of the country who refuse this are not so desirous of punishing rapists as they pretend. The utterances of the leading white men show that with them it is not the crime but the *class*. Bishop Fitzgerald has become apologist for lynchers of the rapists of *white* women only. Governor Tillman, of South Carolina, in the month of June, standing under the tree in Barnwell, S.C., on which eight Afro-Americans were hung last year, declared that he would lead a mob to lynch a *negro* who raped a *white* woman[.]" So say the pulpits, officials and newspapers of the South. But when the victim is a colored woman it is different.

Last winter in Baltimore, Md., three white ruffians assaulted a Miss Camphor, a young Afro-American girl, while out walking with a young man of her own race. They held her escort and outraged the girl. It was a deed dastardly enough to arouse Southern blood, which gives its horror of rape as excuse for lawlessness, but she was an Afro-American. The case went to the courts, an Afro-American lawyer defended the men and they were acquitted.

In Nashville, Tenn., there is a white man, Pat Hanifan, who outraged a little Afro-American girl, and, from the physical injuries received, she has been ruined for life. He was jailed for six months, discharged, and is now a detective in that city. In the same city, last May, a white man outraged an Afro-American girl in a drug store. He was arrested, and released on bail at the trial. It was rumored that five hundred Afro-Americans had organized to lynch him. Two hundred and fifty white citizens armed themselves with Winchesters and guarded him. A cannon was placed in front of his home, and the Buchanan Rifles (State

Militia) ordered to the scene for his protection. The Afro-American mob did not materialize. Only two weeks before Eph. Grizzard, who had only been *charged* with rape upon a white woman, had been taken from the jail, with Governor Buchanan and the police and militia standing by, dragged through the streets in broad daylight, knives plunged into him at every step, and with every fiendish cruelty a frenzied mob could devise, he was at last swung out on the bridge with hands cut to pieces as he tried to climb up the stanchions. A naked, bloody example of the blood-thirstiness of the nineteenth century civilization of the Athens of the South! No cannon or military was called out in his defense. He dared to visit a white woman.

At the very moment these civilized whites were announcing their determination "to protect their wives and daughters," by murdering Grizzard, a white man was in the same jail for raping eight-year-old Maggie Reese, an Afro-American girl. He was not harmed. The "honor" of grown women who were glad enough to be suppported by the Grizzard boys and Ed Coy, as long as the liasion was not known, needed protection; they were white. The outrage upon helpless childhood needed no avenging in this case; she was black.

A white man in Guthrie, Oklahoma Territory, two months ago inflicted such injuries upon another Afro-American child that she died. He was not punished, but an attempt was made in the same town in the month of June to lynch an Afro-American who visited a white woman.

In Memphis, Tenn., in the month of June, Ellerton L. Dorr, who is the husband of Russell Hancock's widow, was arrested for attempted rape on Mattie Cole, a neighbor's cook; he was only prevented from accomplishing his purpose, by the appearance of Mattie's employer. Dorr's friends say he was drunk and not responsible for his actions. The grand jury refused to indict him and he was discharged.

CHAPTER III.   THE NEW CRY

The appeal of Southern whites to Northern sympathy and sanction, the adroit, insiduous plea made by Bishop Fitzgerald for suspension of judgment because those "who condemn lynching express no sympathy for the *white* woman in the case," falls to the ground in the light of the foregoing.

From this exposition of the race issue in lynch law, the whole matter is explained by the well-known opposition growing out of slavery to the progress of the race. This is crystalized in the oft-repeated slogan: "This is a white man's country and the white man must rule." The South resented giving the Afro-American his freedom, the ballot box and the Civil Rights Law. The raids of the Ku-Klux and White Liners[2] to subvert reconstruction government, the Hamburg and Ellerton, S.C., the Copiah County Miss., and the Lafayette Parish, La., massacres[3] were excused as the natural resentment of intelligence against government by ignorance.

Honest white men practically conceded the necessity of intelligence murdering ignorance to correct the mistake of the general government, and the race was left to the tender mercies of the solid South. Thoughtful Afro-Americans with the strong arm of the government withdrawn and with the hope to stop such wholesale massacres urged the race to sacrifice its political rights for sake of peace. They honestly believed the race should fit itself for government, and when that should be done, the objection to race participation in politics would be removed.

But the sacrifice did not remove the trouble, nor move the South to justice. One by one the Southern States have legally (?) disfranchised the Afro-American, and since the repeal of the Civil Rights Bill nearly every Southern State has passed separate car laws with a penalty against their infringement. The race regardless of advancement is penned into filthy, stifling partitions cut off from smoking cars. All this while, although the political cause has been removed, the butcheries of black men at Barnwell, S.C., Carrolton, Miss., Waycross, Ga., and Memphis, Tenn., have gone on; also the flaying alive of a man in Kentucky, the burning of one in Arkansas, the hanging of a fifteen year old girl in Louisiana, a woman in Jackson, Tenn., and one in Hollendale, Miss., until the dark and bloody record of the South shows 728 Afro-Americans lynched during the past 8 years. Not 50 of these were for political causes; the rest were for all manner of accusations from that of rape of white women, to the case of the boy Will Lewis who was hanged at Tullahoma, Tenn., last year for being drunk and "sassy" to white folks.

[2]Secret white supremacist societies such as the Ku Klux Klan and the White Liners flourished after 1867.

[3]Raids by armed whites, as in these three incidents cited by Wells, were typically directed against groups of African Americans rather than individuals. In the Hamburg case, several members of the African American militia were arrested on July 4, 1876, for "blocking traffic" in the course of their parade; they had refused to step aside to allow passage of two buggies driven by whites. In the ensuing riot, several African Americans were killed.

These statistics compiled by the Chicago "Tribune" were given the first of this year (1892). Since then, not less than one hundred and fifty have been known to have met violent death at the hands of cruel bloodthirsty mobs during the past nine months.

To palliate this record (which grows worse as the Afro-American becomes intelligent) and excuse some of the most heinous crimes that ever stained the history of a country, the South is shielding itself behind the plausible screen of defending the honor of its women. This, too, in the face of the fact that only *one-third* of the 728 victims to mobs have been *charged* with rape, to say nothing of those of that one-third who were innocent of the charge. A white correspondent of the Baltimore Sun declares that the Afro-American who was lynched in Chestertown, Md., in May for assault on a white girl was innocent; that the deed was done by a white man who had since disappeared. The girl herself maintained that her assailant was a white man. When that poor Afro-American was murdered, the whites excused their refusal of a trial on the ground that they wished to spare the white girl the mortification of having to testify in court.

This cry has had its effect. It has closed the heart, stifled the conscience, warped the judgment and hushed the voice of press and pulpit on the subject of lynch law throughout this "land of liberty." Men who stand high in the esteem of the public for christian character, for moral and physical courage, for devotion to the principles of equal and exact justice to all, and for great sagacity, stand as cowards who fear to open their mouths before this great outrage. They do not see that by their tacit encouragement, their silent acquiescence, the black shadow of lawlessness in the form of lynch law is spreading its wings over the whole country.

Men who, like Governor Tillman, start the ball of lynch law rolling for a certain crime, are powerless to stop it when drunken or criminal white toughs feel like hanging an Afro-American on any pretext.

Even to the better class of Afro-Americans the crime of rape is so revolting they have too often taken the white man's word and given lynch law neither the investigation nor condemnation it deserved.

They forget that a concession of the right to lynch a man for a certain crime, not only concedes the right to lynch any person for any crime, but (so frequently is the cry of rape now raised) it is in a fair way to stamp us a race of rapists and desperadoes. They have gone on hoping and believing that general education and financial strength would solve the difficulty, and are devoting their energies to the accumulation of both.

The mob spirit has grown with the increasing intelligence of the Afro-American. It has left the out-of-the-way places where ignorance prevails, has thrown off the mask and with this new cry stalks in broad daylight in large cities, the centres of civilization, and is encouraged by the "leading citizens" and the press.

CHAPTER IV. THE MALICIOUS AND UNTRUTHFUL WHITE PRESS

The "Daily Commercial" and "Evening Scimitar" of Memphis, Tenn., are owned by leading business men of that city, and yet, in spite of the fact that there had been no white woman in Memphis outraged by an Afro-American, and that Memphis possessed a thrifty law-abiding, property owning class of Afro-Americans the "Commercial" of May 17th, under the head of "More Rapes, More Lynchings" gave utterance to the following:

["]The lynching of three Negro scoundrels reported in our dispatches from Anniston, Ala., for a brutal outrage committed upon a white woman will be a text for much comment on "Southern barbarism" by Northern newspapers; but we fancy it will hardly prove effective for campaign purposes among intelligent people. The frequency of these lynchings calls attention to the frequency of the crimes which causes lynching. The "Southern barbarism" which deserves the serious attention of all people North and South, is the barbarism which preys upon weak and defenseless women. Nothing but the most prompt, speedy and extreme punishment can hold in check the horrible and beastial propensities of the Negro race. There is a strange similarity about a number of cases of this character which have lately occurred.

In each case the crime was deliberately planned and perpetrated by several Negroes. They watched for an opportunity when the women were left without a protector. It was not a sudden yielding to a fit of passion, but the consummation of a devilish purpose which has been seeking and waiting for the opportunity. This feature of the crime not only makes it the most fiendishly brutal, but it adds to the terror of the situation in the thinly settled country communities. No man can leave his family at night without the dread that some roving Negro ruffian is watching and waiting for this opportunity. The swift punishment which invariably follows these horrible crimes doubtless acts as a deterring effect upon the Negroes in that immediate neighborhood for a short time. But the lesson is not widely learned nor long remembered. Then such crimes, equally atrocious, have happened in quick succession, one in Tennessee, one in Arkansas, and one in Alabama. The facts of the crime appear to appeal more to the Negro's lustful imagination than the facts of the punishment do to his fears. He sets aside all fear of death in any form when opportunity is found for the gratification of his bestial desires. There is small reason to hope for any change for the better. The commission of this crime grows more frequent every year. The generation of Negroes which have grown up since the war have lost in large measure the traditional and wholesome awe of the white race which kept the Negroes in subjection, even when their masters were in the army, and their families left unprotected except by the slaves themselves. There is no longer a restraint upon the brute passion of the Negro.

What is to be done? The crime of rape is always horrible, but the Southern man there is nothing which so fills the soul with horror, loathing and fury as the outraging of a white woman by a Negro. It is the race question in the ugliest, vilest, most dangerous aspect. The Negro as a political factor can be controlled. But neither laws nor lynchings can subdue his lusts. Sooner or later it will force a crisis. We do not know in what form it will come."

In its issue of June 4th, the Memphis "Evening Scimitar" gives the following excuse for lynch law:

"Aside from the violation of white women by Negroes, which is the outcropping of a bestial perversion of instinct, the chief cause of trouble between the races in the South is the Negro's lack of manners. In the the state of slavery he learned politeness from association with white people, who took pains to teach him. Since the emancipation came and the tie of mutual interest and regard between master and servant was broken, the Negro has drifted away into a state which is neither freedom nor bondage. Lacking the proper inspiration of the one and the restraining force of the other he has taken up the idea that boorish insolence is independence, and the exercise of a decent degree of breeding toward white people is identical with servile submission. In consequence of the prevalence of this notion there are many Negroes who use every opportunity to make themselves offensive, particularly when they think it can be done with impunity.

We have had too many instances right here in Memphis to doubt this, and our experience is not exceptional. *The white people won't stand this sort of thing, and whether they be insulted as individuals are as a race, the response will be prompt and effectual.* The bloody riot of 1866,[4] in which so many Negroes perished, was brought on principally by the outrageous conduct of the blacks toward the whites on the streets. It is also a remarkable and discouraging fact that the majority of such scoundrels are Negroes who have received educational advantages at the hands of the white taxpayers. They have got just enough of learning to make them realize how hopelessly their race is behind the other in everything that makes a great people, and they attempt to "get even" by insolence, which is ever the resentment of inferiors. There are well-bred Negroes among us, and it is truly unfortunate that they should have to pay, even in part, the penalty of the offenses committed by the baser sort, but this is the way of the world. The innocent must suffer for the guilty. If the Negroes as a people possessed a hundredth part of the self-respect which is evidenced by the courteous bearing of some that the "Scimitar" could name, the friction between the races would be reduced to a minimum. It will not do to beg the question by pleading that many white men are also stirring up strife. The Caucasian blackguard simply obeys the promptings of a depraved disposition, and he is seldom deliberately rough or offensive toward strangers or unprotected women.

The Negro tough, on the contrary, is given to just that kind of offending, and he almost invariably singles out white people as his victims."

On March 9th, 1892, there were lynched in this same city three of the best specimens of young since-the-war Afro-American manhood. They were peaceful, law-abiding citizens and energetic business men.

They believed the problem was to be solved by eschewing politics and putting money in the purse. They owned a flourishing grocery business in a thickly populated suburb of Memphis, and a white man named Barrett had one on the opposite corner. After a personal difficulty which Barrett sought by going into the "People's Grocery" drawing a pistol and was thrashed by Calvin McDowell, he (Barrett) threatened to "clean them out." These men were a mile beyond the city

---

[4]This Memphis riot, one of the bloodiest of the Reconstruction era, resulted in the deaths of forty-six African Americans (men, women, and children), the injury of many more, and the burning of ninety-one houses, twelve schools, and four churches. The riot was touched off when African American soldiers from Fort Pickering freed a prisoner from the custody of the Memphis police.

limits and police protection; hearing that Barrett's crowd was coming to attack them Saturday night, they mustered forces and prepared to defend themselves against the attack.

When Barrett came he led a *posse* of officers, twelve in number, who afterward claimed to be hunting a man for whom they had a warrant. That twelve men in citizen's clothes should think it necessary to go in the night to hunt one man who had never before been arrested, or made any record as a criminal has never been explained. When they entered the back door the young men thought the threatened attack was on, and fired into them. Three of the officers were wounded, and when the *defending* party found it was officers of the law upon whom they had fired, they ceased and got away.

Thirty-one men were arrested and thrown in jail as "conspirators," although they all declared more than once they did not know they were firing on officers. Excitement was at fever heat until the morning papers, two days after, announced that the wounded deputy sheriffs were out of danger. This hindered rather than helped the plans of the whites. There was no law on the statute books which would execute an Afro-American for wounding a white man, but the "unwritten law" did. Three of these men, the president, the manager and clerk of the grocery—"the leaders of the conspiracy"—were secretly taken from jail and lynched in a shockingly brutal manner. "The Negroes are getting too independent," they say, "we must teach them a lesson."

What lesson? The lesson of subordination. "Kill the leaders and it will cow the Negro who dares to shoot a white man, even in self-defense."

Although the race was wild over the outrage, the mockery of law and justice which disarmed men and locked them up in jails where they could be easily and safely reached by the mob—the Afro-American ministers, newspapers and leaders counselled obedience to the law which did not protect them.

Their counsel was heeded and not a hand was uplifted to resent the outrage; following the advice of the "Free Speech," people left the city in great numbers.

The dailies and associated press reports heralded these men to the country as "toughs," and "Negro desperadoes who kept a low dive." This same press service printed that the Negro who was lynched at Indianola, Miss., in May, had outraged the sheriff's eight-year-old daughter[.] The girl was more than eighteen years old, and was found by her father in this man's room, who was a servant on the place.

Not content with misrepresenting the race, the mob-spirit was not to be satisfied until the paper which was doing all it could to counteract this impression was silenced. The colored people were resenting their bad treatment in a way to make itself felt, yet gave the mob no excuse for further murder, until the appearance of the editorial which is construed as a reflection on the "honor" of the Southern white women. It is not half so libelous as that of the "Commercial" which appeared four days before, and which has been given in these pages. They would have lynched the manager of the "Free Speech" for exercising the right of free speech if they had found him as quickly as they would have hung a rapist, and glad of the excuse to do so. The owners were ordered not to return, "The Free Speech" was suspended with as little compunction as the business of the "People's Grocery" broken up and the proprietors murdered.

CHAPTER V.   THE SOUTH'S POSITION

Henry W. Grady[5] in his well-remembered speeches in New England and New York pictured the Afro-American as incapable of self-government. Through him and other leading men the cry of the South to the country has been "Hands off! Leave us to solve our problem." To the Afro-American the South says, "the white man must and will rule." There is little difference between the Ante-bellum South and the New South.

Her white citizens are wedded to any method however revolting, any measure however extreme, for the subjugation of the young manhood of the race. They have cheated him out of his ballot, deprived him of civil rights or redress therefor in the civil courts, robbed him of the fruits of his labor, and are still murdering, burning and lynching him.

The result is a growing disregard of human life. Lynch law has spread its insiduous influence till men in New York State, Pennsylvania and on the free Western plains feel they can take the law in their own hands with impunity, especially where an Afro-American is concerned. The South is brutalized to a degree not realized by its own inhabitants, and the very foundation of government, law and order, are imperilled.

[5]Henry Grady, nationally renowned journalist and orator, was part owner and editor of the *Atlanta Constitution*.

Public sentiment has had a slight "reaction" though not sufficient to stop the crusade of lawlessness and lynching. The spirit of christianity of the great M. E. Church was aroused to the frequent and revolting crimes against a weak people, enough to pass strong condemnatory resolutions at its General Conference in Omaha last May. The spirit of justice of the grand old party asserted itself sufficiently to secure a denunciation of the wrongs, and a feeble declaration of the belief in human rights in the Republican platform at Minneapolis, June 7th. Some of the great dailies and weeklies have swung into line declaring that lynch law must go. The President of the United States[6] issued a proclamation that it be not tolerated in the territories over which he has jurisdiction. Governor Northern and Chief Justice Bleckley of Georgia have proclaimed against it. The citizens of Chattanooga, Tenn., have set a worthy example in that they not only condemn lynch law, but her public men demanded a trial for Weems, the accused rapist, and guarded him while the trial was in progress. The trial only lasted ten minutes, and Weems chose to plead guilty and accept twenty-one years sentence, than invite the certain death which awaited him outside that cordon of police if he had told the truth and shown the letters he had from the white woman in the case.

Col. A. S. Colyar, of Nashville, Tenn., is so overcome with the horrible state of affairs that he addressed the following earnest letter to the Nashville "American." "Nothing since I have been a reading man has so impressed me with the decay of manhood among the people of Tennssee as the dastardly submission to the mob reign. We have reached the unprecedented low level; the awful criminal depravity of substituting the mob for the court and jury, of giving up the jail keys to the mob whenever they are demanded. We do it in the largest cities and in the country towns; we do it in midday; we do it after full, not to say formal, notice, and so thoroughly and generally is it acquiesced in that the murderers have discarded the formula of masks. They go into the town where everybody knows them, sometimes under the gaze of the governor, in the presence of the courts, in the presence of the sheriff and his deputies, in the presence of the entire police force, take out the prisoner, take his life, often with fiendish glee, and often with acts of cruelty and barbarism which impress the reader with a degeneracy rapidly approaching savage life. That the State is disgraced but faintly expresses the humiliation which has settled upon the once proud people of Tennessee. The State, in its majesty, through its orga-

---

[6]Benjamin Harrison, a Republican from Ohio.

nized life, for which the people pay liberally, makes but one record, but one note, and that a criminal falsehood, 'was hung by persons to the jury unknown.' The murder at Shelbyville is only a verification of what every intelligent man knew would come, because with a mob a rumor is as good as a proof."

These efforts brought forth apologies and a short halt, but the lynching mania was raged again through the past three months with unabated fury.

The strong arm of the law must be brought to bear upon lynchers in severe punishment, but this cannot and will not be done unless a healthy public sentiment demands and sustains such action.

The men and women in the South who disapprove of lynching and remain silent on the perpetration of such outrages, are particeps criminis, accomplices, accessories before and after the fact, equally guilty with the actual law-breakers who would not persist if they did not know that neither the law nor militia would be employed against them.

CHAPTER VI.   SELF HELP

In the creation of this healthier public sentiment, the Afro-American can do for himself what no one else can do for him, The world looks on with wonder that we have conceded so much and remain law-abiding under such great outrage and provocation.

To Northern capital and Afro-American labor the South owes its rehabilitation. If labor is withdrawn capital will not remain. The Afro-American is thus the backbone of the South. A thorough knowledge and judicious exercise of this power in lynching localities could many times effect a bloodless revolution. The white man's dollar is his god, and to stop this will be to stop outrages in many localities.

The Afro Americans of Memphis denounced the lynching of three of their best citizens, and urged and waited for the authorities to act in the matter and bring the lynchers to justice. No attempt was made to do so, and the black men left the city by thousands, bringing about great stagnation in every branch of business. Those who remained so injured the business of the street car company by staying off the cars, that the superintendent, manager and treasurer called personally on the editor of the "Free Speech," asked them to urge our people to give them their patronage again. Other business men became alarmed over the situation and the "Free Speech" was run away that the colored people might be more easily controlled. A meeting of white citizens in

June, three months after the lynching, passed resolutions for the first time, condemning it. *But they did not punish the lynchers.* Every one of them was known by name, because they had been selected to do the dirty work, by some of the very citizens who passed these resolutions. Memphis is fast losing her black population, who proclaim as they go that there is no protection for the life and property of any Afro-American citizen in Memphis who is not a slave.

The Afro-American citizens of Kentucky, whose intellectual and financial improvement has been phenomenal, have never had a separate car law until now. Delegations and petitions poured into the Legislature against it, yet the bill passed and the Jim Crow Car of Kentucky is a legalized institution. Will the great mass of Negroes continue to patronize the railroad? A special from Covington, Ky., says:

Covington, June 13th.—The railroads of the State are beginning to feel very markedly, the effects of the separate coach bill recently passed by the Legislature. No class of people in the State have so many and so largely attended excursions as the blacks. All these have been abandoned, and regular travel is reduced to a minimum. A competent authority says the loss to the various roads will reach $1,000,000 this year.

A call to a State Conference in Lexington, Ky,, last June had delegates from every county in the State. Those delegates, the ministers, teachers, heads of secret and others orders, and the head of every every family should pas the word around for every member of the race in Kentucky to stay off railroads unless obliged to ride[.] If they did so, and their advice was followed persistently the convention would not need to petition the Legislature to repeal the law or raise money to file a suit. The railroad corporations would be so effected they would in self-defense lobby to have the separate car law repealed. On the other hand, as long as the railroads can get Afro-American excursions they will always have plenty of money to fight all the suits brought against them. They will be aided in so doing by the same partisan public sentiment which passed the law. White men passed the law, and white judges and juries would pass upon the suits against the law, and render judgment in line with their prejudices and in deference to the greater financial power.

The appeal to the white man's pocket has ever been more effectual than all the appeals ever made to his conscience. Nothing, absolutely nothing, is to be gained by a further sacrifice of manhood and self-respect. By the right exercise of his power as the industrial factor of the South, the Afro-American can demand and secure his rights, the punishment of lynchers, and a fair trial for accused rapists.

Of the many inhuman outrages of this present year, the only case where the proposed lynching did *not* occur, was where the men armed themselves in Jacksonville, Fla., and Paducah, Ky., and prevented it. The only times an Afro-American who was assaulted got away has been when he had a gun and used it in self-defense.

The lesson this teaches and which every Afro American should ponder well, is that a Winchester rifle should have a place of honor in every black home, and it should be used for that protection which the law refuses to give. When the white man who is always the aggressor knows he runs as great risk of biting the dust every time his Afro-American victim does, he will have greater respect for Afro-American life. The more the Afro-American yields and cringes and begs, the more he has to do so, the more he is insulted, outraged and lynched.

The assertion has been substantiated throughout these pages that the press contains unreliable and doctored reports of lynchings, and one of the most necessary things for the race to do is to get these facts before the public. The people must know before they can act, and there is no educator to compare with the press.

The Afro-American papers are the only ones which will print the truth, and they lack means to employ agents and detectives to get at the facts. The race must rally a mighty host to the support of their journals, and thus enable them to do much in the way of investigation.

A lynching occurred at Port Jarvis, N.Y., the first week in June. A white and colored man were implicated in the assault upon a white girl. It was charged that the white man paid the colored boy to make the assault, which he did on the public highway in broad day time, and was lynched. This, too was done by "parties unknown." The white man in the case still lives. He was imprisoned and promises to fight the case on trial. At the preliminary examination, it developed that he had been a suitor of the girl's. She had repulsed and refused him, yet had given him money, and he had sent threatening letters demanding more.

The day before this examination she was so wrought up, she left home and wandered miles away. When found she said she did so because she was afraid of the man's testimony. Why should she be afraid of the prisoner? Why should she yield to his demands for money if not to prevent him exposing something he knew? It seems explainable only on the hypothesis that a *liason* existed between the colored boy and the girl, and the white man knew of it. The press is singularly silent. Has it a motive? We owe it to ourselves to find out.

The story comes from Larned, Kansas, Oct. 1st, that a young white lady held at bay until daylight, without alarming any one in the house, "a burly Negro" who entered her room and bed. The "burly Negro" was promptly lynched without investigation or examination of inconsistant stories.

A house was found burned down near Montgomery, Ala., in Monroe County, Oct. 13th, a few weeks ago; also the burned bodies of the owners and melted piles of gold and silver.

These discoveries led to the conclusion that the awful crime was not prompted by motives of robbery. The suggestion of the whites was that "brutal lust was the incentive, and as there are nearly 200 Negroes living within a radius of five miles of the place the conclusion was inevitable that some of them were the perpetrators."

Upon this "suggestion" probably made by the real criminal, the mob acted upon the "conclusion" and arrested ten Afro-Americans, four of whom, they tell the world, confessed to the deed of murdering Richard L. Johnson and outraging his daughter, Jeanette. These four men, Berrell Jones, Moses Johnson, Jim and John Packer, none of them 25 years of age, upon this conclusion, were taken from jail, hanged, shot, and burned while yet alive the night of Oct. 12th. The same report says Mr. Johnson was on the best of terms with his Negro tenants.

The race thus outraged must find out the facts of this awful hurling of men into eternity on supposition, and give them to the indifferent and apathetic country. We feel this to be a garbled report, but how can we prove it?

Near Vicksburg, Miss., a murder was committed by a gang of burglars. Of course it must have been done by Negroes, and Negroes were arrested for it. It is believed that 2 men, Smith Tooley and John Adams belonged to a gang controlled by white men and, fearing exposure, on the night of July 4th, they were hanged in the Court House yard by those interested in silencing them. Robberies since committed in the same vicinity have been known to be by white men who had their faces blackened. We strongly believe in the innocence of these murdered men, but we have no proof. No other news goes out to the world save that which stamps us as a race of cut-throats, robbers and lustful wild beasts. So great is Southern hate and prejudice, they legally (?) hung poor little thirteen year old Mildrey Brown at Columbia, S.C., Oct. 7th, on the circumstantial evidence that she poisoned a white infant. If her guilt had been proven unmistakably, had she been white, Mildrey Brown would never have been hung.

The country would have been aroused and South Carolina disgraced forever for such a crime. The Afro American himself did not know as he should have known as his journals should be in a position to have him know and act.

Nothing is more definitely settled than he must act for himself. I have shown how he may employ the boycott, emigration and the press, and I feel that by a combination of all these agencies can be effectually stamped out lynch law, that last relic of barbarism and slavery. "The gods help those who help themselves."

A RED RECORD.

Tabulated Statistics and Alleged Causes of

Lynchings in the United States,

1892–1893–1894.

Respectfully submitted to the Nineteenth Century civilization in "the Land of the Free and the Home of the Brave."

BY
Miss IDA B. WELLS,
128 Clark Street,
CHICAGO.

PREFACE

Hon. Frederick Douglass' Letter[1]

Dear Miss Wells:

Let me give you thanks for your faithful paper on the lynch abomination now generally practiced against colored people in the South. There has been no word equal to it in convincing power. I have spoken, but my word is feeble in comparison. You give us what you know and testify from actual knowledge. You have dealt with the facts with cool, painstaking fidelity, and left those naked and uncontradicted facts to speak for themselves.

Brave woman! you have done your people and mine a service which can neither be weighed nor measured. If the American conscience were only half alive, if the American church and clergy were only half Christianized, if American moral sensibility were not hardened by persistent infliction of outrage and crime against colored people, a scream of horror, shame, and indignation would rise to Heaven wherever your pamphlet shall be read.

But alas! even crime has power to reproduce itself and create conditions favorable to its own existence. It sometimes seems we are deserted by earth and Heaven—yet we must still think, speak and work, and trust in the power of a merciful God for final deliverance

Very truly and gratefully yours,

Cedar Hill, Anacostia, D.C.　　　　　Frederick Douglass.

CONTENTS

[1]This letter was originally written for *Southern Horrors;* Wells reprinted it in *A Red Record.*

CHAPTER I.   THE CASE STATED

The student of American sociology will find the year 1894 marked by a pronounced awakening of the public conscience to a system of anarchy and outlawry which had grown during a series of ten years to be so common, that scenes of unusual brutality failed to have any visible effect upon the humane sentiments of the people of our land.

Beginning with the emancipation of the Negro, the inevitable result of unbribled power exercised for two and a half centuries, by the white man over the Negro, began to show itself in acts of conscienceless outlawry. During the slave regime, the Southern white man owned the Negro body and soul. It was to his interest to dwarf the soul and preserve the body. Vested with unlimited power over his slave, to subject him to any and all kinds of physical punishment, the white man was still restrained from such punishment as tended to injure the slave by abating his physical powers and thereby reducing his financial worth. While slaves were scourged mercilessly, and in countless cases inhumanly treated in other respects, still the white owner rarely permitted his anger to go so far as to take a life, which would entail upon him a loss of several hundred dollars. The slave was rarely killed, he was too valuable; it was easier and quite as effective, for discipline or revenge, to sell him "Down South."

But Emancipation came and the vested interests of the white man in the Negro's body were lost. The white man had no right to scourge the emancipated Negro, still less has he a right to kill him. But the Southern white people had been educated so long in that school of practice, in which might makes right, that they disdained to draw strict lines of action in dealing with the Negro. In slave times the Negro was kept subservient and submissive by the frequency and severity of the scourging, but, with freedom, a new system of intimidation came into vogue; the Negro was not only whipped and scourged; he was killed.

Not all nor nearly all of the murders done by white men, during the past thirty years in the South, have come to light, but the statistics as gathered and preserved by white men, and which have not been questioned, show that during these years more than ten thousand Negroes have been killed in cold blood, without the formality of judicial trial and legal execution. And yet, as evidence of the absolute impunity with which the white man dares to kill a Negro, the same record shows that during all these years, and for all these murders only three white men have been tried, convicted, and executed. As no white man has been lynched for the murder of colored people, these three executions are the only instances of the death penalty being visited upon white men for murdering Negroes.

Naturally enough the commission of these crimes began to tell upon the public conscience, and the Southern white man, as a tribute to the nineteenth century civilization, was in a manner compelled to give excuses for his barbarism. His excuses have adapted themselves to the emergency, and are aptly outlined by that greatest of all Negroes, Frederick Douglass, in an article of recent date, in which he shows that there have been three distinct eras of Southern barbarism, to account for which three distinct excuses have been made.

The first excuse given to the civilized world for the murder of unoffending Negroes was the necessity of the white man to repress and stamp out alleged "race riots." For years immediately succeeding the war there was an appalling slaughter of colored people, and the wires usually conveyed to northern people and the world the intelligence, first, that an insurrection was being planned by Negroes, which, a few hours later, would prove to have been vigorously resisted by white men, and controlled with a resulting loss of several killed and wounded. It was always a remarkable feature in these insurrections and riots that only Negroes were killed during the rioting, and that all the white men escaped unharmed.

From 1865 to 1872, hundreds of colored men and women were mercilessly murdered and the almost invariable reason assigned was that they met their death by being alleged participants in an insurrection or riot. But this story at last wore itself out. No insurrection ever materialized; no Negro rioter was ever apprehended and proven guilty, and no dynamite ever recorded the black man's protest against oppression and wrong. It was too much to ask thoughtful people to believe this transparent story, and the southern white people at last made up their minds that some other excuse must be had.

Then came the second excuse, which had its birth during the turbulent times of reconstruction. By an amendment to the Constitution the Negro was given the right of franchise, and, theoretically at least, his ballot became his invaluable emblem of citizenship. In a government "of the people, for the people, and by the people," the Negro's vote became an important factor in all matters of state and national politics. But this did not last long. The southern white man would not consider that the Negro had any right which a white man was bound to respect, and the idea of a republican form of government in the southern states grew into general contempt. It was maintained that "This is a white man's government," and regardless of numbers the white man should rule. "No Negro domination" became the new legend on the sanguinary banner of the sunny South, and under it rode the Ku Klux Klan, the Regulators, and the lawless mobs, which for any cause chose to murder one man or a dozen as suited their purpose best. It was a long, gory campaign; the blood chills and the heart almost loses faith in Christianity when one thinks of Yazoo, Hamburg, Edgefield, Copiah, and the countless massacres of defenseless Negroes, whose only crime was the attempt to exercise their right to vote.

But it was a bootless strife for colored people. The government which had made the Negro a citizen found itself unable to protect him. It gave him the right to vote, but denied him the protection which should have maintained that right. Scourged from his home; hunted through the swamps; hung by midnight raiders, and openly murdered in the light of day, the Negro clung to his right of franchise with a heroism which would have wrung admiration from the hearts of savages. He believed that in that small white ballot there was a subtle something which stood for manhood as well as citizenship, and thousands of brave black men went to their graves, exemplifying the one by dying for the other.

The white man's victory soon became complete by fraud, violence, intimidation and murder. The franchise vouchsafed to the Negro grew to be a "barren ideality," and regardless of numbers, the colored people found themselves voiceless in the councils of those whose duty it was to rule. With no longer the fear of "Negro Domination" before their eyes, the white man's second excuse became valueless. With the Southern governments all subverted and the Negro actually eliminated from all participation in state and national elections, there could be no longer an excuse for killing Negroes to prevent "Negro Domination."

Brutality still continued; Negroes were whipped, scourged, exiled, shot and hung whenever and wherever it pleased the white man so to treat them, and as the civilized world with increasing persistency held the white people of the South to account for its outlawry, the murderers invented the third excuse—that Negroes had to be killed to avenge their assaults upon women. There could be framed no possible excuse more harmful to the Negro and more unanswerable if true in its sufficiency for the white man. Humanity abhors the assailant of womanhood, and this charge upon the Negro at once placed him beyond the pale of human sympathy. With such unanimity, earnestness and apparent candor was this charge made and reiterated that the world has accepted the story that the Negro is a monster which the Southern white man has painted him. And to-day, the Christian world feels, that while lynching is a crime, and lawlessness and anarchy the certain precursors of a nation's fall, it can not by word or deed, extend sympathy or help to a race of outlaws, who might mistake their plea for justice and deem it an excuse for their continued wrongs.

The Negro has suffered much and is willing to suffer more. He recognizes that the wrongs of two centuries can not be righted in a day, and he tries to bear his burden with patience for to-day and be hopeful for to-morrow. But there comes a time when the veriest worm will turn, and the Negro feels to-day that after all the work he has done, all the sacrifices he has made, and all the suffering he has endured, if he did not, now, defend his name and manhood from this vile accusation, he would be unworthy even of the contempt of mankind. It is to this charge he now feels he must make answer.

If the Southern people in defense of their lawlessness, would tell the truth and admit that colored men and women are lynched for almost any offense, from murder to a misdemeanor, there would not now be the necessity for this defense. But when they intentionally, maliciously and constantly belie the record and bolster up these falsehoods by the words of legislators, preachers, governors and bishops, then the Negro must give to the world his side of the awful story.

A word as to the charge itself. In considering the third reason assigned by the Southern white people for the butchery of blacks, the question must be asked, what the white man means when he charges the black man with rape. Does he mean the crime which the statutes of the civilized states describe as such? Not by any means. With the Southern white man, any mesalliance existing between a white woman and a colored man is a sufficient foundation for the charge of rape. The Southern white man says that it is impossible for a voluntary alliance to exist between a white woman and a colored man, and therefore, the fact of an alliance is a proof of force. In numerous instances where colored men have been lynched on the charge of rape, it was positively known at the time of lynching, and indisputably proven after the victim's death, that the relationship sustained between the man and woman was voluntary and clandestine, and that in no court of law could even the charge of assault have been successfully maintained.

It was for the assertion of this fact, in the defense of her own race, that the writer hereof became an exile; her property destroyed and her return to her home forbidden under penalty of death, for writing the following editorial which was printed in her paper, the Free Speech, in Memphis, Tenn., May 21, 1892:

"Eight Negroes lynched since last issue of the 'Free Speech' one at Little Rock, Ark., last Saturday morning where the citizens broke (?) into the penitentiary and got their man; three near Anniston, Ala., one near New Orleans; and three at Clarksville, Ga., the last three for killing a white man, and five on the same old racket—the new alarm about raping white women. The same programme of hanging, then shooting bullets into the lifeless bodies was carried out to the letter. Nobody in this section of the country believes the old threadbare lie that Negro men rape white women. If Southern white men are not careful, they will over-reach themselves and public sentiment will have a reaction; a conclusion will then be reached which will be very damaging to the moral reputation of their women."

But threats cannot suppress the truth, and while the Negro suffers the soul deformity, resultant from two and a half centuries of slavery, he is no more guilty of this vilest of all vile charges than the white man who would blacken his name.

During all the years of slavery, no such charge was ever made, not even during the dark days of the rebellion, when the white man, following the fortunes of war went to do battle for the maintenance of slavery. While the master was away fighting to forge the fetters upon the slave, he left his wife and children with no protectors save the Negroes themselves. And yet during those years of trust and peril, no Negro proved recreant to his trust and no white man returned to a home that had been dispoiled.

Likewise during the period of alleged "insurrection," and alarming "race riots," it never occurred to the white man, that his wife and children were in danger of assault. Nor in the Reconstruction era, when the hue and cry was against "Negro Domination," was there ever a thought that the domination would ever contaminate a fireside or strike to death the virtue of womanhood. It must appear strange indeed, to every thoughtful and candid man, that more than a quarter of a century elapsed before the Negro began to show signs of such infamous degeneration.

In his remarkable apology for lynching, Bishop Haygood,[2] of Georgia, says: "No race, not the most savage, tolerates the rape of woman, but it may be said without reflection upon any other people that the Southern people are now and always have been most sensitive concerning the honor of their women—their mothers, wives, sisters and daughters." It is not the purpose of this defense to say one word against the white women of the South. Such need not be said, but it is their misfortune that the chivalrous white men of that section, in order to escape the deserved execration of the civilized world, should shield themselves by their cowardly and infamously false excuse, and call into question that very honor about which their distinguished priestly apologist claims they are most sensitive. To justify their own barbarism they assume a chivalry which they do not possess. True chivalry respects all womanhood, and no one who reads the record, as it is written in the faces of the million mulattoes in the South, will for a minute conceive that the southern white man had a very chivalrous regard for the honor due the women of his own race or respect for the womanhood which circumstances placed in his power. That chivalry which is "most sensitive concerning the honor of women" can hope for but little respect from the civilized world, when it confines itself entirely to the women who happen to be white. Virtue knows no color line, and the chivalry which depends upon complexion of skin and texture of hair can command no honest respect.

When emancipation came to the Negroes, there arose in the northern part of the United States an almost divine sentiment among the noblest, purest and best white women of the North, who felt called to a mission to educate and Christianize the millions of southern ex-slaves. From every nook and corner of the North, brave young white women answered that call and left their cultured homes, their happy associations and their lives of ease, and with heroic determination went to the South to carry light and truth to the benighted blacks. It was a heroism no less than that which calls for volunteers for India, Africa and the Isles of the sea. To educate their unfortunate charges; to teach them the Christian virtues and to inspire in them the moral sentiments manifest in their own lives, these young women braved dangers whose record reads more like fiction than fact. They became social outlaws in the South. The peculiar sensitiveness of the southern white men for women, never shed its protecting influence about them.

---

[2]Atticus G. Haygood was president of Emory University when he was named a bishop of the Methodist Church in 1890.

No friendly word from their own race cheered them in their work; no hospitable doors gave them the companionship like that from which they had come. No chivalrous white man doffed his hat in honor or respect. They were "Nigger teachers"—unpardonable offenders in the social ethics of the South, and were insulted, persecuted and ostracised, not by Negroes, but by the white manhood which boasts of its chivalry toward women.

And yet these northern women worked on, year after year, unselfishly, with a heroism which amounted almost to martyrdom. Threading their way through dense forests, working in schoolhouse, in the cabin and in the church, thrown at all times and in all places among the unfortunate and lowly Negroes, whom they had come to find and to serve, these northern women, thousands and thousands of them, have spent more than a quarter of a century in giving to the colored people their splendid lessons for home and heart and soul. Without protection, save that which innocence gives to every good woman, they went about their work, fearing no assault and suffering none. Their chivalrous protectors were hundreds of miles away in their northern homes, and yet they never feared any "great dark faced mobs," they dared night or day to "go beyond their own roof trees." They never complained of assaults, and no mob was ever called into existence to avenge crimes against them. Before the world adjudges the Negro a moral monster, a vicious assailant of womanhood and a menace to the sacred precincts of home, the colored people ask the consideration of the silent record of gratitude, respect, protection and devotion of the millions of the race in the South, to the thousands of northern white women who have served as teachers and missionaries since the war.

The Negro may not have known what chivalry was, but he knew enough to preserve inviolate the womanhood of the South which was entrusted to his hands during the war. The finer sensibilities of his soul may have been crushed out by years of slavery, but his heart was full of gratitude to the white women of the North, who blessed his home and inspired his soul in all these years of freedom. Faithful to his trust in both of these instances, he should now have the impartial ear of the civilized world, when he dares to speak for himself as against the infamy wherewith he stands charged.

It is his regret, that, in his own defense, he must disclose to the world that degree of dehumanizing brutality which fixes upon America the blot of a national crime. Whatever faults and failings other nations may have in their dealings with their own subjects or with other people, no other civilized nation stands condemned before the world with a series of crimes so peculiarly national. It becomes a painful duty of the Negro to reproduce a record which shows that a large portion of the American people avow anarchy, condone murder and defy the contempt of civilization.

These pages are written in no spirit of vindictiveness, for all who give the subject consideration must concede that far too serious is the condition of that civilized government in which the spirit of unrestrained outlawry constantly increases in violence, and casts its blight over a continually growing area of territory. We plead not for the colored people alone, but for all victims of the terrible injustice which puts men and women to death without form of law. During the year 1894, there were 132 persons executed in the United States by due form of law, while in the same year, 197 persons were put to death by mobs who gave the victims no opportunity to make a lawful defense. No comment need be made upon a condition of public sentiment responsible for such alarming results.

The purpose of the pages which follow shall be to give the record which has been made, not by colored men, but that which is the result of compilations made by white men, of reports sent over the civilized world by white men in the South. Out of their own mouths shall the murderers be condemned. For a number of years the Chicago Tribune, admittedly one of the leading journals of America, has made a specialty of the compilation of statistics touching upon lynching. The data compiled by that journal and published to the world January 1st, 1894, up to the present time has not been disputed. In order to be safe from the charge of exaggeration, the incidents hereinafter reported have been confined to those vouched for by the Tribune.

CHAPTER II.   LYNCH LAW STATISTICS

From the record published in the Chicago Tribune, January 1, 1894, the following computation of lynching statistics is made referring only to the colored victims of Lynch Law during the year 1893:

ARSON

Sept. 15, Paul Hill, Carrollton, Ala.; Sept. 15, Paul Archer, Carrollton, Ala.; Sept. 15, William Archer, Carrollton, Ala.; Sept. 15, Emma Fair, Carrollton, Ala.

SUSPECTED ROBBERY

Dec. 23, unknown negro, Fannin, Miss.

ASSAULT

Dec. 25, Calvin Thomas, near Brainbridge, Ga.

ATTEMPTED ASSAULT

Dec. 28, Tillman Green, Columbia, La.

INCENDIARISM

Jan. 26, Patrick Wells, Quincy, Fla.; Feb. 9, Frank Harrell, Dickery, Miss.; Feb. 9, William Filder, Dickery, Miss.

ATTEMPTED RAPE

Feb. 21, Richard Mays, Springville, Mo.; Aug. 14, Dug Hazleton, Carrollton, Ga.; Sept. 1, Judge McNeil, Cadiz, Ky.; Sept. 11, Frank Smith, Newton, Miss.; Sept. 16, William Jackson, Nevada, Mo.; Sept. 19, Riley Gulley, Pine Apple, Ala.; Oct. 9, John Davis, Shorterville, Ala.; Nov. 8, Robert Kennedy, Spartansburg, S.C.

BURGLARY

Feb. 16, Richard Forman, Granada, Miss.

WIFE BEATING

Oct. 14, David Jackson, Covington, La.

ATTEMPTED MURDER

Sept. 21, Thomas Smith, Roanoke, Va.

ATTEMPTED ROBBERY

Dec. 12, four unknown negroes, near Selma, Ala.

RACE PREJUDICE

Jan. 30, Thomas Carr, Kosciusko, Miss.; Feb. 7, William Butler, Hickory Creek, Texas; Aug. 27, Charles Tart, Lyons Station, Miss.; Dec. 7, Robert Greenwood, Cross county, Ark.; July 14, Allen Butler, Lawrenceville, Ill.

THIEVES

Oct. 24, two unknown negroes, Knox Point, La.

ALLEGED BARN BURNING

Nov. 4, Edward Wagner, Lynchburg, Va.; Nov. 4, William Wagner, Lynchburg, Va.; Nov. 4, Samuel Motlow, Lynchburg, Va.; Nov. 4, Eliza Motlow, Lynchburg, Va.

ALLEGED MURDER

Jan. 21, Robert Landry, St. James Parish, La.; Jan. 21, Chicken George, St. James Parish, La.; Jan. 21, Richard Davis, St. James Parish, La.; Dec. 8, Benjamin Menter, Berlin, Ala.; Dec. 8, Robert Wilkins, Berlin, Ala.; Dec. 8, Joseph Gevhens, Berlin, Ala.

ALLEGED COMPLICITY IN MURDER

Sept. 16, Valsin Julian, Jefferson Parish, La.; Sept. 16, Basil Julian, Jefferson Parish, La.; Sept. 16, Paul Julian, Jefferson Parish, La.; Sept. 16, John Willis, Jefferson Parish, La.

MURDER

June 29, Samuel Thorp, Savannah, Ga.; June 29, George S. Riechen, Waynesboro, Ga.; June 30, Joseph Bird, Wilberton, I. T.;[3] July 1, James Lamar, Darien, Ga.; July 28, Henry Miller, Dallas, Texas; July 28, Ada Hiers, Walterboro, S.C.; July 28, Alexander Brown, Bastrop, Texas; July 30, W. G. Jamison, Quincy, Ill.; Sept. 1, John Ferguson, Lawrens, S.C.; Sept. 1, Oscar Johnston, Berkeley, S.C.; Sept. 1, Henry Ewing, Berkeley, S.C.; Sept. 8, William Smith, Camden, Ark.; Sept. 15, Staples Green, Livingston, Ala.; Sept. 29, Hiram Jacobs, Mount Vernon, Ga.; Sept. 29, Lucien Mannet, Mount Vernon, Ga.; Sept. 29, Hire Bevington, Mount Vernon, Ga.; Sept. 29, Weldon Gordon, Mount Vernon, Ga.; Sept. 29, Parse Strickland, Mount Vernon, Ga.; Oct. 20, William Dalton, Cartersville, Ga.; Oct. 27, M. B. Taylor, Wise Court House, Va.; Oct. 27, Isaac Williams, Madison, Ga.; Nov. 10, Miller Davis, Center Point, Ark.; Nov. 14, John Johnston, Auburn, N.Y.

Sept. 27, Calvin Stewart, Langley, S.C.; Sept. 29, Henry Coleman, Benton, La.; Oct. 18, William Richards, Summerfield, Ga.; Oct. 18, James Dickson, Summerfield, Ga.; Oct. 27, Edward Jenkins, Clayton county, Ga.; Nov. 9, Henry Boggs, Fort White, Fla.; Nov. 14, three unknown negroes, Lake City Junction, Fla.; Nov. 14, D. T. Nelson, Varney, Ark.; Nov. 29, Newton Jones, Baxley, Ga.; Dec. 2, Lucius Holt, Concord, Ga.; Dec. 10, two unknown negroes, Richmond, Ala.; July 12,

---

[3] Indian Territory.

Henry Fleming, Columbus, Miss.; July 17, unknown negro, Briar Field, Ala.; July 18, Meredith Lewis, Roseland, La.; July 29, Edward Bill, Dresden, Tenn.; Aug. 1, Henry Reynolds, Montgomery, Tenn.; Aug. 9, unknown negro, McCreery, Ark.; Aug. 12, unknown negro, Brantford, Fla.; Aug. 18, Charles Walton, Morganfield, Ky.; Aug. 21, Charles Tait, near Memphis, Tenn.; Aug. 28, Leonard Taylor, New Castle, Ky.; Sept. 8, Benjamin Jackson, Quincy, Miss.; Sept. 14, John Williams, Jackson, Tenn.

SELF DEFENSE

July 30, unknown negro[,] Wingo, Ky.

POISONING WELLS

Aug. 18, two unknown negroes, Franklin Parish, La.

ALLEGED WELL POISONING

Sept. 15, Benjamin Jackson, Jackson, Miss.; Sept. 15, Mahala Jackson, Jackson, Miss; Sept. 15, Louisa Carter, Jackson, Miss.; Sept. 15, W. A. Haley, Jackson, Miss.; Sept. 15, Rufus Bigley, Jackson, Miss.

INSULTING WHITES

Feb. 18, John Hughes, Moberly, Mo.; June 2, Isaac Lincoln, Fort Madison, S.C.

MURDEROUS ASSAULT

April 20, Daniel Adams, Selina, Kan.

NO OFFENSE

July 21, Charles Martin, Shelby Co., Tenn.; July 30, William Steen, Paris, Miss.; August 31, unknown negro, Yarborough, Tex.; Sept. 30, unknown negro, Houston, Tex.; Dec. 28, Mack Segars, Brantley, Ala.

ALLEGED RAPE

July 7, Charles T. Miller, Bardwell, Ky.; Aug. 10, Daniel Lewis, Waycross, Ga.; Aug. 10, James Taylor, Waycross, Ga.; Aug. 10, John Chambers, Waycross, Ga.

ALLEGED STOCK POISONING

Dec. 16, Henry G. Givens, Nebro, Ky.

SUSPECTED MURDER

Dec. 23, Sloan Allen, West Mississippi.

SUSPICION OF RAPE

Feb. 14, Andy Blount, Chattanooga, Tenn.

TURNING STATE'S EVIDENCE

Dec. 19, William Ferguson, Adele, Ga.

RAPE

Jan. 19, James Williams, Pickens Co., Ala.; Feb. 11, unknown negro, Forest Hill, Tenn.; Feb. 26, Joseph Hayne, or Paine, Jellico, Tenn.; Nov. 1, Abner Anthony, Hot Springs, Va.; Nov. 1, Thomas Hill, Spring Place, Ga.; April 24, John Peterson, Denmark, S.C.; May 6, Samuel Gaillard, ——, S.C.; May 10, Haywood Banks, or Marksdale, Columbia, S.C.; May 12, Israel Halliway, Napoleonville, La.; May 12, unknown negro, Wytheville, Va.; May 31, John Wallace, Jefferson Springs, Ark.; June 3, Samuel Bush, Decatur, Ill.; June 8, L. C. Dumas, Gleason, Tenn.; June 13, William Shorter, Winchester, Va.; June 14, George Williams, near Waco, Tex.; June 24, Daniel Edwards, Selina or Selma, Ala.; June 27, Ernest Murphy, Daleville, Ala.; July 6, unknown negro, Poplar Head, La.; July 6, unknown negro, Poplar Head, La.; July 12, Robert Larkin, Oscola, Tex.; July 17, Warren Dean, Stone Creek, Ga.; July 21, unknown negro, Brantford, Fla.; July 17, John Cotton, Connersville, Ark.; July 22, Lee Walker, New Albany, Miss.; July 26, —— Handy, Suansea, S.C.; July 30, William Thompson, Columbia, S.C.; July 28, Isaac Harper, Calera, Ala.; July 30, Thomas Preston, Columbia, S.C.; July 30, Handy Kaigler, Columbia, S.C.; Aug. 13, Monroe Smith, Springfield, Ala.; Aug. 19, negro tramp, near Paducah, Ky.; Aug. 21, John Nilson, near Leavenworth, Kan.; Aug. 23, Jacob Davis, Green Wood, S.C.; Sept. 2, William Arkinson, McKenney, Ky.; Sept. 16, unknown negro, Centerville, Ala.; Sept. 16, Jessie Mitchell, Amelia C. H., Va.; Sept 25, Perry Bratcher, New Boston, Tex.; Oct. 9, William Lacey, Jasper, Ala.; Oct. 22, John Gamble. Pikesville, Tenn.

OFFENSES CHARGED ARE AS FOLLOWS

Rape, 39; attempted rape, 8; alleged rape, 4; suspicion of rape, 1; murder, 44; alleged murder, 6; alleged complicity in murder, 4; murderous assault, 1; attempted murder, 1; attempted robbery, 4; arson, 4; incendiarism, 3; alleged stock poisoning, 1; poisoning wells, 2; alleged poisoning wells, 5; burglary, 1; wife beating, 1; self defense, 1; suspected robbery, 1; assault and battery, 1; insulting whites, 2; malpractice, 1; alleged barn burning, 4; stealing, 2; unknown offense, 4; no offense, 1; race prejudice, 4; total, 159.

LYNCHINGS BY STATES

Alabama, 25; Arkansas, 7; Florida, 7; Georgia, 24; Indian Territory, 1; Illinois, 3; Kansas, 2; Kentucky, 8; Louisiana, 18; Mississippi, 17; Missouri, 3; New York, 1; South Carolina, 15; Tennessee, 10; Texas, 8; Virginia, 10.

RECORD FOR THE YEAR 1892

While it is intended that the record here presented shall include specially the lynchings of 1893, it will not be amiss to give the record for the year preceding. The facts contended for will always appear manifest—that not one-third of the victims lynched were charged with rape, and further that the charges made embraced a range of offenses from murders to misdemeanors.

In 1892 there were 241 persons lynched. The entire number is divided among the following states:

Alabama, 22; Arkansas, 25; California, 3; Florida, 11; Georgia, 17; Idaho, 8; Illinois, 1; Kansas, 3; Kentucky, 9; Louisiana, 29; Maryland, 1; Mississippi, 16; Missouri, 6; Montana, 4; New York, 1; North Carolina, 5; North Dakota, 1; Ohio, 3; South Carolina, 5; Tennessee, 28; Texas, 15; Virginia, 7; West Virginia, 5; Wyoming, 9; Arizona Territory, 3; Oklahoma, 2.

Of this number 160 were of Negro descent. Four of them were lynched in New York, Ohio and Kansas; the remainder were murdered in the South. Five of this number were females. The charges for which they were lynched cover a wide range. They are as follows:

Rape, 46; murder, 58; rioting, 3; race prejudice, 6; no cause given, 4; incendiarism, 6; robbery, 6; assault and battery, 1; attempted rape, 11; suspected robbery, 4; larceny, 1; self defense, 1; insulting women, 2; desperadoes, 6; fraud, 1; attempted murder, 2; no offense stated, boy and girl, 2.

In the case of the boy and girl above referred to, their father, named Hastings, was accused of the murder of a white man; his fourteen-year-old daughter and sixteen-year-old son were hanged and their bodies filled with bullets, then the father was also lynched. This was in November, 1892, at Jonesville, Louisiana.

CHAPTER III. LYNCHING IMBECILES

(An Arkansas Butchery)

The only excuse which capital punishment attempts to find is upon the theory that the criminal is past the power of reformation and his life is a constant menace to the community. If, however, he is mentally unbalanced, irresponsible for his acts, there can be no more inhuman act conceived of than the wilful sacrifice of his life. So thoroughly is that principle grounded in the law, that all civilized society surrounds human life with a safeguard, which prevents the execution of a criminal who is insane, even if sane at the time of his criminal act. Should he become insane after its commission the law steps in and protects him during the period of his insanity. But Lynch Law has no such regard for human life. Assuming for itself an absolute supremacy over the law of the land, it has time and again dyed its hands in the blood of men who were imbeciles. Two or three noteworthy cases will suffice to show with what inhuman ferocity irresponsible men have been put to death by this system of injustice.

An instance occurred during the year 1892 in Arkansas, a report of which is given in full in the Arkansas Democrat, published at Little Rock, in that state, on the 11th day of February of that year. The paper mentioned is perhaps one of the leading weeklies in that state and the account given in detail has every mark of a careful and conscientious investigation. The victims of this tragedy were a colored man, named Hamp Biscoe, his wife and a thirteen year-old son. Hamp Biscoe, it appears, was a hard working, thrifty farmer, who lived near England, Arkansas, upon a small farm with his family. The investigation of the tragedy was conducted by a resident of Arkansas named R. B. Carlee, a white man, who furnished the account to the Arkansas Democrat over his own signature. He says the original trouble which led to the lynching was a quarrel between Biscoe and a white man about a debt. About six years after Biscoe pre-empted his land, a white man made a demand of $100 upon him for services in showing him the land and making the sale. Biscoe denied the service and refused to pay the demand. The white man, however, brought suit, obtained judgment for the hundred dollars and Biscoe's farm was sold to pay the judgment.

The suit, judgment and subsequent legal proceedings appear to have driven Biscoe almost crazy and brooding over his wrongs he grew to be a confirmed imbecile. He would allow but few men[,] white or colored, to come upon his place, as he suspected every stranger to be planning to steal his farm. A week preceding the tragedy, a white man named Venable, whose farm adjoined Biscoe's, let down the fence and proceeded to drive through Biscoe's field. The latter saw him; grew very excited, cursed him and drove him from his farm with bitter oaths and violent threats. Venable went away and secured a warrant for Biscoe's arrest. This warrant was placed in the hands of a constable named John Ford, who took a colored deputy and two white men out to Biscoe's farm to make the arrest. When they arrived at the house Biscoe refused to be arrested and warned them he would shoot if they persisted in their attempt to arrest him. The warning was unheeded by Ford, who entered upon the premises, when Biscoe, true to his word, fired upon him. The load tore a part of his clothes from his body, one shot going through his arm and entering his breast. After he had fallen, Ford drew his revolver and shot Biscoe in the head and his wife through the arm. The Negro deputy then began firing and struck Biscoe in the small of the back. Ford's wound was not dangerous and in a few days he was able to be around again. Biscoe, however, was so severely shot that he was unable to stand after the firing was over.

Two other white men hearing the exchange of shots went to the rescue of the officers, forced open the door of Biscoe's cabin and arrested him, his wife and thirteen-year-old son, and took them, together with a babe at the breast, to a small frame house near the depot and put them under guard. The subsequent proceedings were briefly told by Mr. Carlee in the columns of the Arkansas Democrat above mentioned, from whose account the following excerpt is taken:

"It was rumored here that the Negroes were to be lynched that night, but I do not think it was generally credited, as it was not believed that Ford was greatly hurt and the Negro was held to be fatally injured and crazy at that. But that night, about 8 o'clock, a party of perhaps twelve or fifteen men, a number of whom were known to the guards, came to the house and told the Negro guards they would take care of the prisoners now, and for them to leave; as they did not obey at once they were persuaded to leave with words that did not admit of delay.

"The woman began to cry and said, 'You intend to kill us to get our money.' They told her to hush (she was heavy with child and had a child at her breast) as they intended to give her a nice present. The guards heard no more, but hastened to a Negro church near by and urged the preacher to go up and stop the mob. A few minutes after, the shooting began, perhaps about forty shots being fired. The white men then left rapidly and the Negroes went to the house. Hamp Biscoe and his wife were killed, the baby had a slight wound across the upper lip; the boy was still alive and lived until after midnight, talking rationally and telling who did the shooting.

"He said when they came in and shot his father, he attempted to run out of doors and a young man shot him in the bowels and that he fell. He saw another man shoot his mother and a taller young man, whom he did not know, shoot his father. After they had killed them, the young man who had shot his mother pulled off her stockings and took $220 in currency that she had hid there. The men then came to the door where the boy was lying and one of them turned him over and put his pistol to his breast and shot him again. This is the story the dying boy told as near as I can get it. It is quite singular that the guards and those who had conversed with him were not required to testify. The woman was known to have the money as she had exposed it that day. She also had $36 in silver, which the plunderer of the body did not get. The Negro was undoubtedly insane and had been for several years. The citizens of this community condemn the murder and have no sympathy with it. The Negro was a well to do farmer, but had become crazed because he was convinced some plot had been made to steal his land and only a few days ago declared that he expected to die in defense of his home in a short time and he did not care how soon. The killing of a woman with the child at her breast and in her condition, and also a young boy, was extremely brutal. As for Hamp Biscoe he was dangerous and should long have been confined in the insane asylum. Such were the facts as near as I can get them and you can use them as you see fit, but I would prefer you would suppress the names charged by the Negroes with the killing."

Perhaps the civilized world will think, that with all these facts laid before the public, by a writer who signs his name to his communication, in a land where grand juries are sworn to investigate, where judges and juries are sworn to administer the law and sheriffs are paid to execute the decrees of the courts, and where, in fact, every instrument of civilization is supposed to work for the common good of all citizens, that this matter was duly investigated, the criminals apprehended and the punishment meted out to the murderers. But this is a mistake; nothing of the kind was done or attempted. Six months after the publication, above referred to, an investigator, writing to find out what had been done in the matter, received the following reply:

OFFICE OF
S. S. GLOVER,
SHERIFF AND COLLECTOR,
LONOKE COUNTY.

Lonoke, Ark., 9-12-1892.

Geo. Washington, Esq.,
Chicago, Ill.

DEAR SIR:—The parties who killed Hamp Briscoe February the 9th, have never been arrested. The parties are still in the county. It was done by some of the citizens, and those who know will not tell.

S. S. GLOVER, Sheriff.

Thus acts the mob with the victim of its fury, conscious that it will never be called to an account. Not only is this true, but the moral support of those who are chosen by the people to execute the law, is frequently given to the support of lawlessness and mob violence. The press and even the pulpit, in the main either by silence or open apology, have condoned and encouraged this state of anarchy.

Tortured and Burned in Texas

Never in the history of civilization has any Christian people stooped to such shocking brutality and indescribable barbarism as that which characterized the people of Paris, Texas, and adjacent communities on the 1st of February, 1893. The cause of this awful outbreak of human passion was the murder of a four year old child, daughter of a man named Vance. This man, Vance, had been a police officer in Paris for years, and was known to be a man of bad temper, overbearing manner and given to harshly treating the prisoners under his care. He had arrested Smith and, it is said, cruelly mistreated him. Whether or not the murder of his child was an act of fiendish revenge, it has not been shown, but many persons who know of the incident have suggested that the secret of the attack on the child lay in a desire for revenge against its father.

In the same town there lived a Negro, named Henry Smith, a well known character, a kind of roustabout, who was generally considered a harmless, weak-minded fellow, not capable of doing any important work, but sufficiently able to do chores and odd jobs around the houses of the white people who cared to employ him. A few days before the final tragedy, this man, Smith, was accused of murdering Myrtle Vance. The crime of murder was of itself bad enough, and to prove that against Smith would have been amply sufficient in Texas to have committed him to the gallows, but the finding of the child so exasperated the father and his friends, that they at once shamefully exaggerated the facts and declared that the babe had been ruthlessly assaulted and then killed. The truth was bad enough, but the white people of the community made it a point to exaggerate every detail of the awful affair, and to inflame the public mind so that nothing less than immediate and violent death would satisfy the populace. As a matter of fact, the child was not brutally assaulted as the world has been told in excuse for the awful barbarism of that day. Persons who saw the child after its death, have stated, under the most solemn pledge to truth, that there was no evidence of such an assault as was published at that time, only a slight abrasion and discoloration was noticeable and that mostly about the neck. In spite of this fact, so eminent a man as Bishop Haygood[4] deliberately and, it must also appear, maliciously falsified the fact by stating that the child was torn limb from limb, or to quote his own words, "First outraged with demoniacal cruelty and then taken by her heels and torn asunder in the mad wantonness of gorilla ferocity."

Nothing is farther from the truth than that statement. It is a cold blooded, deliberate, brutal falsehood which this Christian (?) Bishop uses to bolster up the infamous plea that the people of Paris were driven to insanity by learning that the little child had been viciously assaulted, choked to death, and then torn to pieces by a demon in human form. It was a brutal murder, but no more brutal than hundreds of murders which occur in this country, and which have been equalled every year in fiendishness and brutality, and for which the death penalty is prescribed by law and inflicted only after the person has been legally adjudged guilty of the crime. Those who knew Smith, believe that Vance had at some time given him cause to seek revenge and that this fearful crime was the outgrowth of his attempt to avenge himself of some real or fancied wrong. That the murderer was known as an imbecile, had no effect whatever upon the people who thirsted for his blood. They determined to make an example of him and proceeded to carry out their purpose with unspeakably greater ferocity than that which characterized the half crazy object of their revenge.

For a day or so after the child was found in the woods, Smith remained in the vicinity as if nothing had happened, and when finally

[4]See note p. 80.

becoming aware that he was suspected, he made an attempt to escape. He was apprehended, however, not far from the scene of his crime and the news flashed across the country that the white Christian people of Paris, Texas and the communities thereabout had deliberately determined to lay aside all forms of law and inaugurate an entirely new form of punishment for the murder. They absolutely refused to make any inquiry as to the sanity or insanity of their prisoner, but set the day and hour when in the presence of assembled thousands they put their helpless victim to the stake, tortured him, and then burned him to death for the delectation and satisfaction of Christian people.

Lest it might be charged that any description of the deeds of that day are exaggerated, a white man's description which was published in the white journals of this country is used. The New York Sun of February 2d, 1893, contains an account, from which we make the following excerpt:

PARIS, Tex., Feb. 1, 1893.—Henry Smith, the negro ravisher of 4-year-old Myrtle Vance, has expiated in part his awful crime by death at the stake. Ever since the perpetration of his awful crime this city and the entire surrounding country has been in a wild frenzy of excitement. When the news came last night that he had been captured at Hope, Ark., that he had been identified by B. B. Sturgeon, James T. Hicks, and many other of the Paris searching party, the city was wild with joy over the apprehension of the brute. Hundreds of people poured into the city from the adjoining country and the word passed from lip to lip that the punishment of the fiend should fit the crime— that death by fire was the penalty Smith should pay for the most atrocious murder and terrible outrage in Texas history. Curious and sympathizing alike, they came on train and wagons, on horse, and on foot to see if the frail mind of a man could think of a way to sufficiently punish the perpetrator of so terrible a crime. Whisky shops were closed, unruly mobs were dispersed, schools were dismissed by a proclamation from the mayor, and everything was done in a business-like manner.

Meeting of Citizens

About 2 o'clock Friday a mass meeting was called at the courthouse and captains appointed to search for the child. She was found mangled beyond recognition, covered with leaves and brush as above mentioned. As soon as it was learned upon the recovery of the body that the crime was so atrocious the whole town turned out in the chase. The railroads put up bulletins offering free transportation to all who would join in the search. Posses went in every direction, and not a stone was left unturned. Smith was tracked to Detroit on foot, where he jumped on a freight train and left for his old home in Hempstead county, Arkansas. To this county he was tracked and yesterday captured at Clow, a flag station on the Arkansas & Louisiana railway about twenty miles north of Hope. Upon being questioned the fiend denied everything, but upon being stripped for examination his undergarments were seen to be spattered with blood and a part of his shirt was torn off. He was kept under heavy guard at Hope last night, and later on confessed the crime.

This morning he was brought through Texarkana, where 5,000 people awaited the train, anxious to see a man who had received the fate of Ed. Coy. At that place speeches were made by prominent Paris citizens, who asked that the prisoner be not molested by Texarkana people, but that the guard be allowed to deliver him up to the outraged and indignant citizens of Paris. Along the road the train gathered strength from the various towns, the people crowded upon the platforms and tops of coaches anxious to see the lynching and the negro who was soon to be delivered to an infuriated mob.

Burned at the Stake

Arriving here at 12 o'clock the train was met by a surging mass of humanity 10,000 strong. The negro was placed upon a carnival float in mockery of a king upon his throne, and, followed by an immense crowd, was escorted through the city so that all might see the most inhuman monster known in current history. The line of march was up Main street to the square, around the square down Clarksville street to Church street, thence to the open prairies about 300 yards from the Texas & Pacific depot. Here Smith was placed upon a scaffold, six feet square and ten feet high, securely bound, within the view of all beholders. Here the victim was tortured for fifty minutes by red-hot iron brands thrust against his quivering body. Commencing at the feet the brands were placed against him inch by inch until they were thrust against the face. Then, being apparently dead, kerosene was poured upon him, cottonseed hulls placed beneath him and set on fire. In less time than it takes to relate it, the tortured man was wafted beyond the grave to another fire, hotter and more terrible than the one just experienced.

Curiosity seekers have carried away already all that was left of the memorable event, even to pieces of charcoal. The cause of the crime was that Henry Vance when a deputy policeman, in the course of his duty was called to arrest Henry Smith for being drunk and disorderly. The Negro was unruly, and Vance was forced to use his club. The Negro swore vengeance, and several times assaulted Vance. In his greed for revenge, last Thursday, he grabbed up the little girl and committed the crime. The father is prostrated with grief and the mother now lies at death's door, but she has lived to see the slayer of her innocent babe suffer the most horrible death that could be conceived.

Torture beyond Description

Words to describe the awful torture inflicted upon Smith cannot be found. The Negro, for a long time after starting on the journey to Paris, did not realize his plight. At last when he was told that he must die by slow torture he begged for protection. His agony was awful. He pleaded and writhed in bodily and mental pain. Scarcely had the train reached Paris than this torture commenced. His clothes were torn off piecemeal and scattered in the crowd, people catching the shreds and putting them away as mementos. The child's father, her brother, and two uncles then gathered about the Negro as he lay fastened to the torture platform and thrust hot irons into his quivering flesh. It was horrible—the man dying by slow torture in the midst of smoke from his own burning flesh. Every groan from the fiend, every contortion of his body was cheered by the thickly packed crowd of 10,000 persons. The mass of beings 600 yards in diameter, the scaffold being the center. After burning the feet and legs, the hot irons—plenty of fresh ones being at hand—were rolled up and down Smith's stomach, back, and arms. Then the eyes were burned out and irons were thrust down his throat.

The men of the Vance family having wreaked vengeance, the crowd piled all kinds of combustible stuff around the scaffold, poured oil on it and set it afire. The Negro rolled and tossed out of the mass, only to be pushed back by the people nearest him. He tossed out again, and was roped and pulled back. Hundreds of people turned away, but the vast crowd still looked calmly on. People were here from every part of this section. They came from Dallas, Fort Worth, Sherman, Denison, Bonham, Texarkana, Fort Smith, Ark., and a party of fifteen came from Hempstead county, Arkansas, where he was captured. Every train that came in was loaded to its utmost capacity, and there were demands at many points for special trains to bring the people here to see the unparalleled punishment for an unparalleled crime. When the news of the burning went over the country like wildfire, at every country town anvils boomed forth the announcement.

Should Have Been in an Asylum

It may not be amiss in connection with this awful affair, in proof of our assertion that Smith was an imbecile, to give the testimony of a well known colored minister, who lived at Paris, Texas, at the time of the lynching. He was a witness of the awful scenes there enacted, and attempted, in the name of God and humanity, to interfere in the programme. He barely escaped with his life, was driven out of the city and became an exile because of his actions. Reverend King was in New York about the middle of February, and he was there interviewed for a daily paper for that city, and we quote his account as an eye witness of the affair. Said he:

"I was ridden out of Paris on a rail because I was the only man in Lamar county to raise my voice against the lynching of Smith. I opposed the illegal measures before the arrival of Henry Smith as a prisoner, and I was warned that I might meet his fate if I was not careful; but the sense of justice made me bold, and when I saw the poor wretch trembling with fear, and got so near him that I could hear his teeth chatter, I determined to stand by him to the last.

"I hated him for his crime, but two crimes do not make a virtue; and in the brief conversation I had with Smith I was more firmly convinced than ever that he was irresponsible.

"I had known Smith for years, and there were times when Smith was out of his head for weeks. Two years ago I made an effort to have him put in an asylum, but the white people were trying to fasten the murder of a young colored girl upon him, and would not listen. For days before the murder of the little Vance girl, Smith was out of his head and dangerous. He had just undergone an attack of delirium tremens and was in no condition to be allowed at large. He realized his condition, for I spoke with him not three weeks ago, and in answer to my exhortations, he promised to reform. The next time I saw him was on the day of his execution.

" 'Drink did it! drink did it;' he sobbed. Then bowing his face in his hands, he asked: 'Is it true, did I kill her? Oh, my God, my God!' For a moment he seemed to forget the awful fate that awaited him, and his body swayed to and fro with grief. Some one seized me by the shoulder and hurled me back, and Smith fell writhing to the ground in terror as four men seized his arms to drag him to the float on which he was to be exhibited before he was finally burned at the stake.

"I followed the procession and wept aloud as I saw little children of my own race follow the unfortunate man and taunt him with jeers. Even at the stake, children of both sexes and colors gathered in groups, and when the father of the murdered child raised the hissing iron with which he was about to torture the helpless victim, the children became as frantic as the grown people and struggled forward to obtain places of advantage.

"It was terrible. One little tot scarcely older than little Myrtle Vance clapped her baby hands as her father held her on his shoulders above the heads of the people.

" 'For God's sake,' I shouted, 'send the children home.'

" 'No, no,' shouted a hundred maddened voices; 'let them learn a lesson.'

"I love children, but as I looked about the little faces distorted with passion and the bloodshot eyes of the cruel parents who held them high in their arms, I thanked God that I have none of my own.

"As the hot iron sank deep into poor Henry's flesh a hideous yell rent the air, and, with a sound as terrible as the cry of lost souls on judgment day, 20,000 maddened people took up the victim's cry of agony and a prolonged howl of maddened glee rent the air.

"No one was himself now. Every man, woman and child in that awful crowd was worked up to a greater frenzy than that which actuated Smith's horrible crime. The people were capable of any new atrocity now, and as Smith's yells became more and more frequent, it was difficult to hold the crowd back, so anxious were the savages to participate in the sickening tortures.

"For half an hour I tried to pray as the beads of agony rolled down my forehead and bathed my face.

"For an instant a hush spread over the people. I could stand no more, and with a superhuman effort dashed through the compact mass of humanity and stood at the foot of the burning scaffold.

" 'In the name of God,' I cried, 'I command you to cease this torture.'

"The heavy butt of a Winchester rifle descended on my head and I fell to the ground. Rough hands seized me and angry men bore me away, and I was thankful.

"At the outskirts of the crowd I was attacked again, and then several men, no doubt glad to get away from the fearful place, escorted me to my home, where I was allowed to take a small amount of clothing. A jeering crowd gathered without, and when I appeared at the door ready hands seized me and I was placed upon a rail, and, with curses and oaths, taken to the railway station and placed upon a train. As the train moved out some one thrust a roll of bills into my hand and said, 'God bless you, but it was no use.' "

When asked if he should ever return to Paris, Mr. King said: "I shall never go south again. The impressions of that awful day will stay with me forever."

CHAPTER IV.　LYNCHING OF INNOCENT MEN

(Lynched on Account of Relationship)

If no other reason appealed to the sober sense of the American people to check the growth of Lynch Law, the absolute unreliability and reck-lessness of the mob in inflicting punishment for crimes done, should do so. Several instances of this spirit have occurred in the year past. In Louisiana, near New Orleans, in July, 1893, Roselius Julian, a colored man, shot and killed a white judge, named Victor Estopinal. The cause of the shooting has never been definitely ascertained. It is claimed that the Negro resented an insult to his wife, and the killing of the white man was an act of a Negro (who dared) to defend his home. The judge was killed in the court house, and Julian, heavily armed, made his escape to the swamps near the city. He has never been appre-hended, nor has any information ever been gleaned as to his where-abouts. A mob determined to secure the fugitive murderer and burn him alive. The swamps were hunted through and through in vain, when, being unable to wreak their revenge upon the murderer, the mob turned its attention to his unfortunate relatives. Dispatches from New Orleans, dated September 19, 1893, described the affair as fol-lows:

"Posses were immediately organized and the surrounding country was scoured, but the search was fruitless so far as the real criminal was concerned. The mother, three brothers and two sisters of the Negro were arrested yesterday at the Black Ridge in the rear of the city by the police and taken to the little jail on Judge Estopinal's place about Southport, because of the belief that they were succoring the fugitive.

"About 11 o'clock twenty-five men, some armed with rifles and shotguns, came up to the jail. They unlocked the door and held a conference among themselves as to what they should do. Some were in favor of hanging the five, while others insisted that only two of the brothers should be strung up. This was finally agreed to, and the two doomed negroes were hurried to a pasture one hundred yards distant, and there asked to take their last chance of saving their lives by making a confession, but the Negroes made no reply. They were then told to kneel down and pray. One did so, the other remained standing, but both prayed fervently. The taller Negro was then hoisted up. The shorter Negro stood gazing at the horrible death of his brother without flinching. Five minutes later he was also hanged. The mob decided to take the remaining brother out to Camp Parapet and hang him there. The other two were to be taken out and flogged, with an order to get out of the parish in less than half an hour. The third brother, Paul, was taken out to the camp, which is about a mile distant in the interior, and there he was hanged to a tree."

Another young man, who was in no way related to Julian, who perhaps did not even know the man and who was entirely innocent of any offense in connection therewith, was murdered by the same mob. The same paper says:

"During the search for Julian on Saturday one branch of the posse visited the house of a Negro family in the neighborhood of Camp Parapet, and failing to find the object of their search, tried to induce John Willis, a young Negro, to disclose the whereabouts of Julian. He refused to do so, or could not do so, and was kicked to death by the gang."

An Indiana Case

Almost equal to the ferocity of the mob which killed the three brothers, Julian and the unoffending, John Willis, because of the murder of Judge Estopinal, was the action of a mob near Vincennes, Ind. In this case a wealthy colored man, named Allen Butler, who was well known in the community, and enjoyed the confidence and respect of the entire country, was made the victim of a mob and hung because his son had become unduly intimate with a white girl who was a servant around his house. There was no pretense that the facts were otherwise than as here stated. The woman lived at Butler's house as a servant, and she and Butler's son fell in love with each other, and later it was found that the girl was in a delicate condition. It was claimed, but with how much truth no one has ever been able to tell, that the father had procured an abortion, or himself had operated on the girl, and that she had left the house to go back to her home. It was never claimed that the father was in any way responsible for the action of his son, but the authorities procured the arrest of both father and son, and at the preliminary examination the father gave bail to appear before the Grand Jury when it should convene. On the same night, however, the mob took the matter in hand and with the intention of hanging the son. It assembled near Sumner, while the boy, who had been unable to give bail, was lodged in jail at Lawrenceville. As it was impossible to reach Lawrenceville and hang the son, the leaders of the mob concluded they would go to Butler's house and hang him. Butler was found at his home, taken out by the mob and hung to a tree. This was in the law-abiding state of Indiana, which furnished the United States its last president and which claims all the honor, pride and glory of northern civilization. None of the leaders of the mob were apprehended, and no steps whatever were taken to bring the murderers to justice.

Killed for His Stepfather's Crime

An account has been given of the cremation of Henry Smith, at Paris, Texas, for the murder of the infant child of a man named Vance. It would appear that human ferocity was not sated when it vented itself upon a human being by burning his eyes out, by thrusting a red hot iron down his throat, and then by burning his body to ashes. Henry Smith, the victim of these savage orgies, was beyond all the power of torture, but a few miles outside of Paris, some members of the community concluded that it would be proper to kill a stepson named William Butler as a partial penalty for the original crime. This young man, against whom no word has ever been said, and who was in fact an orderly, peaceable boy, had been watched with the severest scrutiny by members of the mob who believed he knew something of the whereabouts of Smith. He declared from the very first that he did not know where his stepfather was, which statement was well proven to be a fact after the discovery of Smith in Arkansas, whence he had fled through swamps and woods and unfrequented places. Yet Butler was apprehended, placed under arrest, and on the night of February 6th, taken out on Hickory Creek, five miles southeast of Paris, and hung for his stepfather's crime. After his body was suspended in the air, the mob filled it with bullets.

Lynched Because the Jury Acquitted Him

The entire system of the judiciary of this country is in the hands of white people. To this add the fact of the inherent prejudice against colored people, and it will be clearly seen that a white jury is certain to find a Negro prisoner guilty if there is the least evidence to warrant such a finding.

Meredith Lewis was arrested in Roseland, La., in July of last year. A white jury found him not guilty of the crime of murder wherewith he stood charged. This did not suit the mob. A few nights after the verdict was rendered, and he declared to be innocent, a mob gathered in his vicinity and went to his house. He was called, and suspecting nothing, went outside. He was seized and hurried off to a convenient spot and hanged by the neck until he was dead for the murder of a woman of which the jury had said he was innocent.

Lynched as a Scapegoat

Wednesday, July 5th, about 10 o'clock in the morning, a terrible crime was committed within four miles of Wickliffe, Ky. Two girls, Mary and Ruby Ray, were found murdered a short distance from their home. The news of this terrible cowardly murder of two helpless young girls spread like wild fire, and searching parties scoured the territory surrounding Wickliffe and Bardwell. Two of the searching party, the Clark brothers, saw a man enter the Dupoyster cornfield; they got their guns and fired at the fleeing figure, but without effect; he got away, but they said he was a white man or nearly so. The search continued all day without effect, save the arrest of two or three strange Negroes. A bloodhound was brought from the penitentiary and put on the trail which he followed from the scene of the murder to the river and into the boat of a fisherman named Gordon. Gordon stated that he had ferried one man and only one across the river about about half past six the evening of July 5th; that his passenger sat in front of him, and he was a white man or a very bright mulatto, who could not be told from a white man. The bloodhound was put across the river in the boat, and he struck a trail again at Bird's Point on the Missouri side, ran about three hundred yards to the cottage of a white farmer named Grant and there lay down refusing to go further.

Thursday morning a brakesman on a freight train going out of Sikeston, Mo., discovered a Negro stealing a ride; he ordered him off and had hot words which terminated in a fight. The brakesman had the Negro arrested. When arrested, between 11 and 12 o'clock, he had on a dark woolen shirt, light pants and coat, and no vest. He had twelve dollars in paper, two silver dollars and ninety-five cents in change; he had also four rings in his pockets, a knife and a razor which were rusted and stained. The Sikeston authorities immediately jumped to the conclusion that this man was the murderer for whom the Kentuckians across the river were searching. They telegraphed to Bardwell that their prisoner had on no coat, but wore a blue vest and pants which would perhaps correspond with the coat found at the scene of the murder, and that the names of the murdered girls were in the rings found in his possession.

As soon as this news was received, the sheriffs of Ballard and Carlisle counties and a posse (?) of thirty well armed and determined Kentuckians, who had pledged their word the prisoner should be taken back to the scene of the supposed crime, to be executed there if proved to be the guilty man, chartered a train and at nine o'clock Thursday night started for Sikeston. Arriving there two hours later, the sheriff at Sikeston, who had no warrant for the prisoner's arrest and detention, delivered him into the hands of the mob without authority for so doing, and accompanied them to Bird's Point. The prisoner gave his name as Miller, his home at Springfield, and said he had never been in Kentucky in his life, but the sheriff turned him over to the mob to be taken to Wickliffe, that Frank Gordon, the fisherman, who had put a man across the river might identify him.

In other words, the protection of the law was withdrawn from C. J. Miller, and he was given to a mob by this sheriff at Sikeston, who knew that the prisoner's life depended on one man's word. After an altercation with the train men, who wanted another $50 for taking the train back to Bird's Point, the crowd arrived there at three o'clock, Friday morning. Here was anchored "The Three States," a ferry boat plying between Wickliffe, Ky., Cairo, Ill., and Bird's Point, Mo. This boat left Cairo at twelve o'clock, Thursday, with nearly three hundred of Cairo's best (?) citizens and thirty kegs of beer on board. This was consumed while the crowd and the bloodhound waited for the prisoner.

When the prisoner was on board "The Three States" the dog was turned loose, and after moving aimlessly around followed the crowd to where Miller sat handcuffed and there stopped. The crowd closed in on the pair and insisted that the brute had identified him because of that action. When the boat reached Wickliffe, Gordon, the fisherman, was called on to say whether the prisoner was the man he ferried over the river the day of the murder.

The sheriff of Ballard county informed him, sternly that if the prisoner was not the man, he (the fisherman) would be held responsible as knowing who the guilty man was. Gordon stated before, that the man he ferried across was a white man or a bright colored man; Miller was a dark brown skinned man, with kinky hair, "neither yellow nor black," says the Cairo Evening Telegram of Friday, July 7th. The fisherman went up to Miller from behind, looked at him without speaking for fully five minutes, then slowly said, "Yes, that's the man I crossed over." This was about six o'clock, Friday morning, and the crowd wished to hang Miller then and there. But Mr. Ray, the father of the girls, insisted that he be taken to Bardwell, the county seat of Ballard, and twelve miles inland. He said he thought a white man committed the crime, and that he was not satisfied that was the man. They took him to Bardwell and at ten o'clock, this same excited, unauthorized mob undertook to determine Miller's guilt. One of the Clark brothers who shot at a fleeing man in the Dupoyster cornfield, said the prisoner was the same man; the other said he was not, but the testimony of the first was accepted. A colored woman who had said she gave breakfast to a colored man clad in a blue flannel suit the morning of the murder, said positively that she had never seen Miller before. The gold rings found in his possession had no names in them, as had been asserted, and Mr. Ray said they did not belong to his daughters. Meantime a funeral pyre for the purpose of burning Miller to death had been erected in the center of the village. While the crowd swayed by passion was clamoring that he be burnt, Miller stepped forward and made the following statement: "My name is C. J. Miller. I am from Springfield, Ill.; my wife lives at 716 N. 2d street. I am here among you today, looked upon as one of the most brutal men before the people. I stand here surrounded by men who are excited, men who are not willing to let the law take its course, and as far as the crime is concerned, I have committed no crime, and certainly no crime gross enough to deprive me of my life and liberty to walk upon the green earth."

A telegram was sent to the chief of the police at Springfield, Ill., asking if one C. J. Miller lived there. An answer in the negative was returned. A few hours after, it was ascertained that a man named Miller, and his wife, did live at the number the prisoner gave in his speech, but the information came to Bardwell too late to do the pris-

Lynching of C. J. Miller, at Bardwell, Kentucky, July 7th, 1893. [This and all subsequent images were part of the original pamphlets.—ED.]

oner any good. Miller was taken to jail, every stitch of clothing literally torn from his body and examined again. On the lower left side of the bosom of his shirt was found a dark reddish spot about the size of a dime. Miller said it was paint which he had gotten on him at Jefferson Barracks. This spot was only on the right side, and could not be seen from the under side at all, thus showing it had not gone through the cloth as blood or any liquid substance would do.

Chief-of-Police Mahaney, of Cairo, Ill., was with the prisoner, and he took his knife and scraped at the spot, particles of which came off in his hand. Miller told them to take his clothes to any expert, and if the spot was shown to be blood, they might do anything they wished with him. They took his clothes away and were gone some time. After a while they were brought back and thrown into the cell without a word. It is needless to say that if the spot had been found to be blood, that fact would have been announced, and the shirt retained as evidence. Meanwhile numbers of rough, drunken men crowded into the cell and tried to force a confession of the deed from the prisoner's lips. He refused to talk save to reiterate his innocence. To Mr. Mahaney, who talked seriously and kindly to him, telling him the mob meant to burn and torture him at three o'clock, Miller said: "Burning and torture here lasts but a little while, but if I die with a lie on my soul, I shall be tortured forever. I am innocent." For more than three hours, all sorts of pressure in the way of threats, abuse and urging, was brought to bear to force him to confess to the murder and thus justify the mob in its deed of murder. Miller remained firm; but as the hour drew near, and the crowd became more impatient, he asked for a priest. As none could be procured, he then asked for a Methodist minister, who came, prayed with the doomed man, baptized him and exhorted Miller to confess. To keep up the flagging spirits of the dense crowd around the jail, the rumor went out more than once, that Miller had confessed. But the solemn assurance of the minister, chief-of-police, and leading editor—who were with Miller all along—is that this rumor is absolutely false.

At three o'clock the mob rushed to the jail to secure the prisoner. Mr. Ray had changed his mind about the promised burning; he was still in doubt as to the prisoner's guilt. He again addressed the crowd to that effect, urging them not to burn Miller, and the mob heeded him so far, that they compromised on hanging instead of burning, which was agreed to by Mr. Ray. There was a loud yell, and a rush was made for the prisoner. He was stripped naked, his clothing literally torn from his body, and his shirt was tied around his loins. Some one declared the rope was a "white man's death," and a log-chain, nearly a hundred feet in length, weighing over one hundred pounds, was placed round Miller's neck and body, and he was led and dragged through the streets of the village in that condition followed by thousands of people. He fainted from exhaustion several times, but was supported to the platform where they first intended burning him.

The chain was hooked around his neck, a man climbed the telegraph pole and the other end of the chain was passed up to him and made fast to the cross-arm. Others brought a long forked stick which Miller was made to straddle. By this means he was raised several feet from the ground and then let fall. The first fall broke his neck, but he was raised in this way and let fall a second time. Numberless shots were fired into the dangling body, for most of that crowd were heavily armed, and had been drinking all day.

Miller's body hung thus exposed from three to five o'clock, during which time, several photographs of him as he hung dangling at the end of the chain were taken, and his toes and fingers were cut off. His body was taken down, placed on the platform, the torch applied, and in a few moments there was nothing left of C. J. Miller save a few bones and ashes. Thus perished another of the many victims of Lynch Law, but it is the honest and sober belief of many who witnessed the scene that an innocent man has been barbarously and shockingly put to death in the glare of the 19th century civilization, by those who profess to believe in Christianity, law and order.

CHAPTER V.
LYNCHED FOR ANYTHING OR NOTHING

(Lynched for Wife Beating)

In nearly all communities wife beating is punishable with a fine, and in no community is it made a felony. Dave Jackson, of Abita, La., was a colored man who had beaten his wife. He had not killed her, nor seriously wounded her, but as Louisiana lynchers had not filled out their quota of crimes, his case was deemed of sufficient importance to apply the method of that barbarous people. He was in the custody of the officials, but the mob went to the jail and took him out in front of the prison and hanged him by the neck until he was dead. This was in Nov. 1893.

Hanged for Stealing Hogs

Details are very meagre of a lynching which occurred near Knox Point, La., on the 24th of October, 1893. Upon one point, however, there was no uncertainty, and that is, that the persons lynched were Negroes. It was claimed that they had been stealing hogs, but even this claim had not been subjected to the investigation of a court. That matter was not considered necessary. A few of the neighbors who had lost hogs suspected these men were responsible for their loss, and made up their minds to furnish an example for others to be warned by. The two men were secured by a mob and hanged.

Lynched for No Offense

Perhaps the most characteristic feature of this record of lynch law for the year 1893, is the remarkable fact that five human beings were lynched and that the matter was considered of so little importance that the powerful press bureaus of the country did not consider the matter of enough importance to ascertain the causes for which they were hanged. It tells the world, with perhaps greater emphasis than any other feature of the record, that Lynch Law has become so common in the United States that the finding of the dead body of a Negro, suspended between heaven and earth to the limb of a tree, is of so slight importance that neither the civil authorities nor press agencies consider the matter worth investigating. July 21st, in Shelby county, Tenn., a colored man by the name of Charles Martin was lynched. July 30th, at Paris, Mo., a colored man named William Steen shared the same fate. December 28th, Mack Segars was announced to have been lynched at Brantley, Alabama. August 31st, at Yarborough, Texas, and on September 19th, at Houston, a colored man was found lynched, but so little attention was paid to the matter that not only was no record made as to why these last two men were lynched, but even their names were not given. The dispatches simply stated that an unknown Negro was found lynched in each case.

There are friends of humanity who feel their souls shrink from any compromise with murder, but whose deep and abiding reverence for womanhood causes them to hesitate in giving their support to this crusade against Lynch Law, out of fear that they may encourage the miscreants whose deeds are worse than murder. But to these friends it must appear certain that these five men could not have been guilty of any terrible crime. They were simply lynched by parties of men who had it in their power to kill them, and who chose to avenge some fancied wrong by murder, rather than submit their grievances to court.

Lynched Because They Were Saucy

At Moberly, Mo., February 18th and at Fort Madison, S.C., June 2d, both in 1892, a record was made in the line of lynching which should certainly appeal to every humanitarian who has any regard for the sacredness of human life. John Hughes, of Moberly, and Isaac Lincoln, of Fort Madison, and Will Lewis in Tullahoma, Tenn., suffered death for no more serious charge than that they "were saucy to white people." In the days of slavery it was held to be a very serious matter for a colored person to fail to yield the sidewalk at the demand of a white person, and it will not be surprising to find some evidence of this intolerance existing in the days of freedom. But the most that could be expected as a penalty for acting or speaking saucily to a white person would be a slight physical chastisement to make the Negro "know his place" or an arrest and fine. But Missouri, Tennessee and South Carolina chose to make precedents in their cases and as a result both men, after being charged with their offense and apprehended, were taken by a mob and lynched. The civil authorities, who in either case would have been very quick to satisfy the aggrieved white people had they complained and brought the prisoners to court, by imposing proper penalty upon them, did not feel it their duty to make any investigation after the Negroes were killed. They were dead and out of the way and as no one would be called upon to render an account for their taking off, the matter was dismissed from the public mind.

Lynched for a Quarrel

One of the most notable instances of lynching for the year 1893, occurred about the 20th of September. It was notable for the fact that the mayor of the city exerted every available power to protect the victim of the lynching from the mob. In his splendid endeavor to uphold the law, the mayor called out the troops, and the result was a deadly fight between the militia and mob, nine of the mob being killed.

The trouble occurred at Roanoke, Va. It is frequently claimed that lynchings occur only in sparsely settled districts, and, in fact, it is a favorite plea of governors and reverend apologists to couple two arrant falsehoods, stating that lynchings occur only because of assaults upon white women, and that these assaults occur and the lynchings follow in thinly inhabited districts where the power of the law is entirely inadequate to meet the emergency. This Roanoke case is a double refutation, for it not only disproves the alleged charge that the Negro assaulted a white woman, as was telegraphed all over the country at the time, but it also shows conclusively that even in one of the largest cities of the old state of Virginia, one of the original thirteen colonies, which prides itself of being the mother of presidents, it was possible for a lynching to occur in broad daylight under circumstances of revolting savagery.

When the news first came from Roanoke of the contemplated lynching, it was stated that a big burly Negro had assaulted a white woman, that he had been apprehended and that the citizens were determined to summarily dispose of his case. Mayor Trout was a man who believed in maintaining the majesty of the law, and who at once gave notice that no lynching would be permitted in Roanoke, and that the Negro, whose name was Smith, being in the custody of the law, should be dealt with according to law; but the mob did not pay any attention to the brave words of the mayor. It evidently thought that it was only another case of swagger, such as frequently characterizes lynching episodes. Mayor Trout, finding immense crowds gathering about the city, and fearing an attempt to lynch Smith, called out the militia and stationed them at the jail.

It was known that the woman refused to accuse Smith of assaulting her, and that his offense consisted in quarreling with her about the change of money in a transaction in which he bought something from her market booth. Both parties lost their temper, and the result was a row from which Smith had to make his escape. At once the old cry was sounded that the woman had been assaulted, and in a few hours all the town was wild with people thirsting for the assailant's blood. The further incidents of that day may well be told by a dispatch from Roanoke under date of the 21st of September and published in the Chicago Record. It says:

"It is claimed by members of the military company that they frequently warned the mob to keep away from the jail, under penalty of being shot. Capt. Bird told them he was under orders to protect the prisoner whose life the mob so eagerly sought, and come what may he would not allow him to be taken by the mob. To this the crowd replied with hoots and derisive jeers. The rioters appeared to become frenzied at the determined stand taken by the men and Captain Bird, and finally a crowd of excited men made a rush for the side door of the jail. The captain directed his men to drive the would-be lynchers back.

"At this moment the mob opened fire on the soldiers. This appeared for a moment to startle the captain and his men. But it was only for a moment. Then he coolly gave the command: 'Ready! aim! fire!' The company obeyed to the instant, and poured a volley of bullets into that part of the mob which was trying to batter down the side door of the jail.

"The rioters fell back before the fire of the militia, leaving one man writhing in the agonies of death at the doorstep. There was a lull for a moment. Then the word was quickly passed through the throng in front of the jail and down the street that a man was killed. Then there was an awful rush toward the little band of soldiers. Excited men were yelling like demons.

"The fight became general, and ere it was ended nine men were dead and more than forty wounded."

This stubborn stand on behalf of law and order disconcerted the crowd and it fell back in disorder. It did not long remain inactive but assembled again for a second assault. Having only a small band of militia, and knowing they would be absolutely at the mercy of the thousands who were gathering to wreak vengeance upon them, the mayor ordered them to disperse and go to their homes, and he himself, having been wounded, was quietly conveyed out of the city.

The next day the mob grew in numbers and its rage increased in its intensity. There was no longer any doubt that Smith, innocent as he was of any crime, would be killed, for with the mayor out of the city and the governor of the state using no effort to control the mob, it was only a question of a few hours when the assault would be repeated and its victim put to death. All this happened as per programme. The description of that morning's carnival appeared in the paper above quoted and reads as follows:

"A squad of twenty men took the negro Smith from three policemen just before five o'clock this morning and hanged him to a hickory limb on Ninth avenue, in the residence section of the city. They riddled his body with bullets and put a placard on it saying: 'This is Mayor Trout's friend.' A coroner's jury of Bismel was summoned and viewed the body and rendered a verdict of death at the hands of unknown men. Thousands of persons visited the scene of the lynching between daylight and eight o'clock when the body was cut down. After the jury had completed its work the body was placed in the hands of officers, who were unable to keep back the mob. Three hundred men tried to drag the body through the streets of the town, but the Rev. Dr. Campbell of the First Presbyterian church and Capt. R. B. Moorman, with pleas and by force prevented them.

"Capt. Moorman hired a wagon and the body was put in it. It was then conveyed to the bank of the Roanoke, about two miles from the scene of the lynching. Here the body was dragged from the wagon by ropes for about 200 yards and burned. Piles of dry brushwood were brought, and the body was placed upon it, and more brushwood piled on the body, leaving only the head bare. The whole pile was then saturated with coal oil and a match was applied. The body was consumed within an hour. The cremation was witnessed by several thousand people. At one time the mob threatened to burn the Negro in Mayor Trout's yard."

Thus did the people of Roanoke, Va., add this measure of proof to maintain our contention that it is only necessary to charge a Negro with a crime in order to secure his certain death. It was well known in the city before he was killed that he had not assaulted the woman with whom he had had the trouble, but he dared to have an altercation with a white woman, and he must pay the penalty. For an offense which would not in any civilized community have brought upon him a punishment greater than a fine of a few dollars, this unfortunate Negro was hung, shot and burned.

Suspected, Innocent and Lynched

Five persons, Benjamin Jackson, his wife, Mahala Jackson, his mother-in-law, Lou Carter, Rufus Bigley, were lynched near Quincy, Miss., the charge against them being suspicion of well poisoning. It appears from the newspaper dispatches at that time that a family by the name of Woodruff was taken ill in September of 1892. As a result of their illness one or more of the family are said to have died, though that matter is not stated definitely. It was suspected that the cause of their illness was the existence of poison in the water, some miscreant having placed poison in the well. Suspicion pointed to a colored man named Benjamin Jackson who was at once arrested. With him also were arrested his wife and mother-in-law and all were held on the same charge.

The matter came up for judicial investigation, but as might have been expected, the white people concluded it was unnecessary to wait the result of the investigation—that it was preferable to hang the accused first and try him afterward. By this method of procedure, the desired result was always obtained—the accused was hanged. Accordingly Benjamin Jackson was taken from the officers by a crowd of about two hundred people, while the inquest was being held, and hanged. After the killing of Jackson, the inquest was continued to ascertain the possible connection of the other persons charged with the crime. Against the wife and mother-in-law of the unfortunate man there was not the slightest evidence and the coroner's jury was fair enough to give them their liberty. They were declared innocent and returned to their homes. But this did not protect the women from the demands of the Christian white people of that section of the country. In any other land and with any other people, the fact that these two accused persons were women would have pleaded in their favor for protection and fair play, but that had no weight with the Mississippi Christians nor the further fact that a jury of white men had declared them innocent. The hanging of one victim on an unproven charge did not begin to satisfy the mob in its bloodthirsty demands and the result was that even after the women had been discharged, they were at once taken in charge by a mob, which hung them by the neck until they were dead.

Still the mob was not satisfied. During the coroner's investigation the name of a fourth person, Rufus Bigley, was mentioned. He was acquainted with the Jacksons and that fact, together with some testimony adduced at the inquest, prompted the mob to decide that he should die also. Search was at once made for him and the next day he was apprehended. He was not given over into the hands of the civil authorities for trial nor did the coroner's inquest find that he was guilty, but the mob was quite sufficient in itself. After finding Bigley, he was strung up to a tree and his body left hanging, where it was found next day. It may be remarked here in passing that this instance of the moral degradation of the people of Mississippi did not excite any interest in the public at large. American Christianity heard of this awful affair and read of its details and neither press nor pulpit gave the matter more than a passing comment. Had it occurred in the wilds of interior Africa, there would have been an outcry from the humane people of this country against the savagery which would so mercilessly put men and women to death. But it was an evidence of American civilization to be passed by unnoticed, to be denied or condoned as the requirements of any future emergency might determine.

Lynched for an Attempted Assault

With only a little more aggravation than that of Smith who quarreled at Roanoke with the market woman, was the assault which operated as the incentive to a most brutal lynching in Memphis, Tenn. Memphis is one of the queen cities of the south, with a population of about seventy thousand souls—easily one of the twenty largest, most progressive and wealthiest cities of the United States. And yet in its streets there occurred a scene of shocking savagery which would have disgraced the Congo. No woman was harmed, no serious indignity suffered. Two women driving to town in a wagon, were suddenly accosted by Lee Walker. He claimed that he demanded something to eat. The women claimed that he attempted to assault them. They gave such an alarm that he ran away. At once the dispatches spread over the entire country that a big, burly Negro had brutally assaulted two women. Crowds began to search for the alleged fiend. While hunting him they shot another Negro dead in his tracks for refusing to stop when ordered to do so. After a few days Lee Walker was found, and put in jail in Memphis until the mob there was ready for him.

The Memphis Commercial of Sunday, July 23, contains a full account of the tragedy from which the following extracts are made:

At 12 o'clock last night, Lee Walker, who attempted to outrage Miss Mollie McCadden, last Tuesday morning, was taken from the county jail and hanged to a telegraph pole just north of the prison. All day rumors were afloat that with nightfall an attack would be made upon the jail, and as everyone anticipated that a vigorous resistance would be made, a conflict between the mob and the authorities was feared.

At 10 o'clock Capt. O'Haver, Sergt. Horan and several patrolmen were on hand, but they could do nothing with the crowd. An attack by the mob was made on the door in the south wall, and it yielded. Sheriff McLendon and several of his men threw themselves into the breach, but two or three of the storming party shoved by. They were seized by the police, but were not subdued, the officers refraining from using their clubs. The entire mob might at first have been dispersed by ten policemen who would use their clubs, but the sheriff insisted that no violence be done.

The mob got an iron rail and used it as a battering ram against the lobby doors. Sheriff McLendon tried to stop them, and some one of the mob knocked him down with a chair. Still he counseled moderation and would not order his deputies and the police to disperse the crowd by force. The pacific policy of the sheriff impressed the mob with the idea that the officers were afraid, or at least would do them no harm, and they redoubled their efforts, urged on by a big switchman. At 12 o'clock the door of the prison was broken in with a rail.

As soon as the rapist was brought out of the door calls were heard for a rope; then some one shouted, "Burn him!" But there was no time to make a fire. When Walker got into the lobby a dozen of the men began beating and stabbing him. He was half dragged, half carried to the corner of Front street and the alley between Sycamore and Mill, and hung to a telegraph pole.

Walker made a desperate resistance. Two men entered his cell first and ordered him to come forth. He refused, and they failing to drag him out, others entered. He scratched and bit his assailants, wounding several of them severely with his teeth. The mob retaliated by striking and cutting him with fists and knives. When he reached the steps leading down to the door he made another stand and was stabbed again and again. By the time he reached the lobby his power to resist was gone, and he was shoved along through the mob of yelling, cursing men and boys, who beat, spat upon and slashed the wretch-like demon. One of the leaders of the mob fell, and the crowd walked ruthlessly over him. He was badly hurt—a jawbone fractured and internal injuries inflicted. After the lynching friends took charge of him.

The mob proceeded north on Front street with the victim, stopping at Sycamore street to get a rope from a grocery. "Take him to the iron bridge on Main street," yelled several men. The men who had hold of the Negro were in a hurry to finish the job, however, and when they reached the telephone pole at the corner of Front street and the first alley north of Sycamore they stopped. A hastily improvised noose was slipped over the Negro's head, and several young men mounted a pile of lumber near the pole and threw the rope over one of the iron stepping pins. The Negro was lifted up until his feet were three feet above the ground, the rope was made taut, and a corpse dangled in midair. A big fellow who helped lead the mob pulled the Negro's legs until his neck cracked. The wretch's clothes had been torn off, and, as he swung, the man who pulled his legs mutilated the corpse.

One or two knife cuts, more or less, made little difference in the appearance of the dead rapist, however, for before the rope was around his neck his skin was cut almost to ribbons. One pistol shot was fired while the corpse was hanging. A dozen voices protested against the use of firearms, and there was no more shooting. The body was permitted to hang for half an hour, then it was cut down and the rope divided among those who lingered around the scene of the tragedy. Then it was suggested that the corpse be burned, and it was done. The entire performance, from the assault on the jail to the burning of the dead Negro was witnessed by a score or so of policemen and as many deputy sheriffs, but not a hand was lifted to stop the proceedinges after the jail door yielded.

As the body hung to the telegraph pole, blood streaming down from the knife wounds in his neck, his hips and lower part of his legs also slashed with knives, the crowd hurled expletives at him, swung the body so that it was dashed against the pole, and, so far from the ghastly sight proving trying to the nerves, the crowd looked on with complaisance, if not with real pleasure. The Negro died hard. The neck was not broken, as the body was drawn up without being given a fall, and death came by strangulation. For fully ten minutes after he was strung up the chest heaved occasionally, and there were convulsive movements of the limbs. Finally he was pronounced dead, and a few minutes later Detective Richardson climbed on a pile of staves and cut the rope. The body fell in a ghastly heap, and the crowd laughed at the sound and crowded around the prostrate body, a few kicking the inanimate carcass.

Detective Richardson, who is also a deputy coroner, then proceeded to impanel the following jury of inquest: J. S. Moody, A. C. Waldran, B. J. Childs, J. N. House, Nelson Bills, T. L. Smith, and A. Newhouse. After viewing the body the inquest was adjourned without any testimony being taken until 9 o'clock this morning. The jury will meet at the coroner's office, 51 Beale street, up stairs, and decide on a verdict. If no witnesses are forthcoming, the jury will be able to arrive at a verdict just the same, as all members of it saw the lynching. Then some one raised the cry of "Burn him!" It was quickly taken up and soon resounded from a hundred throats. Detective Richardson, for a long time, single-handed, stood the crowd off. He talked and begged the men not to bring disgrace on the city by burning the body, arguing that all the vengeance possible had been wrought.

While this was going on a small crowd was busy starting a fire in the middle of the street. The material was handy. Some bundles of staves were taken from the adjoining lumber yard for kindling. Heavier wood was obtained from the same source, and coal oil from a neighboring grocery. Then the cries of "Burn him! Burn him!" were redoubled.

Half a dozen men seized the naked body. The crowd cheered. They marched to the fire, and giving the body a swing, it was landed in the middle of the fire. There was a cry for more wood, as the fire had begun to die owing to the long delay. Willing hands procured the wood, and it was piled up on the Negro, almost, for a time, obscuring him from view. The head was in plain view, as also were the limbs, and one arm which stood out high above the body, the elbow crooked, held in that position by a stick of wood. In a few moments the hands began to swell, then came great blisters over all the exposed parts of the body; then in places the flesh was burned away and the bones began to show through. It was a horrible sight, one which, perhaps, none there had ever witnessed before. It proved too much for a large part of the crowd and the majority of the mob left very shortly after the burning began.

But a large number stayed, and were not a bit set back by the sight of a human body being burned to ashes. Two or three white women, accompanied by their escorts, pushed to the front to obtain an unobstructed view, and looked on with astonishing coolness and nonchalance. One man and woman brought a little girl, not over 12 years old, apparently their daughter, to view a scene which was calculated to drive sleep from the child's eyes for many nights, if not to produce a permanent injury to her nervous system. The comments of the crowd were varied. Some remarked on the efficacy of this style of cure for rapists, others rejoiced that men's wives and daughters were now safe from this wretch. Some laughed as the flesh cracked and blistered, and while a large number pronounced the burning of a dead body as a useless episode, not in all that throng was a word of sympathy heard for the wretch himself.

The rope that was used to hang the Negro, and also that which was used to lead him from the jail, were eagerly sought by relic hunters. They almost fought for a chance to cut off a piece of rope, and in an incredibly short time both ropes had disappeared and were scattered in the pockets of the crowd in sections of from an inch to six inches long. Others of the relic hunters remained until the ashes cooled to obtain such ghastly relics as the teeth, nails, and bits of charred skin of the immolated victim of his own lust. After burning the body the mob tied a rope around the charred trunk and dragged it down Main street to the court house, where it was hanged to a center pole. The rope broke and the corpse dropped with a thud, but it was again hoisted, the charred legs barely touching the ground. The teeth were knocked out and the finger nails cut off as souvenirs. The crowd made so much noise that the police interfered. Undertaker Walsh was telephoned for, who took charge of the body and carried it to his establishment, where it will be prepared for burial in the potter's field today.

A prelude to this exhibition of 19th century barbarism was the following telegram received by the Chicago Inter Ocean, at 2 o'clock, Saturday afternoon—ten hours before the lynching:

"MEMPHIS, TENN., July 22, To Inter-Ocean, Chicago.

"Lee Walker, colored man, accused of raping white women, in jail here, will be taken out and burned by whites to-night. Can you send Miss Ida Wells to write it up? Answer. R. M. Martin, with Public Ledger."

The Public Ledger is one of the oldest evening daily papers in Memphis, and this telegram shows that the intentions of the mob were well known long before they were executed. The personnel of the mob is given by the Memphis Appeal-Avalanche. It says, "At first it seemed as if a crowd of roughs were the principals, but as it increased in size, men in all walks of life figured as leaders, although the majority were young men."

This was the punishment meted out to a Negro, charged, not with rape, but attempted assault, and without any proof as to his guilt, for the women were not given a chance to identify him. It was only a little less horrible than the burning alive of Henry Smith, at Paris, Texas, February 1st, 1893, or that of Edward Coy, in Texarkana, Texas, February 20, 1892. Both were charged with assault on white women, and both were tied to the stake and burned while yet alive, in the presence of ten thousand persons. In the case of Coy, the white woman in the case, applied the match, even while the victim protested his innocence.

The cut which is here given [p. 118] is the exact reproduction of the photograph taken at the scene of the lynching at Clanton, Alabama, August, 1891. The cause for which the man was hanged is given in the words of the mob which were written on the back of the photograph, and they are also given. This photograph was sent to Judge A. W. Tourgee, of Mayville, N.Y.

In some of these cases the mob affects to believe in the Negro's guilt. The world is told that the white woman in the case identifies him, or the prisoner "confesses." But in the lynching which took place in Barnwell County, South Carolina, April 24, 1893, the mob's victim, John Peterson, escaped and placed himself under Governor Tillman's protection; not only did he declare his innocence, but offered to prove an alibi, by white witnesses. Before his witnesses could be brought, the mob arrived at the Governor's mansion and demanded the prisoner. He was given up, and although the white woman in the case said he was not the man, he was hanged 24 hours after, and over a thousand bullets fired into his body, on the declaration that "a crime had been committed and some one had to hang for it."

CHAPTER VI.
HISTORY OF SOME CASES OF RAPE

It has been claimed that the Southern white women have been slandered because, in defending the Negro race from the charge that all colored men, who are lynched, only pay penalty for assaulting women. It is certain that lynching mobs have not only refused to give the Negro a chance to defend himself, but have killed their victim with a

Scene of lynching
at Clanton,
Alabama, Aug. 1891.

full knowledge that the relationship of the alleged assailant with the woman who accused him, was voluntary and clandestine. As a matter of fact, one of the prime causes of the Lynch Law agitation has been a necessity for defending the Negro from this awful charge against him. This defense has been necessary because the apologists for outlawry insist that in no case has the accusing woman been a willing consort of her paramour, who is lynched because overtaken in wrong. It is well known, however, that such is the case. In July of this year, 1894, John Paul Bocock, a Southern white man living in New York, and assistant editor of the New York Tribune, took occasion to defy the publication of any instance where the lynched Negro was the victim of a white woman's falsehood. Such cases are not rare, but the press and people conversant with the facts, almost invariably suppress them.

Facsimile of the
back of the
photograph.

The New York Sun of July 30th, 1894, contained a synopsis of interviews with leading congressmen and editors of the South. Speaker Crisp, of the House of Representatives, who was recently a Judge of the Supreme Court of Georgia, led in declaring that lynching seldom or never took place, save for vile crime against women and children. Dr. Hoss, editor of the leading organ of the Methodist Church South, published in its columns that it was his belief that more than three hundred women had been assaulted by Negro men within three months. When asked to prove his charges, or give a single case upon which his "belief" was founded, he said that he could do so, but the details were unfit for publication. No other evidence but his "belief" could be adduced to substantiate this grave charge, yet Bishop Haygood,[5] in the Forum of October, 1893, quotes this "belief" in apology for lynching, and voluntarily adds: "It is my opinion that this is an underestimate." The "opinion" of this man, based upon a "belief," had greater weight coming from a man who has posed as a friend to "Our Brother in Black," and was accepted as authority. An interview of Miss Frances E. Willard, the great apostle of temperance, the daughter of abolitionists and a personal friend and helper of many individual colored people, has been quoted in support of the utterance of this calumny against a weak and defenseless race. In the New York Voice of October 23, 1890, after a tour in the South, where she was told all these things by the "best white people," she said: "The grogshop is the Negro's center of power. Better whisky and more of it is the rallying cry of great, dark-faced mobs. The colored race multiplies like the locusts of Egypt. The grogshop is its center of power. The safety of woman, of childhood, the home, is menaced in a thousand localities at this moment, so that men dare not go beyond the sight of their own roof-tree."

These charges so often reiterated, have had the effect of fastening the odium upon the race of a peculiar propensity for this foul crime. The Negro is thus forced to a defense of his good name, and this chapter will be devoted to the history of some of the cases where assault upon white women by Negroes is charged. He is not the aggressor in this fight, but the situation demands that the facts be given, and they will speak for themselves. Of the 1,115 Negro men, women and children hanged, shot and roasted alive from January 1st, 1882, to January 1st, 1894, inclusive, only 348 of that number were charged with rape. Nearly 700 of these persons were lynched for any other reason which could be manufactured by a mob wishing to indulge in a lynching bee.

A White Woman's Falsehood

The Cleveland, Ohio, Gazette, January 16, 1892, gives an account of one of these cases of "rape."

Mrs. J. C. Underwood, the wife of a minister of Elyria, Ohio, accused an Afro-American of rape. She told her husband that during his absence in 1888, stumping the state for the Prohibition Party, the man came to the kitchen door, forced his way in the house and

[5]See note p. 80.

insulted her. She tried to drive him out with a heavy poker, but he overpowered and chloroformed her, and when she revived her clothing was torn and she was in a horrible condition. She did not know the man, but could identify him. She subsequently pointed out William Offett, a married man, who was arrested, and, being in Ohio, was granted a trial.

The prisoner vehemently denied the charge of rape, but confessed he went to Mrs. Underwood's residence at her invitation and was criminally intimate with her at her request. This availed him nothing against the sworn testimony of a minister's wife, a lady of the highest respectability. He was found guilty, and entered the penitentiary, December 14, 1888, for fifteen years. Sometime afterwards the woman's remorse led her to confess to her husband that the man was innocent. These are her words: "I met Offett at the postoffice. It was raining. He was polite to me, and as I had several bundles in my arms he offered to carry them home for me, which he did. He had a strange fascination for me, and I invited him to call on me. He called, bringing chestnuts and candy for the children. By this means we got them to leave us alone in the room. Then I sat on his lap. He made a proposal to me and I readily consented. Why I did so I do not know, but that I did is true. He visited me several times after that and each time I was indiscreet. I did not care after the first time. In fact I could not have resisted, and had no desire to resist."

When asked by her husband why she told him she had been outraged, she said: "I had several reasons for telling you. One was the neighbors saw the fellow here, another was, I was afraid I had contracted a loathsome disease, and still another was that I feared I might give birth to a Negro baby. I hoped to save my reputation by telling you a deliberate lie." Her husband, horrified by the confession, had Offett, who had already served four years, released and secured a divorce.

There have been many such cases throughout the South, with the difference that the Southern white men in insensate fury wreak their vengeance without intervention of law upon the Negro who consorts with their women.

Tried to Manufacture an Outrage

The Memphis (Tenn.) Ledger, of June 8, 1892, has the following: "If Lillie Bailey, a rather pretty white girl, seventeen years of age, who is now at the city hospital, would be somewhat less reserved about her disgrace there would be some very nauseating details in the story of her life. She is the mother of a little coon. The truth might reveal fearful depravity or the evidence of a rank outrage. She will not divulge the name of the man who has left such black evidence of her disgrace, and in fact says it is a matter in which there can be no interest to the outside world. She came to Memphis nearly three months ago, and was taken in at the Woman's Refuge in the southern part of the city. She remained there until a few weeks ago when the child was born. The ladies in charge of the Refuge were horrified. The girl was at once sent to the city hospital, where she has been since May 30th. She is a country girl. She came to Memphis from her father's farm, a short distance from Hernando, Miss. Just when she left there she would not say. In fact she says she came to Memphis from Arkansas, and says her home is in that state. She is rather good looking, has blue eyes, a low forehead and dark red hair. The ladies at the Woman's Refuge do not know anything about the girl further than what they learned when she was an inmate of the institution; and she would not tell much. When the child was born an attempt was made to get the girl to reveal the name of the Negro who had disgraced her, she obstinately refused and it was impossible to elicit any information from her on the subject."

Note the wording: "The truth might reveal fearful depravity or rank outrage." If it had been a white child or if Lillie Bailey had told a pitiful story of Negro outrage, it would have been a case of woman's weakness or assault and she could have remained at the Woman's Refuge. But a Negro child and to withhold its father's name and thus prevent the killing of another Negro "rapist" was a case of "fearful depravity." Had she revealed the father's name, he would have been lynched and his taking off charged to an assault upon a white woman.

Burned Alive for Adultery

In Texarkana, Arkansas, Edward Coy was accused of assaulting a white woman. The press dispatches of February 18, 1892, told in detail how he was tied to a tree, the flesh cut from his body by men and boys, and after coal oil was poured over him, the woman he had assaulted gladly set fire to him, and 15,000 persons saw him burn to death. October 1st, the Chicago Inter Ocean contained the following account of that horror from the pen of the "Bystander"—Judge Albion W. Tourgee—as the result of his investigations:

"1. The woman who was paraded as victim of violence was of bad character; her husband was a drunkard and a gambler.

"2. She was publicly reported and generally known to have been criminally intimate with Coy for more than a year previous.

"3. She was compelled by threats, if not by violence, to make the charge against the victim.

"4. When she came to apply the match Coy asked her if she would burn him after they had 'been sweethearting' so long.

"5. A large majority of the 'superior' white men prominent in the affair are the reputed fathers of mulatto children.

"These are not pleasant facts, but they are illustrative of the vital phase of the so-called 'race question,' which should properly be designated an earnest inquiry as to the best methods by which religion, science, law and political power may be employed to excuse injustice, barbarity and crime done to a people because of race and color. There can be no possible belief that these people were inspired by any consuming zeal to vindicate God's law against miscegenationists of the most practical sort. The woman was a willing partner in the victim's guilt, and being of the 'superior' race must naturally have been more guilty."

Not Identified but Lynched

February 11th, 1893, there occurred in Shelby county, Tennessee, the fourth Negro lynching within fifteen months. The three first were lynched in the city of Memphis for firing on white men in self-defense. This Negro, Richard Neal, was lynched a few miles from the city limits, and the following is taken from the Memphis (Tenn.) Scimitar:

"As the Scimitar stated on Saturday the Negro, Richard Neal, who raped Mrs. Jack White near Forest Hill, in this county, was lynched by a mob of about 200 white citizens of the neighborhood. Sheriff McLendon, accompanied by Deputies Perkins, App and Harvey and a Scimitar reporter, arrived on the scene of the execution about 3:30 in the afternoon. The body was suspended from the first limb of a post oak tree by a new quarter inch grass rope. A hangman's knot, evidently tied by an expert, fitted snugly under the left ear of the corpse, and a new hame string pinioned, the victim's arms behind him. His legs were not tied. The body was perfectly limber when the Sheriff's posse cut it down and retained enough heat to warm the feet of Deputy Perkins, whose road cart was converted into a hearse. On arriving with the body at Forest Hill the Sheriff made a bargain with a stalwart young man with a blonde mustache and deep blue eyes, who told the Scimitar reporter that he was the leader of the mob, to haul the body to Germantown for $3.

"When within half-a-mile of Germantown the Sheriff and posse were overtaken by Squire McDonald of Collierville, who had come down to hold the inquest. The Squire had his jury with him, and it was agreed for the convenience of all parties that he should proceed with the corpse to Germantown and conduct the inquiry as to the cause of death. He did so, and a verdict of death from hanging by parties unknown was returned in due form.

"The execution of Neal was done deliberately and by the best people of the Collierville, Germantown and Forest Hill neighborhoods, without passion or exhibition of anger.

"He was arrested on Friday about ten o'clock, by Constable Bob Cash, who carried him before Mrs. White. She said: 'I think he is the man. I am almost certain of it. If he isn't the man he is exactly like him.'

"The Negro's coat was torn also, and there were other circumstances against him. The committee returned and made its report, and the chairman put the question of guilt or innocence to a vote.

"All who thought the proof strong enough to warrant execution were invited to cross over to the other side of the road. Everybody but four or five negroes crossed over.

"The committee then placed Neal on a mule with his arms tied behind him, and proceeded to the scene of the crime, followed by the mob. The rope, with a noose already prepared, was tied to the limb nearest the spot where the unpardonable sin was committed, and the doomed man's mule was brought to a standstill beneath it.

"Then Neal confessed. He said he was the right man, but denied that he used force or threats to accomplish his purpose. It was a matter of purchase, he claimed, and said the price paid was twenty-five cents. He warned the colored men present to beware of white women and resist temptation, for to yield to their blandishments or to the passions of men, meant death.

"While he was speaking, Mrs. White came from her home and calling Constable Cash to one side, asked if he could not save the Negro's life. The reply was, 'No,' and Mrs. White returned to the house.

"When all was in readiness, the husband of Neal's victim leaped upon the mule's back and adjusted the rope around the Negro's neck. No cap was used, and Neal showed no fear, nor did he beg for mercy.

The mule was struck with a whip and bounded out from under Neal, leaving him suspended in the air with his feet about three feet from the ground."

Delivered to the Mob
by the Governor of the State

John Peterson, near Denmark, S.C., was suspected of rape, but escaped, went to Columbia, and placed himself under Gov. Tillman's protection, declaring he too could prove an alibi by white witnesses. A white reporter hearing his declaration volunteered to find these witnesses, and telegraphed the governor that he would be in Columbia with them on Monday. In the meantime the mob at Denmark, learning Peterson's whereabouts, went to the governor and demanded the prisoner. Gov. Tillman, who had during his canvass for re-election the year before, declared that he would lead a mob to lynch a Negro that assaulted a white woman, gave Peterson up to the mob. He was taken back to Denmark, and the white girl in the case as positively declared that he was not the man. But the verdict of the mob was that "the crime had been committed and somebody had to hang for it, and if he, Peterson, was not guilty of that he was of some other crime," and he was hung, and his body riddled with 1,000 bullets.

Lynched as a Warning

Alabama furnishes a case in point. A colored man named Daniel Edwards, lived near Selma, Alabama, and worked for a family of a farmer near that place. This resulted in an intimacy between the young man and a daughter of the householder, which finally developed in the disgrace of the girl. After the birth of the child, the mother disclosed the fact that Edwards was its father. The relationship had been sustained for more than a year, and yet this colored man was apprehended, thrown into jail from whence he was taken by a mob of one hundred neighbors and hung to a tree and his body riddled with bullets. A dispatch which describes the lynching, ends as follows. "Upon his back was found pinned this morning the following: 'Warning to all Negroes that are too intimate with white girls. This the work of one hundred best citizens of the South Side.'"

There can be no doubt from the announcement made by this "one hundred best citizens" that they understood full well the character of the relationship which existed between Edwards and the girl, but when the dispatches were sent out, describing the affair, it was claimed that Edwards was lynched for rape.

Suppressing the Truth

In a county in Mississippi during the month of July the Associated Press dispatches sent out a report that the sheriff's eight year old daughter had been assaulted by a big, black, burly brute who had been promptly lynched. The facts which have since been investigated show that the girl was more than eighteen years old and that she was discovered by her father in this young man's room who was a servant on the place. But these facts the Associated Press has not given to the world, nor did the same agency acquaint the world with the fact that a Negro youth who was lynched in Tuscumbia, Ala., the same year on the same charge told the white girl who accused him before the mob, that he had met her in the woods often by appointment. There is a young mulatto in one of the State prisons of the South to-day who is there by charge of a young white woman to screen herself. He is a college graduate and had been corresponding with, and clandestinely visiting her until he was surprised and run out of her room en deshabille[6] by her father. He was put in prison in another town to save his life from the mob and his lawyer advised that it were better to save his life by pleading guilty to charges made and being sentenced for years, than to attempt a defense by exhibiting the letters written him by this girl. In the latter event, the mob would surely murder him, while there was a chance for his life by adopting the former course. Names, places and dates are not given for the same reason.

The excuse has come to be so safe, it is not surprising that a Philadelphia girl, beautiful and well educated, and of good family, should make a confession published in all the daily papers of that city October, 1894, that she had been stealing for some time, and that to cover one of her thefts, she had said she had been bound and gagged in her father's house by a colored man, and money stolen therefrom by him. Had this been done in many localities, it would only have been necessary for her to "identify" the first Negro in that vicinity, to have brought about another lynching bee[.]

[6]Undressed.

A Vile Slander with
Scant Retraction

The following published in the Cleveland (Ohio) Leader of Oct. 23d, 1894, only emphasizes our demand that a fair trial shall be given those accused of crime, and the protection of the law be extended until time for a defense be granted.

"The sensational story sent out last night from Hicksville that a Negro had outraged a little four-year-old girl proves to be a base canard. The correspondents who went into the details should have taken the pains to investigate, and the officials should have known more of the matter before they gave out such grossly exaggerated information.

"The Negro, Charles O'Neil, had been working for a couple of women and, it seems, had worked all winter without being remunerated. There is a little girl, and the girl's mother and grandmother evidently started the story with idea of frightening the Negro out of the country and thus balancing accounts. The town was considerably wrought up and for a time things looked serious. The accused had a preliminary hearing to-day and not an iota of evidence was produced to indicate that such a crime had been committed, or that he had even attempted such an outrage. The village marshal was frightened nearly out of his wits and did little to quiet the excitement last night.

"The affair was an outrage on the Negro, at the expense of innocent childhood, a brainless fabrication from start to finish."

The original story was sent throughout this country and England, but the Cleveland Leader, so far as known, is the only journal which has published these facts in refutation of the slander so often published against the race.

Not only is it true that many of the alleged cases of rape against the Negro, are like the foregoing, but the same crime committed by white men against Negro women and girls, is never punished by mob or the law. A leading journal in South Carolina openly said some months ago that "it is not the same thing for a white man to assault a colored woman as for a colored man to assault a white woman, because the colored woman had no finer feelings nor virtue to be outraged!" Yet colored women have always had far more reason to complain of white men in this respect than ever white women have had of Negroes.

Illinois Has a Lynching

In the month of June, 1893, the proud commonwealth of Illinois joined the ranks of Lynching States. Illinois, which gave to the world the immortal heroes, Lincoln, Grant and Logan,[7] trailed its banner of justice in the dust—dyed its hands red in the blood of a man not proven guilty of crime.

June 3, 1893, the country about Decatur, one of the largest cities of the state was startled with the cry that a white woman had been assaulted by a colored tramp. Three days later a colored man named Samuel Bush was arrested and put in jail. A white man testified that Bush, on the day of the assault, asked him where he could get a drink and he pointed to the house where the farmer's wife was subsequently said to have been assaulted. Bush said he went to the well but did not go near the house, and did not assault the woman. After he was arrested the alleged victim did not see him to identify him—he was presumed to be guilty.

The citizens determined to kill him. The mob gathered, went to the jail, met with no resistance, took the suspected man, dragged him out tearing every stitch of clothing from his body, then hanged him to a telegraph pole. The grand jury refused to indict the lynchers though the names of over twenty persons who were leaders in the mob were well known. In fact twenty-two persons were indicted, but the grand jurors and the prosecuting attorney disagreed as to the form of the indictments, which caused the jurors to change their minds. All indictments were reconsidered and the matter was dropped. Not one of the dozens of men prominent in that murder have suffered a whit more inconvenience for the butchery of that man, than they would have suffered for shooting a dog.

Color Line Justice

In Baltimore, Maryland, a gang of white ruffians assaulted a respectable colored girl who was out walking with a young man of her own race. They held her escort and outraged the girl. It was a deed dastardly enough to arouse Southern blood, which gives its horror of rape as excuse for lawlessness, but she was a colored woman. The case went to the courts and they were acquitted.

[7]John Alexander Logan (1826–1886) was a Union general in the Civil War who went on to serve in both houses of Congress. As a Radical Republican congressman he was active in the impeachment trial of President Andrew Johnson.

In Nashville, Tennessee, there was a white man, Pat Hanifan, who outraged a little colored girl, and from the physical injuries received she was ruined for life. He was jailed for six months, discharged, and is now a detective in that city. In the same city, last May, a white man outraged a colored girl in a drug store. He was arrested and released on bail at the trial. It was rumored that five hundred colored men had organized to lynch him. Two hundred and fifty white citizens armed themselves with Winchesters and guarded him. A cannon was placed in front of his home, and the Buchanan Rifles (State Militia) ordered to the scene for his protection. The colored mob did not show up. Only two weeks before, Eph. Grizzard, who had only been charged with rape upon a white woman, had been taken from the jail, with Governor Buchanan and the police and militia standing by, dragged through the streets in broad daylight, knives plunged into him at every step, and with every fiendish cruelty that a frenzied mob could devise, he was at last swung out on the bridge with hands cut to pieces as he tried to climb up the stanchions. A naked, bloody example of the bloodthirstiness of the nineteenth century civilization of the Athens of the South! No cannon nor military were called out in his defense. He dared to visit a white woman.

At the very moment when these civilized whites were announcing their determination "to protect their wives and daughters," by murdering Grizzard, a white man was in the same jail for raping eight-year-old Maggie Reese, a colored girl. He was not harmed. The "honor" of grown women who were glad enough to be supported by the Grizzard boys and Ed Coy, as long as the liaison was not known, needed protection; they were white. The outrage upon helpless childhood needed no avenging in this case; she was black.

A white man in Guthrie, Oklahoma Territory, two months after inflicted such injuries upon another colored girl that she died. He was not punished, but an attempt was made in the same town in the month of June to lynch a colored man who visited a white woman.

In Memphis, Tennessee, in the month of June, Ellerton L. Dorr, who is the husband of Russell Hancock's widow, was arrested for attempted rape on Mattie Cole, a neighbor's cook; he was only prevented from accomplishing his purpose by the appearance of Mattie's employer. Dorr's friends say he was drunk and not responsible for his actions. The grand jury refused to indict him and he was discharged.

In Tallahassee, Florida, a colored girl, Charlotte Gilliam, was assaulted by white men. Her father went to have a warrant for their arrest issued, but the judge refused to issue it.

In Bowling Green, Virginia, Moses Christopher, a colored lad, was charged with assault, September 10. He was indicted, tried, convicted and sentenced to death in one day. In the same state at Danville, two weeks before—August 29, Thomas J. Penn, a white man, committed a criminal assault upon Lina Hanna, a twelve-year-old colored girl, but he has not been tried, certainly not killed either by the law or the mob.

In Surrey county, Virginia, C. L. Brock, a white man, criminally assaulted a ten-year-old colored girl, and threatened to kill her if she told. Notwithstanding, she confessed to her aunt, Mrs. Alice Bates, and the white brute added further crime by killing Mrs. Bates when she upbraided him about his crime upon her niece. He emptied the contents of his revolver into her body as she lay. Brock has never been apprehended, and no effort has been made to do so by the legal authorities.

But even when punishment is meted out by law to white villians for this horrible crime, it is seldom or never that capital punishment is invoked. Two cases just clipped from the daily papers will suffice to show how this crime is punished when committed by white offenders and black.

LOUISVILLE, KY., October 19.—Smith Young, colored, was to-day sentenced to be hanged. Young criminally assaulted a six-year-old child about six months ago.

Jacques Blucher, the Pontiac Frenchman who was arrested at that place for a criminal assault on his daughter Fanny on July 29 last, pleaded nolo contendere when placed on trial at East Greenwich, near Providence, R.I., Tuesday, and was sentenced to five years in State Prison.

Charles Wilson was convicted of assault upon seven-year-old Mamie Keys in Philadelphia, in October, and sentenced to ten years in prison. He was white. Indianapolis courts sentenced a white man in September to eight years in prison for assault upon a twelve-year old white girl.

April 24, 1893, a lynching was set for Denmark, S.C., on the charge of rape. A white girl accused a Negro of assault, and the mob was about to lynch him. A few hours before the lynching three reputable white men rode into the town and solemnly testified that the accused Negro was at work with them 25 miles away on the day and at the hour the crime had been committed. He was accordingly set free. A white person's word is taken as absolutely for as against a Negro.

CHAPTER VII. THE CRUSADE JUSTIFIED

(Appeal from America to the World)

It has been urged in criticism of the movement appealing to the English people for sympathy and support in our crusade against Lynch Law that our action was unpatriotic, vindictive and useless. It is not a part of the plan of this pamphlet to make any defense for that crusade nor to indict any apology for the motives which led to the presentation of the facts of American lynchings to the world at large. To those who are not willfully blind and unjustly critical, the record of more than a thousand lynchings in ten years is enough to justify any peaceable movement tending to ameliorate the conditions which led to this unprecedented slaughter of human beings.

If America would not hear the cry of men, women and children whose dying groans ascended to heaven praying for relief, not only for them but for others who might soon be treated as they, then certainly no fair-minded person can charge disloyalty to those who make an appeal to the civilization of the world for such sympathy and help as it is possible to extend. If stating the facts of these lynchings, as they appeared from time to time in the white newspapers of America—the news gathered by white correspondents, compiled by white press bureaus and disseminated among white people—shows any vindictiveness, then the mind which so charges is not amenable to argument.

But it is the desire of this pamphlet to urge that the crusade started and thus far continued has not been useless, but has been blessed with the most salutary results. The many evidences of the good results can not here be mentioned, but the thoughtful student of the situation can himself find ample proof. There need not here be mentioned the fact that for the first time since lynching began, has there been any occasion for the governors of the several states to speak out in reference to these crimes against law and order.

No matter how heinous the act of the lynchers may have been, it was discussed only for a day or so and then dismissed from the attention of the public. In one or two instances the governor has called attention to the crime, but the civil processes entirely failed to bring the murderers to justice. Since the crusade against lynching was started, however, governors of states, newspapers, senators and representatives and bishops of churches have all been compelled to take cognizance of the prevalence of this crime and to speak in one way or another in the defense of the charge against this barbarism in the United States. This has not been because there was any latent spirit of justice voluntarily asserting itself, especially in those who do the lynching, but because the entire American people now feel, both North and South, that they are objects in the gaze of the civilized world and that for every lynching humanity asks that America render its account to civilization and itself.

Awful Barbarism Ignored

Much has been said during the months of September and October of 1894 about the lynching of six colered men who on suspicion of incendiarism were made the victims of a most barbarous massacre. They were arrested, one by one, by officers of the law; they were handcuffed and chained together and by the officers of the law loaded in a wagon and deliberately driven into an ambush where a mob of lynchers awaited them. At the time and upon the chosen spot, in the darkness of the night and far removed from the habitation of any human soul, the wagon was halted and the mob fired upon the six manacled men, shooting them to death as no humane person would have shot dogs. Chained together as they were, in their awful struggles after the first volley, the victims tumbled out of the wagon upon the ground and there in the mud, struggling in their death throes, the victims were made the target of the murderous shotguns, which fired into the writhing, struggling, dying mass of humanity, until every spark of life was gone. Then the officers of the law who had them in charge, drove away to give the alarm and to tell the world that they had been waylaid and their prisoners forcibly taken from them and killed.

It has been claimed that the prompt, vigorous and highly commendable steps of the governor of the State of Tennessee and the judge having jurisdiction over the crime, and of the citizens of Memphis generally, was the natural revolt of the humane conscience in that section of the country, and the determination of honest and honorable men to rid the community of such men as those who were guilty of this terrible massacre. It has further been claimed that this vigorous uprising of the people and this most commendably prompt action of the civil authorities, is ample proof that the American people will not tolerate the lynching of innocent men, and that in cases where brutal lynchings have not been promptly dealt with, the crimes on the part of the victims were such as to put them outside the pale of humanity and that the world considered their death a necessary sacrifice for the good of all.

But this line of argument can in no possible way be truthfully sustained. The lynching of the six men in 1894, barbarous as it was, was in no way more barbarous than took nothing more than a passing notice. It was only the other lynchings which preceded it, and of which the public[8] fact that the attention of the civilized world has been called to lynching in America which made the people of Tennessee feel the absolute necessity for a prompt, vigorous and just arraignment of all the murderers connected with that crime. Lynching is no longer "Our Problem," it is the problem of the civilized world, and Tennessee could not afford to refuse the legal measures which Christianity demands shall be used for the punishment of crime.

Memphis Then and Now

Only two years prior to the massacre of the six men near Memphis, that same city took part in a massacre in every way as bloody and brutal as that of September last. It was the murder of three young colored men and who were known to be among the most honorable, reliable, worthy and peaceable colored citizens of the community. All of them were engaged in the mercantile business, being members of a corporation which conducted a large grocery store, and one of the three being a letter carrier in the employ of the government. These three men were arrested for resisting an attack of a mob upon their store, in which melee none of the assailants, who had armed themselves for their devilish deeds by securing court processes, were killed or even seriously injured. But these three men were put in jail, and on three or four nights after their incarceration a mob of less than a dozen men, by collusion with the civil authorities, entered the jail, took the three men from the custody of the law and shot them to death. Memphis knew of this awful crime, knew then and knows today who the men were who committed it, and yet not the first step was ever taken to apprehend the guilty wretches who walk the streets today with the brand of murder upon their foreheads, but as safe from harm as the

---

[8]For sense, the preceding sentence should read: The lynching of the six men in 1894, barbarous as it was, was in no way more barbarous than other lynchings which preceded it, and of which the public took nothing more than a passing notice. It was only the fact. . . .

most upright citizen of that community. Memphis would have been
just as calm and complacent and self-satisfied over the murder of the
six colored men in 1894 as it was over these three colored men in
1892, had it not recognized the fact that to escape the brand of barbarism it had not only to speak its denunciation but to act vigorously
in vindication of its name.

An Alabama Horror Ignored

A further instance of this absolute disregard of every principle of justice and the indifference to the barbarism of Lynch Law may be cited
here, and is furnished by white residents in the city of Carrolton,
Alabama. Several cases of arson had been discovered, and in their
search for the guilty parties, suspicion was found to rest upon three
men and a woman. The four suspects were Paul Hill, Paul Archer,
William Archer, his brother, and a woman named Emma Fair. The
prisoners were apprehended, earnestly asserted their innocence, but
went to jail without making any resistance. They claimed that they
could easily prove their innocence upon trial.

One would suspect that the civilization which defends itself against
the barbarisms of Lynch Law by stating that it lynches human beings
only when they are guilty of awful attacks upon women and children,
would have been very careful to have given these four prisoners, who
were simply charged with arson, a fair trial, to which they were entitled upon every principle of law and humanity. Especially would this
seem to be the case when it is considered that one of the prisoners
charged was a woman, and if the Nineteenth Century has shown any
advancement upon any lines of human action, it is pre-eminently
shown in its reverence, respect and protection of its womanhood. But
the people of Alabama failed to have any regard for womanhood whatever.

The three men and the woman were put in jail to await trial. A few
days later it was rumored that they were to be subjects of Lynch Law,
and, sure enough, at night a mob of lynchers went to the jail, not to
avenge any awful crime against womanhood, but to kill four people
who had been suspected of setting a house on fire. They were caged
in their cells, helpless and defenseless; they were at the mercy of civilized white Americans, who, armed with shotguns, were there to maintain the majesty of American law. And most effectively was their duty
done by these splendid representatives of Governor Fishback's brave
and honorable white southerners, who resent "outside interference."

They lined themselves up in the most effective manner and poured volley after volley into the bodies of their helpless, pleading victims, who in their bolted prison cells could do nothing but suffer and die. Then these lynchers went quietly away and the bodies of the woman and three men were taken out and buried with as little ceremony as men would bury hogs.

No one will say that the massacre near Memphis in 1894 was any worse than this bloody crime of Alabama in 1892. The details of this shocking affair were given to the public by the press, but public sentiment was not moved to action in the least; it was only a matter of a day's notice and then went to swell the list of murders which stand charged against the noble, Christian people of Alabama.

America Awakened

But there is now an awakened conscience throughout the land, and Lynch Law can not flourish in the future as it has in the past. The close of the year 1894 witnessed an aroused interest, an assertative humane principle which must tend to the extirpation of that crime. The awful butchery last mentioned failed to excite more than a passing comment in 1894, but far different is it today. Gov. Jones, of Alabama, in 1893 dared to speak out against the rule of the mob in no uncertain terms. His address indicated a most helpful result of the present agitation. In face of the many denials of the outrages on the one hand and apologies for lynchers on the other, Gov. Jones admits the awful lawlessness charged and refuses to join in the infamous plea made to condone the crime. No stronger nor more effective words have been said than those following from Gov. Jones.

"While the ability of the state to deal with open revolts against the supremacy of its laws has been ably demonstrated, I regret that deplorable acts of violence have been perpetrated, in at least four instances, within the past two years by mobs, whose sudden work and quick dispersions rendered it impossible to protect their victims. Within the past two years nine prisoners, who were either in jail or in the custody of the officers, have been taken from them without resistance, and put to death. There was doubt of the guilt of the defendants in most of these cases, and few of them were charged with capital offenses. None of them involved the crime of rape. The largest rewards allowed by law were offered for the apprehension of the offenders, and officers were charged to a vigilant performance of their duties, and aided in some instances by the services of skilled detectives; but not a single arrest has been made and the grand juries in these counties have returned no bills of indictment. This would indicate either that local public sentiment approved these acts of violence or was too weak to punish them, or that the officers charged with that duty were in some way lacking in their performance. The evil cannot be cured or remedied by silence as to its existence. Unchecked, it will continue until it becomes a reproach to our good name, and a menace to our prosperity and peace; and it behooves you to exhaust all remedies within your power to find better preventives for such crimes."

A Friendly Warning

From England comes a friendly voice which must give to every patriotic citizen food for earnese thought. Writing from London, to the Chicago Inter Ocean, Nov. 25, 1894, the distinguished compiler of our last census, Hon. Robert P. Porter, gives the American people a most interesting review of the anti-lynching crusade in England, submitting editorial opinions from all sections of England and Scotland, showing the consensus of British opinion on this subject. It hardly need be said, that without exception, the current of English thought deprecates the rule of mob law, and the conscience of England is shocked by the revelation made during the present crusade. In his letter Mr. Porter says:

"While some English journals have joined certain American journals in ridiculing the well-meaning people who have formed the anti-lynching committee, there is a deep under current on this subject which is injuring the Southern States far more than those who have not been drawn into the question of English investment for the South as I have can surmise. This feeling is by no means all sentiment. An Englishman whose word and active co-operation could send a million sterling to any legitimate Southern enterprise said the other day: "I will not invest a farthing in States where these horrors occur. I have no particular sympathy with the anti-lynching committee, but such outrages indicate to my mind that where life is held to be of such little value there is even less assurance that the laws will protect property. As I understand it the States, not the national government, control in such matters, and where those laws are strongest there is the best field for British capital."

Probably the most bitter attack on the anti-lynching committee has come from the London Times. Those Southern Governors who had their bombastic letters published in the Times, with favorable editorial comment, may have had their laugh at the anti-lynchers here too soon. A few days ago, in commenting on an interesting communication from Richard H. Edmonds, editor of the Manufacturer's Record, setting forth the industrial advantages of the Southern States, which was published in its columns, the Times says: "Without in any way countenancing the impertinence of 'anti-lynching' committee, we may say that a state of things in which the killing of Negroes by blood-thirsty mobs is an incident of not unfrequent occurrence is not conducive to success in industry. Its existence, however, is a serious obstacle to the success of the South in industry; for even now Negro labor, which means at best inefficient labor, must be largely relied on there, and its efficiency must be still further diminished by spasmodic terrorism.

"Those interested in the development of the resources of the Southern States, and no one in proportion to his means has shown more faith in the progress of the South than the writer of this article, must take hold of this matter earnestly and intelligently. Sneering at the anti-lynching committee will do no good. Back of them, in fact, if not in form, is the public opinion of Great Britain. Even the Times cannot deny this. It may not be generally known in the United States, but while the Southern and some of the Northern newspapers are making a target of Miss Wells, the young colored woman who started this English movement, and cracking their jokes at the expense of Miss Florence Balgarnie, who, as honorable secretary, conducts the committee's correspondence, the strongest sort of sentiment is really at the back of the movement. Here we have crystallized every phase of political opinion. Extreme Unionists like the Duke of Argyll and advanced home rulers such as Justin McCarthy; Thomas Burt, the labor leader; Herbert Burrows, the Socialist, and Tom Mann, representing all phases of the Labor party, are co-operating with conservatives like Sir T. Eldon Gorst. But the real strength of this committee is not visible to the casual observer. As a matter of fact it represents many of the leading and most powerful British journals. A. E. Fletcher is editor of the London Daily Chronicle; P. W. Clayden is prominent in the counsels of the London Daily News; Professor James Stuart is Gladstone's[9] great friend and editor of the London Star; William Byles is editor and proprietor of the Bradford Observer; Sir Hugh Gilzen Reid is a leading Birmingham editor; in short, this committee has secured if not the leading editors, certainly important and warm

---

[9] A highly respected statesman, William Ewart Gladstone served as prime minister of Great Britain on four occasions: 1868–74, 1880–85, 1886, and 1892–94 (during the time of Wells's speaking tours of Great Britain).

friends, representing the Manchester Guardian, the Leeds Mercury, the Plymouth Western News, Newcastle Leader, the London Daily Graphic, the Westminster Gazette, the London Echo, a host of minor papers all over the kingdom, and practically the entire religious press of the kingdom.

"The greatest victory for the anti-lynchers comes this morning in the publication in the London Times of William Lloyd Garrison's letter. This letter will have immense effect here. It may have been printed in full in the United States, but nevertheless I will quote a paragraph which will strengthen the anti-lynchers greatly in their crusade here:

" 'A year ago the South derided and resented Northern protests; today it listens, explains and apologizes for its uncovered cruelties. Surely a great triumph for a little woman to accomplish! It is the power of truth simply and unreservedly spoken, for her language was inadequate to describe the horrors exposed.'

"If the Southern states are wise, and I say this with the earnestness of a friend and one who has built a home in the mountain regions of the South and thrown his lot in with them, they will not only listen, but stop lawlessness of all kinds. If they do, and thus secure the confidence of Englishmen, we may in the next decade realize some of the hopes for the new South we have so fondly cherished."

CHAPTER VIII.
MISS WILLARD'S ATTITUDE

No class of American citizens stands in greater need of the humane and thoughtful consideration of all sections of our country than do the colored people, nor does any class exceed us in the measure of grateful regard for acts of kindly interest in our behalf. It is, therefore, to us, a matter of keen regret that a Christian organization so large and influential as the Woman's Christian Temperance Union, should refuse to give its sympathy and support to our oppressed people who ask no further favor than the promotion of public sentiment which shall guarantee to every person accused of crime the safeguard of a fair and impartial trial, and protection from butchery by brutal mobs. Accustomed as we are to the indifference and apathy of Christian people, we would bear this instance of ill fortune in silence, had not Miss Willard gone out of her way to antagonize the cause so dear to our hearts by including in her Annual Address to the W. C. T. U. Convention at Cleveland, November 5, 1894, a studied, unjust and wholly unwarranted attack upon our work.

In her address Miss Willard said:

The zeal for her race of Miss Ida B. Wells, a bright young colored woman, has, it seems to me, clouded her perception as to who were her friends and well-wishers in all high-minded and legitimate efforts to banish the abomination of lynching and torture from the land of the free and the home of the brave. It is my firm belief that in the statements made by Miss Wells concerning white women having taken the initiative in nameless acts between the races she has put an imputation upon half the white race in this country that is unjust, and, save in the rarest exceptional instances, wholly without foundation. This is the unanimous opinion of the most disinterested and observant leaders of opinion whom I have consulted on the subject, and I do not fear to say that the laudable efforts she is making are greatly handicapped by statements of this kind, nor to urge her as a friend and well-wisher to banish from her vocabulary all such allusions as a source of weakness to the cause she has at heart.

This paragraph, brief as it is, contains two statements which have not the slightest foundation in fact. At no time, nor in any place, have I made statements "concerning white women having taken the initiative in nameless acts between the races." Further, at no time, or place nor under any circumstance, have I directly or inferentially "put an imputation upon half the white race in this country" and I challenge this "friend and well-wisher" to give proof of the truth of her charge. Miss Willard protests against lynching in one paragraph and then, in the next, deliberately misrepresents my position in order that she may criticise a movements, whose only purpose is to protect our oppressed race from vindictive slander and Lynch Law.

What I have said and what I now repeat—in answer to her first charge—is, that colored men have been lynched for assault upon women, when the facts were plain that the relationship between the victim lynched and the alleged victim of his assault was voluntary, clandestine and illicit. For that very reason we maintain, that, in every section of our land, the accused should have a fair, impartial trial, so that a man who is colored shall not be hanged for an offense, which, if he were white, would not be adjudged a crime. Facts cited in another chapter—"History of Some Cases of Rape"—amply maintain this position. The publication of these facts in defense of the good name of the race casts no "imputation upon half the white race in this country" and no such imputation can be inferred except by persons deliberately determined to be unjust.

But this is not the only injury which this cause has suffered at the hands of our "friend and well-wisher." It has been said that the Women's Christian Temperance Union, the most powerful organization of women in America, was misrepresented by me while I was in England. Miss Willard was in England at the time and knowing that no such misrepresentation came to her notice, she has permitted that impression to become fixed and widespread, when a word from her would have made the facts plain.

I never at any time or place or in any way misrepresented that organization. When asked what concerted action had been taken by churches and great moral agencies in America to put down Lynch Law, I was compelled in truth to say that no such action had occurred, that pulpit, press and moral agencies in the main were silent and for reasons known to themselves, ignored the awful conditions which to the English people appeared so abhorent. Then the question was asked what the great moral reformers like Miss Frances Willard and Mr. Moody[10] had done to suppress Lynch Law and again I answered—nothing. That Mr. Moody had never said a word against lynching in any of his trips to the South, or in the North either, so far as was known, and that Miss Willard's only public utterance on the situation had condoned lynching and other unjust practices of the South against the Negro. When proof of these statements was demanded, I sent a letter containing a copy of the New York Voice, Oct. 23, 1890, in which appeared Miss Willard's own words of wholesale slander against the colored race and condonation of Southern white people's outrages against us. My letter in part reads as follows:

But Miss Willard, the great temperance leader, went even further in putting the seal of her approval upon the southerners' method of dealing with the Negro. In October, 1890, the Women's Christian Temperance Union held its national meeting at Atlanta, Georgia. It was the first time in the history of the organization that it had gone south for a national meeting, and met the southerners in their own homes. They were welcomed with open arms. The governor of the state and the legislature gave special audiences in the halls of state legislation to the temperance work-

---

[10]Rev. Dwight L. Moody, an internationally recognized evangelist from Northfield, Massachusetts, is perhaps best known as the founder of the Chicago Bible Institute (now the Moody Bible Institute).

ers. They set out to capture the northerners to their way of seeing things, and without troubling to hear the Negro side of the question, these temperance people accepted the white man's story of the problem with which he had to deal. State organizers were appointed that year, who had gone through the southern states since then, but in obedience to southern prejudices have confined their work to white persons only. It is only after Negroes are in prison for crimes that efforts of these temperance women are exerted without regard to "race, color, or previous condition." No "ounce of prevention" is used in their case; they are black, and if these women went among the Negroes for this work, the whites would not receive them. Except here and there, are found no temperance workers of the Negro race; "the great dark-faced mobs" are left the easy prey of the saloonkeepers.

There was pending in the National Congress at this time a Federal Election Bill, the object being to give the National Government control of the national elections in the several states. Had this bill become a law, the Negro, whose vote has been systematically suppressed since 1875 in the southern states, would have had the protection of the National Government, and his vote counted. The South would have been no longer "solid;" the Southerners saw that the balance of power which they unlawfully held in the House of Representatives and the Electoral College, based on the Negro population, would be wrested from them. So they nick-named the pending elections law the "Force Bill"—probably because it would force them to disgorge their ill-gotten political gains—and defeated it. While it was being discussed, the question was submitted to Miss Willard: "What do you think of the race problem and the Force Bill?"

Said Miss Willard: "Now, as to the 'race problem' in its minified, current meaning, I am a true lover of the southern people—have spoken and worked in, perhaps, 200 of their towns and cities; have been taken into their love and confidence at scores of hospitable firesides; have heard them pour out their hearts in the splendid frankness of their impetuous natures. And I have said to them at such times: 'When I go North there will be wafted to you no word from pen or voice that is not loyal to what we are saying here and now.' Going South, a woman, a temperance woman, and a Northern temperance woman—three great barriers to their good will yonder—I was received by them with a confidence that was one of the most delightful surprises of my life. I think we have wronged the South, though we did not mean to do so. The reason was, in part, that we had irreparably wronged ourselves by putting no safeguards on the ballot box at the

North that would sift out alien illiterates. They rule our cities today; the saloon is their palace, and the toddy stick their sceptre. It is not fair that they should vote, nor is it fair that a plantation Negro, who can neither read nor write, whose ideas are bounded by the fence of his own field and the price of his own mule, should be entrusted with the ballot. We ought to have put an educational test upon that ballot from the first. The Anglo-Saxon race will never submit to be dominated by the Negro so long as his altitude reaches no higher than the personal liberty of the saloon, and the power of appreciating the amount of liquor that a dollar will buy. New England would no more submit to this than South Carolina. 'Better whisky and more of it' has been the rallying cry of great dark-faced mobs in the Southern localities where local option was snowed under by the colored vote. Temperance has no enemy like that, for it is unreasoning and unreasonable. Tonight it promises in a great congregation to vote for temperance at the polls tomorrow; but tomorrow twenty-five cents changes that vote in favor of the liquor-seller.

"I pity the southerners, and I believe the great mass of them are as conscientious and kindly-intentioned toward the colored man as an equal number of white church-members of the North. Would-be demagogues lead the colored people to destruction. Half-drunken white roughs murder them at the polls, or intimidate them so that they do not vote. But the better class of people must not be blamed for this, and a more thoroughly American population than the Christian people of the South does not exist. They have the traditions, the kindness, the probity, the courage of our forefathers. The problem on their hands is immeasurable. The colored race multiplies like the locusts of Egypt. The grog-shop is its center of power. 'The safety of woman, of childhood, of the home, is menaced in a thousand localities at this moment, so that the men dare not go beyond the sight of their own roof-tree.' How little we know of all this, seated in comfort and affluence here at the North, descanting upon the rights of every man to cast one vote and have it fairly counted; that well-worn shibboleth invoked once more to dodge a living issue.

"The fact is that illiterate colored men will not vote at the South until the white population chooses to have them do so; and under similar conditions they would not at the North." Here we have Miss Willard's words in full, condoning fraud, violence, murder, at the ballot box; rapine, shooting, hanging and burning; for all these things are done and being done now by the Southern white people. She does not stop there, but goes a step further to aid them in blackening the good name of an entire race, as shown by the sentences quoted in the paragraph above. These utterances, for which the colored people have never forgiven Miss Willard, and which Frederick Douglass has denounced as false, are to be found in full in the Voice of October 23, 1890, a temperance organ published at New York city.

This letter appeared in the May number of Fraternity, the organ of the first Anti-Lynching society of Great Britain. When Lady Henry Somerset learned through Miss Florence Balgarnie that this letter had been published she informed me that if the interview was published she would take steps to let the public know that my statements must be received with caution. As I had no money to pay the printer to suppress the edition which was already published and these ladies did not care to do so, the May number of Fraternity was sent to its subscribers as usual. Three days later there appeared in the daily Westminster Gazette an "interview" with Miss Willard, written by Lady Henry Somerset, which was so subtly unjust in its wording that I was forced to reply in my own defense. In that reply I made only statements which, like those concerning Miss Willard's Voice interview, have not been and cannot be denied. It was as follows:

Lady Henry Somerset's Interview with Miss Willard

To the Editor of the Westminster Gazette: Sir—The interview published in your columns today hardly merits a reply, because of the indifference to suffering manifested. Two ladies are represented sitting under a tree at Reigate, and, after some preliminary remarks on the terrible subject of lynching, Miss Willard laughingly replies by cracking a joke. And the concluding sentence of the interview shows the object is not to determine how best they may help the Negro who is being hanged, shot and burned, but "to guard Miss Willard's reputation."

With me it is not myself nor my reputation, but the life of my people, which is at stake, and I affirm that this is the first time to my knowledge that Miss Willard has said a single word in denunciation of lynching or demand for law. The year 1890, the one in which the interview appears, had a larger lynching record than any previous year, and the number and territory have increased, to say nothing of the human beings burnt alive.

If so earnest as she would have the English public believe her to be, why was she silent when five minutes were given me to speak last

June at Princes' Hall, and in Holborn Town Hall this May? I should say it was as President of the Women's Christian Temperance Union of America she is timid, because all these unions in the South emphasize the hatred of the Negro by excluding him. There is not a single colored woman admitted to the Southern W. C. T. U., but still Miss Willard blames the Negro for the defeat of Prohibition in the South. Miss Willard quotes from Fraternity, but forgets to add my immediate recognition of her presence on the platform at Holborn Town Hall, when, amidst many other resolutions on temperance and other subjects in which she is interested, time was granted to carry an anti-lynching resolution. I was so thankful for this crumb of her speechless presence that I hurried off to the editor of Fraternity and added a postscript to my article blazoning forth that fact.

Any statements I have made concerning Miss Willard are confirmed by the Hon. Frederick Douglass (late United States minister to Hayti) in a speech delivered by him in Washington in January of this year, which has since been published in a pamphlet. The fact is, Miss Willard is no better or worse than the great bulk of white Americans on the Negro questions. They are all afraid to speak out, and it is only British public opinion which will move them, as I am thankful to see it has already begun to move Miss Willard. I am, etc.,

May 21.   IDA B. WELLS.

Unable to deny the truth of these assertions, the charge has been made that I have attacked Miss Willard and misrepresented the W. C. T. U. If to state facts is misrepresentation, then I plead guilty to the charge.

I said then and repeat now, that in all the ten terrible years of shooting, hanging and burning of men, women and children in America, the Women's Christian Temperance Union never suggested one plan or made one move to prevent those awful crimes. If this statement is untrue the records of that organization would disprove it before the ink is dry. It is clearly an issue of fact and in all fairness this charge of misrepresentation should either be substantiated or withdrawn.

It is not necessary, however, to make any representation concerning the W. C. T. U. and the lynching question. The record of that organization speaks for itself. During all the years prior to the agitation begun against Lynch Law, in which years men, women and children were scourged, hanged, shot and burned, the W. C. T. U. had no word, either of pity or protest; its great heart, which concerns itself about humanity the world over, was, toward our cause, pulseless as a stone. Let those who deny this speak by the record. Not until after the first British campaign, in 1893, was even a resolution passed by the body which is the self constituted guardian for "God, home and native land."

Nor need we go back to other years. The annual session of that organization held in Cleveland in November, 1894, made a record which confirms and emphasizes the silence charged against it. At that session, earnest efforts were made to secure the adoption of a resolution of protest against lynching. At that very time two men were being tried for the murder of six colored men who were arrested on charge of barn burning, chained together, and on pretense of being taken to jail, were driven into the woods where they were ambushed and all six shot to death. The six widows of the butchered men had just finished the most pathetic recital ever heard in any court room, and the mute appeal of twenty-seven orphans for justice touched the stoutest hearts. Only two weeks prior to the session, Gov. Jones of Alabama, in his last message to the retiring state legislature, cited the fact that in the two years just past, nine colored men had been taken from the legal authorities by lynching mobs and butchered in cold blood—and not one of these victims was even charged with an assault upon womanhood.

It was thought that this great organization, in face of these facts, would not hesitate to place itself on record in a resolution of protest against this awful brutality towards colored people. Miss Willard gave assurance that such a resolution would be adopted, and that assurance was relied on. The record of the session shows in what good faith that assurance was kept. After recommending an expression against Lynch Law, the President attacked the anti-lynching movement, deliberately misrepresenting my position, and in her annual address, charging me with a statement I never made.

Further than that, when the committee on resolutions reported their work, not a word was said against lynching. In the interest of the cause I smothered the resentment. I felt because of the unwarranted and unjust attack of the President, and labored with members to secure an expression of some kind, tending to abate the awful slaughter of my race. A resolution against lynching was introduced by Mrs. Fessenden and read, and then that great Christian body, which in its resolutions had expressed itself in opposition to the social amusement of card playing, athletic sports and promiscuous dancing; had protested against the licensing of saloons, inveighed against tobacco, pledged its allegiance to the Prohibition party, and thanked the Populist party in Kansas, the Republican party in California and the Democratic party in the South, wholly ignored the seven millions of colored people of this country whose plea was for a word of sympathy and support for the movement in their behalf. The resolution was not adopted, and the convention adjourned.

In the Union Signal Dec. 6, 1894, among the resolutions is found this one:

Resolved, That the National W. C. T. U., which has for years counted among its departments that of peace and arbitration, is utterly opposed to all lawless acts in any and all parts of our common lands and it urges these principles upon the public, praying that the time may speedily come when no human being shall be condemned without due process of law; and when the unspeakable outrages which have so often provoked such lawlessness shall be banished from the world, and childhood, maidenhood and womanhood shall no more be the victims of atrocities worse than death.

This is not the resolution offered by Mrs. Fessenden. She offered the one passed last year by the W. C. T. U. which was a strong unequivocal denunciation of lynching. But she was told by the chairman of the committee on resolutions, Mrs. Rounds, that there was already a lynching resolution in the hands of the committee. Mrs. Fessenden yielded the floor on that assurance, and no resolution of any kind against lynching was submitted and none was voted upon, not even the one above, taken from the columns of the Union Signal, the organ of the national W. C. T. U.!

Even the wording of this resolution which was printed by the W. C. T. U., reiterates the false and unjust charge which has been so often made as an excuse for lynchers. Statistics show that less than one-third of the lynching victims are hanged, shot and burned alive for "unspeakable outrages against womanhood, maidenhood and childhood;" and that nearly a thousand, including women and children, have been lynched upon any pretext whatsoever; and that all have met death upon the unsupported word of white men and women. Despite these facts this resolution which was printed, cloaks an apology for lawlessness, in the same paragraph which affects to condemn it, where it speaks of "the unspeakable outrages which have so often provoked such lawlessness."

Miss Willard told me the day before the resolutions were offered that the Southern women present had held a caucus that day. This was after I, as fraternal delegate from the Woman's Mite Missionary Society of the A. M. E. Church at Cleveland, O., had been introduced to tender its greetings. In so doing I expressed the hope of the colored women that the W. C. T. U. would place itself on record as opposed to lynching which robbed them of husbands, fathers, brothers and sons and in many cases of women as well. No note was made either in the daily papers or the Union Signal of that introduction and greeting, although every other incident of that morning was published. The failure to submit a lynching resolution and the wording of the one above appears to have been the result of that Southern caucus.

On the same day I had a private talk with Miss Willard and told her she had been unjust to me and the cause in her annual address, and asked that she correct the statement that I had misrepresented the W.C.T.U., or that I had "put an imputation on one-half the white race in this country." She said that somebody in England told her it was a pity that I attacked the white women of America. "Oh," said I, "then you went out of your way to prejudice me and my cause in your annual address, not upon what you had heard me say, but what somebody had told you I said?" Her reply was that I must not blame her for her rhetorical expressions—that I had my way of expressing things and she had hers. I told her I most assuredly did blame her when those expressions were calculated to do such harm. I waited for an honest unequivocal retraction of her statements based on "hearsay." Not a word of retraction or explanation was said in the convention and I remained misrepresented before that body through her connivance and consent.

The editorial notes in the Union Signal, Dec. 6, 1894, however, contains the following:

"In her repudiation of the charges brought by Miss Ida Wells against white women as having taken the initiative in nameless crimes between the races, Miss Willard said in her annual address that this statement 'put an unjust imputation upon half the white race.' But as this expression has been misunderstood she desires to declare that she did not intend a literal interpretation to be given to the language used, but employed it to express a tendency that might ensue in public thought as a result of utterances so sweeping as some that have been made by Miss Wells."

Because this explanation is as unjust as the original offense, I am forced in self-defense to submit this account of differences. I desire no quarrel with the W. C. T. U., but my love for the truth is greater than my regard for an alleged friend who, through ignorance or design misrepresents in the most harmful way the cause of a long suffering race, and then unable to maintain the truth of her attack excuses herself as it were by the wave of the hand, declaring that "she did not intend a literal interpretation to be given to the language used." When the lives of men, women and children are at stake, when the inhuman butchers of innocents attempt to justify their barbarism by fastening upon a whole race the obloque[11] of the most infamous of crimes. It is little less than criminal to apologize for the butchers today and tomorrow to repudiate the apology by declaring it a figure of speech.

CHAPTER IX.
LYNCHING RECORD FOR 1894

The following tables are based on statistics taken from the columns of the Chicago Tribune, Jan. 1, 1895. They are a valuable appendix to the foregoing pages. They show, among other things, that in Louisiana, April 23–28, eight Negroes were lynched because one white man was killed by the Negro, the latter acting in self defense. Only seven of them are given in the list.

Near Memphis, Tenn., six Negroes were lynched—this time charged with burning barns. A trial of the indicted resulted in an acquittal, although it was shown on trial that the lynching was pre-arranged for them. Six widows and twenty-seven orphans are indebted to this mob for their condition, and this lynching swells the number to eleven Negroes lynched in and about Memphis since March 9, 1892.

In Brooks county, Ga., Dec. 23rd, while this Christian country was preparing for Christmas celebration, seven Negroes were lynched in twenty-four hours because they refused, or were unable to tell the whereabouts of a colored man named Pike, who killed a white man. The wives and daughters of these lynched men were horribly and brutally outraged by the murderers of their husbands and fathers. But the mob has not been punished and again women and children are robbed of their protectors whose blood cries unavenged to Heaven and humanity. Georgia heads the list of lynching states.

MURDER

Jan. 9, Samuel Smith, Greenville, Ala., Jan. 11, Sherman Wagoner, Mitchell, Ind.; Jan. 12, Roscoe Parker, West Union, Ohio; Feb. 7, Henry Bruce, Gulch Co., Ark.; March 5, Sylvester Rhodes, Collins, Ga.; March 15, Richard Puryea, Stroudsburg, Pa.; March 29, Oliver Jackson, Montgomery, Ala.; March 30, —— Saybrick, Fisher's Ferry, Miss.; April 14, William Lewis, Lanison, Ala.; April 23, Jefferson

[11]Obloquy.

Luggle, Cherokee, Kan.; April 23, Samuel Slaugate, Tallulah, La.; April 23, Thomas Claxton, Tallulah, La.; April 23, David Hawkins, Tallulah, La.; April 27, Thel Claxton, Tallulah, La.; April 27, Comp Claxton, Tallulah, La.; April 27, Scot Harvey, Tallulah, La.; April 27, Jerry McCly, Tallulah, La.; May 17, Henry Scott, Jefferson, Tex.; May 15, Coat Williams, Pine Grove, Fla.; June 2, Jefferson Crawford, Bethesda, S.C.; June 4, Thondo Underwood, Monroe, La.; June 8, Isaac Kemp, Cape Charles, Va.; June 13, Lon Hall, Sweethouse, Tex.; June 13, Bascom Cook, Sweethouse, Tex.; June 15, Luke Thomas, Biloxi, Miss.; June 29, John Williams, Sulphur, Tex.; June 29, Ulysses Hayden, Monett, Mo.; July 6, —— Hood, Amite, Miss.; July 7, James Bell, Charlotte, Tenn.; Sept. 2, Henderson Hollander, Elkhorn, W.Va.; Sept. 14, Robert Williams, Concordia Parish, La.; Sept. 22, Luke Washington, Meghee, Ark.; Sept. 22, Richard Washington, Meghee, Ark.; Sept. 22, Henry Crobyson, Meghee, Ark.; Nov. 10, Lawrence Younger, Lloyd, Va.; Dec. 17, unknown Negro, Williamston, S.C.; Dec. 23, Samuel Taylor, Brooks County, Ga.; Dec. 23, Charles Frazier, Brooks County, Ga.; Dec. 23, Samuel Pike, Brooks County, Ga.; Dec. 23, Harry Sherard, Brooks County, Ga.; Dec. 23, unknown Negro, Brooks County, Ga.; Dec. 23, unknown Negro, Brooks County, Ga.; Dec. 23, unknown Negro, Brooks County, Ga.; Dec. 26, Daniel McDonald, Winston County, Miss.; Dec. 26, William Carter, Winston County, Miss.

RAPE

Jan. 17, John Buckner, Valley Park, Mo.; Jan. 21, M. G. Cambell, Jellico Mines, Ky.; Jan. 27, unknown, Verona, Mo.; Feb. 11, Henry McCreeg, near Pioneer, Tenn.; April 6, Daniel Ahren, Greensboro, Ga.; April 15, Seymour Newland, Rushsylvania, Ohio; April 26, Robert Evarts, Jamaica, Ga.; April 27, James Robinson, Manassas, Va.; April 27, Benjamin White, Manassas, Va.; May 15, Nim Young, Ocala, Fla.; May 22, unknown, Miller County, Ga.; June 13, unknown, Blackshear, Ga.; June 18, Owen Opliltree, Forsyth, Ga.; June 22, Henry Capus, Magnolia, Ark.; June 26, Caleb Godly, Bowling Green, Ky.; June 28, Fayette Franklin, Mitchell, Ga.; July 2, Joseph Johnson, Hiller's Creek, Mo.; July 6, Lewis Bankhead, Cooper, Ala.; July 16, Marion Howard, Scottsville, Ky.; July 20, William Griffith, Woodville, Tex.; Aug. 12, William Nershbread, Rossville, Tenn.; Aug. 14, Marshall Boston, Frankfort, Ky.; Sept. 19, David Gooseby, Atlanta, Ga.; Oct. 15, Willis Griffey, Princeton, Ky.; Nov. 8, Lee Lawrence, Jasper County, Ga.; Nov. 10, Needham Smith, Tipton County, Tenn.; Nov. 14, Robert Mosely, Dolinite, Ala.; Dec. 4, William Jackson, Ocala, Fla.; Dec. 18, unknown, Marion County, Fla.

UNKNOWN OFFENSES

March 6, Lamsen Gregory, Bell's Depot, Tenn.; March 6, unknown woman, near Marche, Ark.; April 14, Alfred Brenn, Calhoun, Ga.; June 8, Harry Gill, West Lancaster, S.C.; Nov. 23, unknown, Landrum, S.C.; Dec. 5, Mrs. Teddy Arthur, Lincoln County, W.Va.

DESPERADO

Jan. 14, Charles Willis, Ocala, Fla.

SUSPECTED INCENDIARISM

Jan. 18, unknown, Bayou Sarah, La.

SUSPECTED ARSON

June 14, J. H. Dave, Monroe, La.

ENTICING SERVANT AWAY

Feb. 10, —— Collins, Athens, Ga.

TRAIN WRECKING

Feb. 10, Jesse Dillingham, Smokeyville, Tex.

HIGHWAY ROBBERY

June 3, unknown, Dublin, Ga.

INCENDIARISM

Nov. 8, Gabe Nalls, Blackford, Ky.; Nov. 8, Ulysses Nalls, Blackford, Ky.

ARSON

Dec. 20, James Allen, Brownsville, Tex.

ASSAULT

Dec. 23, George King, New Orleans, La.

NO OFFENSE

Dec. 28, Scott Sherman, Morehouse Parish, La.

BURGLARY

May 29, Henry Smith, Clinton, Miss.; May 29, William James, Clinton, Miss.

ALLEGED RAPE

June 4, Ready Murdock, Yazoo, Miss.

ATTEMPTED RAPE

July 14, unknown Negro, Biloxi, Miss.; July 26, Vance McClure, New Iberia, La.; July 26, William Tyler, Carlisle, Ky.; Sept. 14, James Smith, Stark, Fla.; Oct. 8, Henry Gibson, Fairfield, Tex.; Oct. 20, —— Williams, Upper Marlboro, Md.; June 9, Lewis Williams, Hewett Springs, Miss.; June 28, George Linton, Brookhaven, Miss.; June 28, Edward White, Hudson, Ala.; July 6, George Pond, Fulton, Miss.; July 7, Augustus Pond, Tupelo, Miss.

RACE PREJUDICE

June 10, Mark Jacobs, Bienville, La.; July 24, unknown woman, Sampson County, Miss.

INTRODUCING SMALLPOX

June 10, James Perry, Knoxville, Ark.

KIDNAPPING

March 2, Lentige, Harland County, Ky.

CONSPIRACY

May 29, J. T. Burgis, Palatka, Fla.

HORSE STEALING

June 20, Archie Haynes, Mason County, Ky.; June 20, Burt Haynes, Mason County, Ky.; June 20, William Haynes, Mason County, Ky.

WRITING LETTER TO WHITE WOMAN

May 9, unknown Negro, West Texas.

GIVING INFORMATION

July 12, James Nelson, Abbeyville, S.C.

STEALING

Jan. 5, Alfred Davis, Live Oak County, Ark.

LARCENY

April 18, Henry Montgomery, Lewisburg, Tenn.

POLITICAL CAUSES

July 19, John Brownlee, Oxford, Ala.

CONJURING

July 20, Allen Myers, Rankin County, Miss.

ATTEMPTED MURDER

June 1, Frank Ballard, Jackson, Tenn.

ALLEGED MURDER

April 5, Negro, near Selma, Ala.; April 5, Negro, near Selma, Ala.

WITHOUT CAUSE

May 17, Samuel Wood, Gates City, Va.

BARN BURNING

April 22, Thomas Black, Tuscumbia, Ala.; April 22, John Williams, Tuscumbia, Ala.; April 22, Toney Johnson, Tuscumbia, Ala.; July 14, William Bell, Dixon, Tenn.; Sept. 1, Daniel Hawkins, Millington, Tenn.; Sept. 1, Robert Haynes, Millington, Tenn.; Sept. 1, Warner Williams, Millington, Tenn.; Sept. 1, Edward Hall, Millington, Tenn.; Sept. 1, John Haynes, Millington, Tenn.; Sept. 1, Graham White, Millington, Tenn.

ASKING WHITE WOMAN TO MARRY HIM

May 23, William Brooks, Galesline, Ark.

OFFENSES CHARGED FOR LYNCHING

Suspected arson, 2; stealing, 1; political causes, 1; murder, 45; rape, 29; desperado, 1; suspected incendiarism, 1; train wrecking, 1; enticing servant away, 1; kidnapping, 1; unknown offense, 6; larceny, 1; barn burning, 10; writing letters to a white woman, 1; without cause, 1; burglary, 1; asking white woman to marry, 1; conspiracy, 1; attempted murder, 1; horse stealing, 3; highway robbery, 1; alleged rape, 1; attempted rape, 11; race prejudice, 2; introducing smallpox, 1; giving information, 1; conjuring, 1; incendiarism, 2; arson, 1; assault, 1; no offense, 1; alleged murder, 2; total (colored), 134.

LYNCHING STATES

Mississippi, 15; Arkansas, 8; Virginia, 5; Tennessee, 15; Alabama, 12; Kentucky, 12; Texas, 9; Georgia, 19; South Carolina, 5; Florida, 7; Louisiana, 15; Missouri, 4; Ohio, 2; Maryland, 1; West Virginia, 2; Indiana, 1; Kansas, 1; Pennsylvania, 1.

LYNCHING BY THE MONTH

January, 11; February, 17; March, 8; April, 36; May, 16; June, 31; July, 21; August, 4; September, 17; October, 7; November, 9; December, 20; total colored and white, 197.

WOMEN LYNCHED

July 24, unknown woman, race prejudice, Sampson County, Miss.; March 6, unknown, woman, unknown offense, Marche, Ark.; Dec. 5, Mrs. Teddy Arthur, unknown cause, Lincoln County, W.Va.

CHAPTER X. THE REMEDY

It is a well established principle of law that every wrong has a remedy. Herein rests our respect for law. The Negro does not claim that all of the one thousand black men, women and children, who have been hanged, shot and burned alive during the past ten years, were innocent of the charges made against them. We have associated too long with the white man not to have copied his vices as well as his virtues. But we do insist that the punishment is not the same for both classes of criminals. In lynching, opportunity is not given the Negro to defend himself against the unsupported accusations of white men and women. The word of the accuser is held to be true and the excited bloodthirsty mob demands that the rule of law be reversed and instead of proving the accused to be guilty, the victim of their hate and revenge must prove himself innocent. No evidence he can offer will satisfy the mob; he is bound hand and foot and swung into eternity. Then to excuse its infamy, the mob almost invariably reports the monstrous falsehood that its victim made a full confession before he was hanged.

With all military, legal and political power in their hands, only two of the lynching States have attempted a check by exercising the power which is theirs. Mayor Trout, of Roanoke, Virginia, called out the militia in 1893, to protect a Negro prisoner, and in so doing nine men were killed and a number wounded. Then the mayor and militia withdrew, left the Negro to his fate and he was promptly lynched. The business men realized the blow to the town's were given light sentences, the highest being one of twelve financial interests, called the mayor home, the grand jury indicted and prosecuted the ringleaders of the mob. They months in State prison. The day he arrived at the penitentiary, he was pardoned by the governor of the State.[12]

The only other real attempt made by the authorities to protect a prisoner of the law, and which was more successful, was that of Gov.

---

[12]For sense, the passage should read: "The business men realized the blow to the town's financial interests, [and] called the mayor home. The grand jury indicted and prosecuted the ringleaders of the mob. They were given light sentences, the highest being one of twelve months in State prison. The day he arrived at the penitentiary, he was pardoned by the governor of the State."

McKinley,[13] of Ohio, who sent the militia to Washington Courthouse, O., in October, 1894, and five men were killed and twenty wounded in maintaining the principle that the law must be upheld.

In South Carolina, in April, 1893, Gov. Tillman aided the mob by yielding up to be killed, a prisoner of the law, who had voluntarily placed himself under the Governor's protection. Public sentiment by its representatives has encouraged Lynch Law, and upon the revolution of this sentiment we must depend for its abolition.

Therefore, we demand a fair trial by law for those accused of crime, and punishment by law after honest conviction. No maudlin sympathy for criminals is solicited, but we do ask that the law shall punish all alike. We earnestly desire those that control the forces which make public sentiment to join with us in the demand. Surely the humanitarian spirit of this country which reaches out to denounce the treatment of the Russian Jews, the Armenian Christians, the laboring poor of Europe, the Siberian exiles and the native women of India—will not longer refuse to lift its voice on this subject. If it were known that the cannibals or the savage Indians had burned three human beings alive in the past two years, the whole of Christendom would be roused, to devise ways and means to put a stop to it. Can you remain silent and inactive when such things are done in our own community and country? Is your duty to humanity in the United States less binding?

What can you do, reader, to prevent lynching, to thwart anarchy and promote law and order throughout our land?

1st. You can help disseminate the facts contained in this book by bringing them to the knowledge of every one with whom you come in contact, to the end that public sentiment may be revolutionized. Let the facts speak for themselves, with you as a medium.

2d. You can be instrumental in having churches, missionary societies, Y. M. C. A.'s, W. C. T. U.'s and all Christian and moral forces in connection with your religious and social life, pass resolutions of condemnation and protest every time a lynching takes place; and see that they are sent to the place where these outrages occur.

3d. Bring to the intelligent consideration of Southern people the refusal of capital to invest where lawlessness and mob violence hold sway. Many labor organizations have declared by resolution that they would avoid lynch infested localities as they would the pestilence when seeking new homes. If the South wishes to build up its waste

---

[13]William McKinley (Republican) served two terms as governor of Ohio and in 1896 was elected president of the United States. He died in office in 1901.

places quickly, there is no better way than to uphold the majesty of the law by enforcing obedience to the same, and meting out the same punishment to all classes of criminals, white as well as black. "Equality before the law," must become a fact as well as a theory before America is truly the "land of the free and the home of the brave."

4th. Think and act on independent lines in this behalf, remembering that after all, it is the white man's civilization and the white man's government which are on trial. This crusade will determine whether that civilization can maintain itself by itself, or whether anarchy shall prevail; whether this Nation shall write itself down a success at self government, or in deepest humiliation admit its failure complete; whether the precepts and theories of Christianity are professed and practiced by American white people as Golden Rules of thought and action, or adopted as a system of morals to be preached to heathen until they attain to the intelligence which needs the system of Lynch Law.

5th. Congressman Blair[14] offered a resolution in the House of Representatives, August, 1894. The organized life of the country can speedily make this a law by sending resolutions to Congress indorsing Mr. Blair's bill and asking Congress to create the commission. In no better way can the question be settled, and the Negro does not fear the issue. The following is the resolution:

"Resolved, By the House of Representatives and Senate in congress assembled, That the committee on labor be instructed to investigate and report the number, location and date of all alleged assaults by males upon females throughout the country during the ten years last preceding the passing of this joint resolution, for or on account of which organized but unlawful violence has been inflicted or attempted to be inflicted. Also to ascertain and report all facts of organized but unlawful violence to the person, with the attendant facts and circumstances, which have been inflicted upon accused persons alleged to have been guilty of crimes punishable by due process of law which have taken place in any part of the country within the ten years last preceding the passage of this resolution. Such investigation shall be made by the usual methods and agencies of the Department of Labor, and report made to Congress as soon as the work can be satisfactorily done, and the sum of $25,000, or so much thereof as may be necessary, is hereby appropriated to pay the expenses out of any money in the treasury not otherwise appropriated."

[14]Senator Henry W. Blair, Republican from New Hampshire.

The belief has been constantly expressed in England that in the United States, which has produced Wm. Lloyd Garrison, Henry Ward Beecher, James Russell Lowell, John G. Whittier[15] and Abraham Lincoln there must be those of their descendants who would take hold of the work of inaugurating an era of law and order. The colored people of this country who have been loyal to the flag believe the same, and strong in that belief have begun this crusade. To those who still feel they have no obligation in the matter, we commend the following lines of Lowell on "Freedom."

> Men! whose boast it is that ye
> Come of fathers brave and free,
> If there breathe on earth a slave
> Are ye truly free and brave?
> If ye do not feel the chain,
> When it works a brother's pain,
> Are ye not base slaves indeed,
> Slaves unworthy to be freed?
>
> Women! who shall one day bear
> Sons to breathe New England air,
> If ye hear without a blush,
> Deeds to make the roused blood rush
> Like red lava through your veins,
> For your sisters now in chains, —
> Answer! are ye fit to be
> Mothers of the brave and free?
>
> Is true freedom but to break
> Fetters for our own dear sake,
> And, with leathern hearts, forget
> That we owe mankind a debt?
> No! true freedom is to share
> All the chains our brothers wear,
> And, with heart and hand, to be
> Earnest to make others free!

[15]William Lloyd Garrison, publisher of the antislavery newspaper *The Liberator,* was a supporter of several African Americans, including Maria Stewart, the first known African American female political speaker; Charlotte Forten, educator, poet, and clubwoman; and Frederick Douglass. A Congregational minister and distinguished orator, Henry Ward Beecher was an outspoken abolitionist before the Civil War and a supporter of moderate Reconstruction policies afterwards. James Russell Lowell, an influential nineteenth-century poet and literary critic from Massachusetts, served also as minister to Spain and ambassador to Great Britain. John Greenleaf Whittier was a highly respected poet, journalist, and abolitionist from Massachusetts.

There are slaves who fear to speak
For the fallen and the weak;
They are slaves who will not choose
Hatred, scoffing, and abuse,
Rather than in silence shrink
From the truth they needs must think;
They are slaves who dare not be
In the right with two or three.

A Field for Practical Work

The very frequent inquiry made after my lectures by interested friends is, "What can I do to help the cause?" The answer always is, "Tell the world the facts." When the Christian world knows the alarming growth and extent of outlawry in our land, some means will be found to stop it.

The object of this publication is to tell the facts, and friends of the cause can lend a helping hand by aiding in the distribution of these books. When I present our cause to a minister, editor, lecturer, or representative of any moral agency, the first demand is for facts and figures. Plainly, I can not then hand out a book with a twenty-five cent tariff on the information contained. This would be only a new method in the book agents' art. In all such cases it is a pleasure to submit this book for investigation, with the certain assurance of gaining a friend to the cause.

There are many agencies which may be enlisted in our cause by the general circulation of the facts herein contained. The preachers, teachers, editors and humanitarians of the white race, at home and abroad, must have facts laid before them, and it is our duty to supply these facts. The Central Anti-Lynching League, Room 9, 128 Clark st., Chicago, has established a Free Distribution Fund, the work of which can be promoted by all who are interested in this work.

Anti-lynching leagues, societies and individuals can order books from this fund at agents' rates. The books will be sent to their order, or, if desired, will be distributed by the League among those whose co-operative aid we so greatly need. The writer hereof assures prompt distribution of books according to order, and public acknowledgment of all orders through the public press.

MOB RULE

IN

NEW ORLEANS.

Robert Charles

ROBERT CHARLES

AND

His Fight to the Death.

◉◉◉◉◉◉◉

THE STORY OF HIS LIFE.
BURNING HUMAN BEINGS ALIVE.
OTHER LYNCHING STATISTICS.

IDA B. WELLS-BARNETT,

CHICAGO.

PRICE 25 CENTS.

Scene depicting the capture of Robert Charles (from the New Orleans *Times-Democrat*).

INTRODUCTION

Immediately after the awful barbarism which disgraced the State of Georgia in April of last year, during which time more than a dozen colored people were put to death with unspeakable barbarity, I published a full report showing that Sam Hose, who was burned to death during that time, never committed a criminal assault, and that he killed his employer in self-defense.

Since that time I have been engaged on a work not yet finished, which I interrupt now to tell the story of the mob in New Orleans, which, despising all law, roamed the streets day and night, searching for colored men and women, whom they beat, shot and killed at will.

In the account of the New Orleans mob I have used freely the graphic reports of the New Orleans Times-Democrat and the New Orleans Picayune. Both papers gave the most minute details of the week's disorder. In their editorial comment they were at all times most urgent in their defense of law and in the strongest terms they condemned the infamous work of the mob.

It is no doubt owing to the determined stand for law and order taken by these great dailies and the courageous action taken by the best citizens of New Orleans, who rallied to the support of the civic authorities, that prevented a massacre of colored people awful to contemplate.

For the accounts and illustrations taken from the above-named journals, sincere thanks are hereby expressed.

The publisher hereof does not attempt to moralize over the deplorable condition of affairs shown in this publication, but simply presents the facts in a plain, unvarnished, connected way, so that he who runs may read. We do not believe that the American people who have encouraged such scenes by their indifference will read unmoved these accounts of brutality, injustice and oppression. We do not believe that the moral conscience of the nation—that which is highest and best among us—will always remain silent in face of such outrages, for God is not dead, and His Spirit is not entirely driven from men's hearts.

When this conscience wakes and speaks out in thunder tones, as it must, it will need facts to use as a weapon against injustice, barbarism and wrong. It is for this reason that I carefully compile, print and send forth these facts. If the reader can do no more, he can pass this pamphlet on to another, or send to the bureau addresses of those to whom he can order copies mailed.

Besides the New Orleans case, a history of burnings in this country is given, together with a table of lynchings for the past eighteen years. Those who would like to assist in the work of disseminating these facts, can do so by ordering copies, which are furnished at greatly reduced rates for gratuitous distribution. The bureau has no funds and is entirely dependent upon contributions from friends and members in carrying on the work.

Chicago, Sept. 1, 1900.   IDA B. WELLS-BARNETT.

SHOT AN OFFICER

The bloodiest week which New Orleans has known since the massacre of the Italians in 1892[1] was ushered in Monday, July 24th, by the inexcusable and unprovoked assault upon two colored men by police officers of New Orleans. Fortified by the assurance born of long expe-

---

[1] Eleven Italians were lynched after having been charged with the murder of the New Orleans chief of police. The Italian government protested, and the United States government eventually paid $25,000 in indemnities to the king of Italy.

rience in the New Orleans service, three policemen, Sergeant Aucoin, Officer Mora and Officer Cantrelle, observing two colored men sitting on doorsteps on Dryades street, between Washington avenue and 6th streets, determined, without a shadow of authority, to arrest them. One of the colored men was named Robert Charles, the other was a lad of nineteen named Leonard Pierce. The colored men had left their homes, a few blocks distant, about an hour prior, and had been sitting upon the doorsteps for a short time talking together. They had not broken the peace in any way whatever, no warrant was in the policemen's hands justifying their arrest, and no crime had been committed of which they were the suspects. The policemen, however, secure in the firm belief that they could do anything to a Negro that they wished, approached the two men, and in less than three minutes from the time they accosted them attempted to put both colored men under arrest. The younger of the two men, Pierce, submitted to arrest, for the officer, Cantrelle, who accosted him, put his gun in the young man's face ready to blow his brains out if he moved. The other colored man, Charles, was made the victim of a savage attack by Officer Mora, who used a billet and then drew a gun and tried to kill Charles. Charles drew his gun nearly as quickly as the policeman, and began a duel in the street, in which both participants were shot. The policeman got the worst of the duel, and fell helpless to the sidewalk. Charles made his escape. Cantrelle took Pierce, his captive, to the police station, to which place Mora, the wounded officer, was also taken, and a man hunt at once instituted for Charles, the wounded fugitive.

In any law-abiding community Charles would have been justified in delivering himself up immediately to the properly constituted authorities and asking a trial by a jury of his peers. He could have been certain that in resisting an unwarranted arrest he had a right to defend his life, even to the point of taking one in that defense, but Charles knew that his arrest in New Orleans, even for defending his life, meant nothing short of a long term in the penitentiary, and still more probable death by lynching at the hands of a cowardly mob. He very bravely determined to protect his life as long as he had breath in his body and strength to draw a hair trigger on his would-be murderers. How well he was justified in that belief is well shown by the newspaper accounts which were given of this transaction. Without a single line of evidence to justify the assertion, the New Orleans daily papers at once declared that both Pierce and Charles were desperadoes, that they were contemplating a burglary and that they began the assault upon the policemen. It is interesting to note how the two leading papers of New Orleans, the Picayune and the Times-Democrat, exert themselves to justify the policemen in the absolutely unprovoked attack upon the two colored men. As these two papers did all in their power to give an excuse for the action of the policemen, it is interesting to note their versions. The Times-Democrat of Tuesday morning, the 25th, says:

"Two blacks, who are desperate men, and no doubt will be proven burglars, made it interesting and dangerous for three bluecoats on Dryades street, between Washington avenue and Sixth street, the Negroes using pistols first and dropping Patrolman Mora. But the desperate darkies did not go free, for the taller of the two, Robinson, is badly wounded and under cover, while Leonard Pierce is in jail.

"For a long time that particular neighborhood has been troubled with bad Negroes, and the neighbors were complaining to the Sixth Precinct police about them. But of late Pierce and Robinson had been camping on a door step on the street, and the people regarded their actions as suspicious. It got to such a point that some of the residents were afraid to go to bed, and last night this was told Sergeant Aucoin, who was rounding up his men. He had just picked up Officers Mora and Cantrell, on Washington avenue and Dryades street, and catching a glimpse of the blacks on the steps, he said he would go over and warn the men to get away from the street. So the patrolmen followed, and Sergeant Aucoin asked the smaller fellow, Pierce, if he lived there. The answer was short and impertinent, the black saying he did not, and with that both Pierce and Robinson drew up to their full height.

"For the moment the sergeant did not think that the Negroes meant fight, and he was on the point of ordering them away when Robinson slipped his pistol from his pocket. Pierce had his revolver out, too, and he fired twice, point blank at the sergeant, and just then Robinson began shooting at the patrolmen. In a second or so the policemen and blacks were fighting with their revolvers, the sergeant having a duel with Pierce, while Cantrell and Mora drew their line of fire on Robinson, who was working his revolver for all he was worth. One of his shots took Mora in the right hip, another caught his index finger on the right hand, and a third struck the small finger of the left hand. Poor Mora was done for; he could not fight any more, but Cantrell kept up his fire, being answered by the big black. Pierce's revolver broke down, the cartridges snapping, and he threw up his hands, begging for quarter.

"The sergeant lowered his pistol and some citizens ran over to where the shooting was going on. One of the bullets that went at Robinson caught him in the breast and he began running, turning out

Sixth street, with Cantrell behind him, shooting every few steps. He was loading his revolver again, but did not use it after the start he took, and in a little while Officer Cantrell lost the man in the darkness.

"Pierce was made a prisoner and hurried to the Sixth Precinct police station, where he was charged with shooting and wounding. The sergeant sent for an ambulance, and Mora was taken to the hospital, the wound in the hip being serious.

"A search was made for Robinson, but he could not be found, and even at 2 o'clock this morning Captain Day, with Sergeant Aucoin and Corporals Perrier and Trenchard, with a good squad of men, were beating the weeds for the black."

The New Orleans Picayune of the same date described the occurrence, and from its account one would think it was an entirely different affair. Both of the two accounts cannot be true, and the unquestioned fact is that neither of them sets out the facts as they occurred. Both accounts attempt to fix the beginning of hostilities upon the colored men, but both were compelled to admit that the colored men were sitting on the doorsteps quietly conversing with one another when the three policemen went up and accosted them. The Times-Democrat unguardedly states that one of the two colored men tried to run away; that Mora seized him and then drew his billy and struck him on the head; that Charles broke away from him and started to run, after which the shooting began. The Picayune, however, declares that Pierce began the firing and that his two shots point blank at Aucoin were the first shots of the fight. As a matter of fact, Pierce never fired a single shot before he was covered by Aucoin's revolver. Charles and the officers did all the shooting. The Picayune's account is as follows:

"Patrolman Mora was shot in the right hip and dangerously wounded last night at 11:30 o'clock in Dryades street, between Washington and Sixth, by two Negroes, who were sitting on a door step in the neighborhood.

"The shooting of Patrolman Mora brings to memory the fact that he was one of the partners of Patrolman Trimp, who was shot by a Negro soldier of the United States government during the progress of the Spanish-American war. The shooting of Mora by the Negro last night is a very simple story. At the hour mentioned, three Negro women noticed two suspicious men sitting on a door step in the above locality. The women saw the two men making an apparent inspection of the building. As they told the story, they saw the men look over the fence and examine the window blinds, and they paid particular attention to the make-up of the building, which was a two-story affair. About that

time Sergeant J. C. Aucoin and Officers Mora and J. D. Cantrell hove
in sight. The women hailed them and described to them the suspicious actions of the two Negroes, who were still sitting on the step.
The trio of bluecoats, on hearing the facts, at once crossed the street
and accosted the men. The latter answered that they were waiting for
a friend whom they were expecting. Not satisfied with this answer, the
sergeant asked them where they lived, and they replied "down town,"
but could not designate the locality. To other questions put by the officers the larger of the two Negroes replied that they had been in town
just three days.

"As this reply was made, the larger man sprang to his feet, and
Patrolman Mora, seeing that he was about to run away, seized him.
The Negro took a firm hold on the officer, and a scuffle ensued. Mora,
noting that he was not being assisted by his brother officers, drew his
billy and struck the Negro on the head. The blow had but little effect
upon the man, for he broke away and started down the street. When
about ten feet away, the Negro drew his revolver and opened fire on
the officer, firing three or four shots. The third shot struck Mora in
the right hip, and was subsequently found to have taken an upward
course. Although badly wounded, Mora drew his pistol and returned
the fire. At his third shot the Negro was noticed to stagger, but he did
not fall. He continued his flight. At this moment Sergeant Aucoin
seized the other Negro, who proved to be a youth, Leon Pierce. As
soon as Officer Mora was shot he sank to the sidewalk, and the other
officer ran to the nearest telephone, and sent in a call for the ambulance. Upon its arrival the wounded officer was placed in it and conveyed to the hospital. An examination by the house surgeon revealed
the fact that the bullet had taken an upward course. In the opinion of
the surgeon the wound was a dangerous one."

But the best proof of the fact that the officers accosted the two colored men and without any warrant or other justification attempted to
arrest them, and did actually seize and begin to club one of them, is
shown by Officer Mora's own statement. The officer was wounded and
had every reason in the world to make his side of the story as good as
possible. His statement was made to a Picayune reporter and the same
was published on the 25th inst., and is as follows:

"I was in the neighborhood of Dryades and Washington streets,
with Sergeant Aucoin and Officer Cantrell, when three Negro women
came up and told us that there were two suspicious-looking Negroes
sitting on a step on Dryades street, betwen Washington and Sixth. We
went to the place indicated and found two Negroes. We interrogated
them as to who they were, what they were doing and how long they

had been here. They replied that they were working for some one and had been in town three days. At about this stage the larger of the two Negroes got up and I grabbed him. The Negro pulled, but I held fast, and he finally pulled me into the street. Here I began using my billet, and the Negro jerked from my grasp and ran. He then pulled a gun and fired. I pulled my gun and returned the fire, each of us firing about three shots. I saw the Negro stumble several times, and I thought I had shot him, but he ran away and I don't know whether any of my shots took effect. Sergeant Aucoin in the meantime held the other man fast. The man was about ten feet from me when he fired, and the three Negresses who told us about the men stood away about twenty-five feet from the shooting."

Thus far in the proceeding the Monday night episode results in Officer Mora lying in the station wounded in the hip; Leonard Pierce, one of the colored men, locked up in the station, and Robert Charles, the other colored man, a fugitive, wounded in the leg and sought for by the entire police force of New Orleans. Not sought for, however, to be placed under arrest and given a fair trial and punished if found guilty according to the law of the land, but sought for by a host of enraged, vindictive and fearless officers, who were coolly ordered to kill him on sight. This order is shown by the Picayune of the 26th inst., in which the following statement appears:

"In talking to the sergeant about the case, the captain asked about the Negro's fighting ability, and the sergeant answered that Charles, though he called him Robinson then, was a desperate man, and it would be best to shoot him before he was given a chance to draw his pistol upon any of the officers."

This instruction was given before anybody had been killed, and the only evidence that Charles was a desperate man lay in the fact that he had refused to be beaten over the head by Officer Mora for sitting on a step quietly conversing with a friend. Charles resisted an absolutely unlawful attack, and a gun fight followed. Both Mora and Charles were shot, but because Mora was white and Charles was black, Charles was at once declared to be a desperado, made an outlaw, and subsequently a price put upon his head and the mob authorized to shoot him like a dog, on sight.

The New Orleans Picayune of Wednesday morning said:

"But he has gone, perhaps to the swamps, and the disappointment of the bluecoats in not getting the murderer is expressed in their curses, each man swearing that the signal to halt that will be offered Charles will be a shot."

In that same colume of the Picayune it was said:

"Hundreds of policemen were about; each corner was guarded by a squad, commanded either by a sergeant or a corporal, and every man had the word to shoot the Negro as soon as he was sighted. He was a desperate black and would be given no chance to take more life." Legal sanction was given to the mob or any man of the mob to kill Charles at sight by the Mayor of New Orleans, who publicly proclaimed a reward of two hundred and fifty dollars, not for the arrest of Charles, not at all, but the reward was offered for Charles' body, "dead or alive." The advertisement was as follows:

"$250 REWARD.

"Under the authority vested in me by law, I hereby offer, in the name of the city of New Orleans, $250 reward for the capture and delivery, dead or alive, to the authorities of the city, the body of the Negro murderer,

"ROBERT CHARLES,

who, on Tuesday morning, July 24, shot and killed

"Police Captain John T. Day and Patrolman Peter J. Lamb, and wounded

"Patrolman August T. Mora.

"PAUL CAPDEVIELLE, Mayor."

This authority, given by the sergeant to kill Charles on sight, would have been no news to Charles, nor to any colored man in New Orleans, who, for any purpose whatever, even to save his life, raised his hand against a white man. It is now, even as it was in the days of slavery, an unpardonable sin for a Negro to resist a white man, no matter how unjust or unprovoked the white man's attack may be. Charles knew this, and knowing to be captured meant to be killed, he resolved to sell his life as dearly as possible.

The next step in the terrible tragedy occurred between 2:30 and 5 o'clock Tuesday morning, about four hours after the affair on Dryades street. The man hunt, which had been inaugurated soon after Officer Mora had been carried to the station, succeeded in running down Robert Charles, the wounded fugitive, and located him at 2023 4th street. It was nearly 2 o'clock in the morning when a large detail of police surrounded the block with the intent to kill Charles on sight. Capt. Day had charge of the squad of police. Charles, the wounded man, was in his house when the police arrived, fully prepared, as results afterward showed, to die in his own home. Capt. Day started for Charles' room. As soon as Charles got sight of him there was a flash, a report, and Day fell dead in his tracks. In another instant

Charles was standing in the door, and seeing Patrolman Peter J. Lamb, he drew his gun, and Lamb fell dead. Two other officers, Sergeant Aucoin and Officer Trenchard, who were in the squad, seeing their comrades, Day and Lamb, fall dead, concluded to raise the siege, and both disappeared into an adjoining house, where they blew out their lights so that their cowardly carcasses could be safe from Charles' deadly aim. The calibre of their courage is well shown by the fact that they concluded to save themselves from any harm by remaining prisoners in that dark room until daybreak, out of reach of Charles' deadly rifle. Sergeant Aucoin, who had been so brave a few hours before when seeing the two colored men sitting on the steps talking together on Dryades street, and supposing that neither was armed, now showed his true calibre. Now he knew that Charles had a gun and was brave enough to use it, so he hid himself in a room two hours while Charles deliberately walked out of his room and into the street after killing both Lamb and Day. It is also shown, as further evidence of the bravery of some of New Orleans' "finest," that one of them, seeing Capt. Day fall, ran seven blocks before he stopped, afterwards giving the excuse that he was hunting for a patrol box.

At daybreak the officers felt safe to renew the attack upon Charles, so they broke into his room, only to find that—what they probably very well knew—he had gone. It appears that he made his escape by crawling through a hole in the ceiling to a little attic in his house. Here he found that he could not escape except by a window which led into an alley which had no opening on 4th street. He scaled the fence and was soon out of reach.

It was now 5 o'clock Tuesday morning, and a general alarm was given. Sergeant Aucoin and Corporal Trenchard, having received a new supply of courage by returning daylight, renewed their effort to capture the man that they had allowed to escape in the darkness. Citizens were called upon to participate in the man hunt and New Orleans was soon the scene of terrible excitement. Officers were present everywhere, and colored men were arrested on all sides upon the pretext that they were impertinent and "game niggers." An instance is mentioned in the Times-Democrat of the 25th and shows the treatment which unoffending colored men received at the hands of some of the officers. This instance shows Corporal Trenchard, who displayed such remarkable bravery on Monday night in dodging Charles' revolver, in his true light. It shows how brave a white man is when he has a gun attacking a Negro who is a helpless prisoner. The account is as follows:

"The police made some arrests in the neighborhood of the killing of the two officers. Mobs of young darkies gathered everywhere. These Negroes talked and joked about the affair, and many of them were for starting a race war on the spot. It was not until several of these little gangs amalgamated and started demonstrations that the police commenced to act. Nearly a dozen arrests were made within an hour, and everybody in the vicinity was in a tremor of excitement.

"It was about 1 o'clock that the Negroes on Fourth street became very noisy, and George Meyers, who lives on Sixth street, near Rampart, appeared to be one of the prime movers in a little riot that was rapidly developing. Policeman Exnicios and Sheridan placed him under arrest, and owing to the fact that the patrol wagon had just left with a number of prisoners, they walked him toward St. Charles avenue in order to get a conveyance to take him to the Sixth Precinct station.

"A huge crowd of Negroes followed the officers and their prisoners. Between Dryades and Baronne, on Sixth, Corporal Trenchard met the trio. He had his pistol in his hand and he came on them running. The Negroes in the wake of the officers and prisoner took to flight immediately. Some disappeared through gates and some over fences and into yards, for Trenchard, visibly excited, was waving his revolver in the air and was threatening to shoot. He joined the officers in their walk toward St. Charles street, and the way he acted led the white people who were witnessing the affair to believe that his prisonr was the wanted Negro. At every step he would punch him or hit him with the barrel of his pistol, and the onlookers cried, "Lynch him!" "Kill him!" and other expressions until the spectators were thoroughly wrought up. At St. Charles street Trenchard desisted, and, calling an empty ice wagon, threw the Negro into the body of the vehicle and ordered Officer Exnicios to take him to the Sixth Precinct station.

"The ride to the station was a wild one. Exnicios had all he could do to watch his prisoner. A gang climbed into the wagon and administered a terrible thrashing to the black en route. It took a half hour to reach the police station, for the mule that was drawing the wagon was not overly fast. When the station was reached a mob of nearly 200 howling white youths was awaiting it. The noise they made was something terrible. Meyers was howling for mercy before he reached the ground. The mob dragged him from the wagon, the officer with him. Then began a torrent of abuse for the unfortunate prisoner.

"The station door was but thirty feet away, but it took Exnicios nearly five minutes to fight his way through the mob to the door.

There were no other officers present, and the station seemed to be deserted. Neither the doorman nor the clerk paid any attention to the noise on the outside. As the result, the maddened crowd wrought their vengeance on the Negro. He was punched, kicked, bruised and torn. The clothes were ripped from his back, while his face after that few minutes was unrecognizable."

This was the treatment accorded and permitted to a helpless prisoner because he was black. All day Wednesday the man hunt continued. The excitement caused by the deaths of Day and Lamb became intense. The officers of the law knew they were trailing a man whose aim was deadly and whose courage they had never seen surpassed. Commenting upon the marksmanship of the man which the paper styled a fiend, the Times-Democrat of Wednesday said:

"One of the extraordinary features of the tragedy was the marksmanship displayed by the Negro desperado. His aim was deadly and his coolness must have been something phenomenal. The two shots that killed Captain Day and Patrolman Lamb struck their victims in the head, a circumstance remarkable enough in itself, considering the suddenness and fury of the onslaught and the darkness that reigned in the alley way.

"Later on Charles fired at Corporal Perrier, who was standing at least seventy-five yards away. The murderer appeared at the gate, took lightning aim along the side of the house, and sent a bullet whizzing past the officer's ear. It was a close shave, and a few inches' deflection would no doubt have added a fourth victim to the list.

"At the time of the affray there is good reason to believe that Charles was seriously wounded, and at any event he had lost quantities of blood. His situation was as critical as it is possible to imagine, yet he shot like an expert in a target range. The circumstance shows the desperate character of the fiend, and his terrible dexterity with weapons makes him one of the most formidable monsters that has ever been loose upon the community."

Wednesday New Orleans was in the hands of a mob. Charles, still sought for and still defending himself, had killed four policemen, and everybody knew that he intended to die fighting. Unable to vent its vindictiveness and bloodthirsty vengeance upon Charles, the mob turned its attention to other colored men who happened to get in the path of its fury. Even colored women, as has happened many times before, were assaulted and beaten and killed by the brutal hoodlums who thronged the streets. The reign of absolute lawlessness began about 8 o'clock Wednesday night. The mob gathered near the Lee statue and was soon making its way to the place where the officers had been shot by Charles. Describing the mob, the Times-Democrat of Thursday morning says:

"The gathering in the square, which numbered about 700, eventually became in a measure quiet, and a large, lean individual, in poor attire and with unshaven face, leaped upon a box that had been brought for the purpose, and in a voice that under no circumstances could be heard at a very great distance, shouted: 'Gentlemen, I am the Mayor of Kenner.' He did not get a chance for some minutes to further declare himself, for the voice of the rabble swung over his like a huge wave over a sinking craft. He stood there, however, wildly waving his arms and demanded a hearing, which was given him when the uneasiness of the mob was quieted for a moment or so.

" 'I am from Kenner, gentlemen, and I have come down to New Orleans to-night to assist you in teaching the blacks a lesson. I have killed a Negro before, and in revenge of the wrong wrought upon you and yours, I am willing to kill again. The only way that you can teach these Niggers a lesson and put them in their place is to go out and lynch a few of them as an object lesson. String up a few of them, and the others will trouble you no more. That is the only thing to do—kill them, string them up, lynch them! I will lead you, if you will but follow. On to the Parish Prison and lynch Pierce!'

"They bore down on the Parish Prison like an avalanche, but the avalanche split harmlessly on the blank walls of the jail, and Remy Klock[2] sent out a brief message: 'You can't have Pierce, and you can't get in.' Up to that time the mob had had no opposition, but Klock's answer chilled them considerably. There was no deep-seated desperation in the crowd after all, only that wild lawlessness which leads to deeds of cruelty, but not to stubborn battle. Around the corner from the prison is a row of pawn and second-hand shops, and to these the mob took like the ducks to the proverbial mill-pond, and the devastation they wrought upon Mr. Fink's establishment was beautiful in its line.

"Everything from breast pins to horse pistols went into the pockets of the crowd, and in the melee a man was shot down, while just around the corner somebody planted a long knife in the body of a little newsboy for no reason as yet shown. Every now and then a Negro would be flushed somewhere in the outskirts of the crowd and left, beaten to a pulp. Just how many were roughly handled will never be

[2]Presumably, the warden.

known, but the unlucky thirteen had been severely beaten and maltreated up to a late hour, a number of those being in the Charity Hospital under the bandages and courtplaster of the doctors."

The first colored man to meet death at the hands of the mob was a passenger on a street car. The mob had broken itself into fragments after its disappointment at the jail, each fragment looking for a Negro to kill. The bloodthirsty cruelty of one crowd is thus described by the Times-Democrat:

" 'We will get a Nigger down here, you bet!' was the yelling boast that went up from a thousand throats, and for the first time the march of the mob was directed toward the downtown sections. The words of the rioters were prophetic, for just as Canal street was reached a car on the Villere line came along.

" 'Stop that car!' cried half a hundred men. The advance guard, heeding the injunction, rushed up to the slowly moving car, and several, seizing the trolley, jerked it down.

" 'Here's a Negro!' said half a dozen men who sprang upon the car.

"The car was full of passengers at the time, among them several women. When the trolley was pulled down and the car thrown in total darkness, the latter began to scream, and for a moment or so it looked as if the life of every person in the car was in peril, for some of the crowd with demoniacal yells of 'There he goes!' began to fire their weapons indiscriminately. The passengers in the car hastily jumped to the ground and joined the crowd, as it was evidently the safest place to be.

" 'Where's that Nigger?' was the query passed along the line, and with that the search began in earnest. The Negro, after jumping off the car, lost himself for a few moments in the crowd, but after a brief search he was again located. The slight delay seemed, if possible, only to whet the desire of the bloodthirsty crowd, for the reappearance of the Negro was the signal for a chorus of screams and pistol shots directed at the fugitive. With the speed of a deer, the man ran straight from the corner of Canal and Villere to Customhouse street. The pursuers, closely following, kept up a running fire, but notwithstanding the fact that they were right at the Negro's heels their aim was poor and their bullets went wide of the mark.

"The Negro, on reaching Customhouse street, darted from the sidewalk out into the middle of the street. This was the worst maneuver that he could have made, as it brought him directly under the light from an arc lamp, located on a nearby corner. When the Negro came plainly in view of the foremost of the closely following mob they directed a volley at him. Half a dozen pistols flashed simultaneously, and one of the bullets evidently found its mark, for the Negro stopped short, threw up his hands, wavered for a moment, and then started to run again. This stop, slight as it was, proved fatal to the Negro's chances, for he had not gotten twenty steps farther when several of the men in advance of the others reached his side. A burly fellow, grabbing him with one hand, dealt him a terrible blow on the head with the other. The wounded man sank to the ground. The crowd pressed around him and began to beat him and stamp him. The men in the rear pressed forward and those beating the man were shoved forward. The half-dead Negro, when he was freed from his assailants, crawled over to the gutter. The men behind, however, stopped pushing when those in front yelled, 'We've got him,' and then it was that the attack on the bleeding Negro was resumed. A vicious kick directed at the Negro's head sent him into the gutter, and for a moment the body sank from view beneath the muddy, slimy water. 'Pull him out; don't let him drown,' was the cry, and instantly several of the men around the half-drowned Negro bent down and drew the body out. Twisting the body around they drew the head and shoulders up on the street, while from the waist down the Negro's body remained under the water. As soon as the crowd saw that the Negro was still alive they again began to beat and kick him. Every few moments they would stop and striking matches look into the man's face to see if he still lived. To better see if he was dead they would stick lighted matches to his eyes. Finally, believing he was dead, they left him and started out to look for other Negroes. Just about this time some one yelled, 'He ain't dead,' and the men came back and renewed the attack. While the men were beating and pounding the prostrate form with stones and sticks a man in the crowd ran up, and crying, 'I'll fix the d—— Negro,' poked the muzzle of a pistol almost against the body and fired. This shot must have ended the man's life, for he lay like a stone, and realizing that they were wasting energy in further attacks, the men left their victim lying in the street."

The same paper, on the same day, July 26th, describes the brutal butchery of an aged colored man early in the morning:

"Baptiste Philo, a Negro, 75 years of age, was a victim of mob violence at Kerlerec and North Peters streets about 2:30 o'clock this morning. The old man is employed about the French Market, and was on his way there when he was met by a crowd and desperately shot. The old man found his way to the Third Precinct police station, where it was found that he had received a ghastly wound in the abdomen.

The ambulance was summoned and he was conveyed to the Charity Hospital. The students pronounced the wound fatal after a superficial examination."

Mob rule continued Thursday, its violence increasing every hour, until 2 P.M., when the climax seemed to be reached. The fact that colored men and women had been made the victims of brutal mobs, chased through the streets, killed upon the highways and butchered in their homes, did not call the best element in New Orleans to active exertion in behalf of law and order. The killing of a few Negroes more or less by irresponsible mobs does not cut much figure in Louisiana. But when the reign of mob law exerts a depressing influence upon the stock market and city securities begin to show unsteady standing in money centers, then the strong arm of the good white people of the South asserts itself and order is quickly brought out of chaos.

It was so with New Orleans on that Thursday. The better element of the white citizens began to realize that New Orleans in the hands of a mob would not prove a promising investment for Eastern capital, so the better element began to stir itself, not for the purpose of punishing the brutality against the Negroes who had been beaten, or bringing to justice the murderers of those who had been killed, but for the purpose of saving the city's credit. The Times-Democrat, upon this phase of the situation, on Friday morning says:

"When it became known later in the day that State bonds had depreciated from a point to a point and a half on the New York market a new phase of seriousness was manifest to the business community. Thinking men realized that a continuance of unchecked disorder would strike a body blow to the credit of the city and in all probability would complicate the negotiation of the forthcoming improvement bonds. The bare thought that such a disaster might be brought about by a few irresponsible boys, tramps and ruffians, inflamed popular indignation to fever pitch. It was all that was needed to bring to the aid of the authorities the active personal co-operation of the entire better element."

With the financial credit of the city at stake, the good citizens rushed to the rescue, and soon the Mayor was able to mobilize a posse of 1,000 willing men to assist the police in maintaining order, but rioting still continued in different sections of the city. Colored men and women were beaten, chased and shot whenever they made their appearance upon the street. Late in the night a most despicable piece of villainy occurred on Rousseau street, where an aged colored woman was killed by the mob. The Times-Democrat thus describes the murder:

"Hannah Mabry, an old Negress, was shot and desperately wounded shortly after midnight this morning while sleeping in her home at No. 1929 Rousseau street. It was the work of a mob, and was evidently well planned so far as escape was concerned, for the place was reached by police officers and a squad of the volunteer police within a very short time after the reports of the shots, but not a prisoner was secured. The square was surrounded, but the mob had scattered in several directions, and, the darkness of the neighborhood aiding them, not one was taken.

"At the time the mob made the attack on the little house there were also in it David Mabry, the 62-year-old husband of the wounded woman; her son, Harry Mabry; his wife, Fannie, and an infant child. The young couple with their babe could not be found after the whole affair was over, and they either escaped or were hustled off by the mob. A careful search of the whole neighborhood was made, but no trace of them could be found.

"The little place occupied by the Mabry family is an old cottage on the swamp side of Rousseau street. It is furnished with slat shutters to both doors and windows. These shutters had been pulled off by the mob and the volleys fired through the glass doors. The younger Mabrys, father, mother and child, were asleep in the first room at the time. Hannah Mabry and her old husband were sleeping in the next room. The old couple occupied the same bed, and it is miraculous that the old man did not share the fate of his spouse.

"Officer Bitterwolf, who was one of the first on the scene, said that he was about a block and a half away with Officers Fordyce and Sweeney. There were about twenty shots fired, and the trio raced to the cottage. They saw twenty or thirty men running down Rousseau street. Chase was given and the crowd turned toward the river and scattered into several vacant lots in the neighborhood.

"The volunteer police stationed at the Sixth Precinct had about five blocks to run before they arrived. They also moved on the reports of the firing, and in a remarkably short time the square was surrounded, but no one could be taken. As they ran to the scene they were assailed on every hand with vile epithets and the accusation of 'Nigger lovers.'

"Rousseau street, where the cottage is situated, is a particularly dark spot, and no doubt the members of the mob were well acquainted with the neighborhood, for the officers said that they seemed to sink into the earth, so completely and quickly did they disappear after they had completed their work, which was complete with the firing of the volley.

"Hannah Mabry was taken to the Charity Hospital in the ambulance, where it was found on examination that she had been shot through the right lung, and that the wound was a particularly serious one.

"Her old husband was found in the little wrecked home well nigh distracted with fear and grief. It was he who informed the police that at the time of the assault the younger Mabrys occupied the front room. As he ran about the little home as well as his feeble condition would permit he severely lacerated his feet on the glass broken from the windows and door. He was escorted to the Sixth Precinct station, where he was properly cared for. He could not realize why his little family had been so murderously attacked, and was inconsolable when his wife was driven off in the ambulance piteously moaning in her pain.

"The search for the perpetrators of the outrage was thorough, but both police and armed force of citizens had only their own efforts to rely on. The residents of the neighborhood were aroused by the firing, but they would give no help in the search and did not appear in the least concerned over the affair. Groups were on almost every doorstep, and some of them even jeered in a quiet way at the men who were voluntarily attempting to capture the members of the mob. Absolutely no information could be had from any of them, and the whole affair had the appearance of being the work of roughs who either lived in the vicinity, or their friends."

DEATH OF CHARLES

Friday witnessed the final act in the bloody drama begun by the three police officers, Aucoin, Mora and Cantrelle. Betrayed into the hands of the police, Charles, who had already sent two of his would-be murderers to their death, made a last stand in a small building, 1210 Saratoga street, and, still defying his pursuers, fought a mob of twenty thousand people, single-handed and alone, killing three more men, mortally wounding two more and seriously wounding nine others. Unable to get to him in him stronghold, the besiegers set fire to his house of refuge. While the building was burning Charles was shooting, and every crack of his death-dealing rifle added another victim to the price which he had placed upon his own life. Finally, when fire and smoke became too much for flesh and blood to stand, the long sought for fugitive appeared in the door, rifle in hand, to charge the countless guns that were drawn upon him. With a courage which was indescribable, he raised his gun to fire again, but this time it failed, for a hundred shots riddled his body, and he fell dead face fronting to the mob. This last scene in the terrible drama is thus described in the Times-Democrat of July 26th:

"Early yesterday afternoon, at 3 o'clock or thereabouts, Police Sergeant Gabriel Porteus was instructed by Chief Gaster to go to a house at No. 1210 Saratoga street, and search it for the fugitive murderer, Robert Charles. A private 'tip' had been received at the headquarters that the fiend was hiding somewhere on the premises.

"Sergeant Porteus took with him Corporal John R. Lally and Officers Zeigel and Essey. The house to which they were directed is a small, double frame cottage, standing flush with Saratoga street, near the corner of Clio. It has two street entrances and two rooms on each side, one in front and one in the rear. It belongs to the type of cheap little dwellings commonly tenanted by Negroes.

"Sergeant Porteus left Ziegel and Essey to guard the outside and went with Corporal Lally to the rear house, where he found Jackson and his wife in the large room on the left. What immediately ensued is only known by the Negroes. They say the sergeant began to question them about their lodgers and finally asked them whether they knew anything about Robert Charles. They strenuously denied all knowledge of his whereabouts.

"The Negroes lied. At that very moment the hunted and desperate murderer lay concealed not a dozen feet away. Near the rear, left-hand corner of the room is a closet or pantry, about three feet deep, and perhaps eight feet long. The door was open and Charles was crouching, Winchester in hand, in the dark further end.

"Near the closet door was a bucket of water, and Jackson says that Sergeant Porteus walked toward it to get a drink. At the next moment a shot rang out and the brave officer fell dead. Lally was shot directly afterward. Exactly how and where will never be known, but the probabilities are that the black fiend sent a bullet into him before he recovered from his surprise at the sudden onslaught. Then the murderer dashed out of the back door and disappeared.

"The neighborhood was already agog with the tragic events of the two preceding days, and the sound of the shots was a signal for wild and instant excitement. In a few moments a crowd had gathered and people were pouring in by the hundred from every point of the compass. Jackson and his wife had fled and at first nobody knew what had happened, but the surmise that Charles had recommenced his bloody work was on every tongue and soon some of the bolder found their way to the house in the rear. There the bleeding forms of the two policemen told the story.

"Lally was still breathing, and a priest was sent for to administer the last rites. Father Fitzgerald responded, and while he was bending over the dying man the outside throng was rushing wildly through the surrounding yards and passage-ways searching for the murderer. 'Where is he?' 'What has become of him?' were the questions on every lip.

"Suddenly the answer came in a shot from the room directly overhead. It was fired through a window facing Saratoga street, and the bullet struck down a young man named Alfred J. Bloomfield, who was standing in the narrow passage-way between the two houses. He fell on his knees and a second bullet stretched him dead.

"When he fled from the closet Charles took refuge in the upper story of the house. There are four windows on that floor, two facing toward Saratoga street and two toward Rampart. The murderer kicked several breaches in the frail central partition, so he could rush from side to side, and like a trapped beast, prepared to make his last stand.

"Nobody had dreamed that he was still in the house, and when Bloomfield was shot there was a headlong stampede. It was some minutes before the exact situation was understood. Then rifles and pistols began to speak, and a hail of bullets poured against the blind frontage of the old house. Every one hunted some coign of vantage, and many climbed to adjacent roofs. Soon the glass of the four upper windows was shattered by flying lead. The fusillade sounded like a battle, and the excitement upon the streets was indescribable.

"Throughout all this hideous uproar Charles seems to have retained a certain diabolical coolness. He kept himself mostly out of sight, but now and then he thrust the gleaming barrel of his rifle through one of the shattered window panes and fired at his besiegers. He worked the weapon with incredible rapidity, discharging from three to five cartridges each time before leaping back to a place of safety. These replies came from all four windows indiscriminately, and showed that he was keeping a close watch in every direction. His wonderful marksmanship never failed him for a moment, and when he missed it was always by the narrowest margin only.

"On the Rampart street side of the house there are several sheds, commanding an excellent range of the upper story. Detective Littleton, Andrew Van Kuren of the Workhouse force and several others climbed upon one of these and opened fire on the upper windows, shooting whenever they could catch a glimpse of the assassin. Charles responded with his rifle, and presently Van Kuren climbed down to find a better position. He was crossing the end of the shed when he was killed.

"Another of Charles' bullets found its billet in the body of Frank Evans, an ex-member of the police force. He was on the Rampart street side firing whenever he had an opportunity. Officer J. W. Bofill and A. S. Leclerc were also wounded in the fusillade.

"While the events thus briefly outlined were transpiring time was a-wing, and the cooler headed in the crowd began to realize that some quick and desperate expedient must be adopted to insure the capture of the fiend and to avert what might be a still greater tragedy than any yet enacted. For nearly two hours the desperate monster had held his besiegers at bay, darkness would soon be at hand and no one could predict what might occur if he made a dash for liberty in the dark.

"At this critical juncture it was suggested that the house be fired. The plan came as an inspiration, and was adopted as the only solution of the situation. The wretched old rookery counted for nothing against the possible continued sacrifice of human life, and steps were immediately taken to apply the torch. The fire department had been summoned to the scene soon after the shooting began; its officers were warned to be ready to prevent a spread of the conflagration, and several men rushed into the lower right-hand room and started a blaze in one corner.

"They first fired an old mattress, and soon smoke was pouring out in dense volumes. It filled the interior of the ramshackle structure, and it was evident that the upper story would soon become untenable. An interval of tense excitement followed, and all eyes were strained for a glimpse of the murderer when he emerged.

"Then came the thrilling climax. Smoked out of his den, the desperate fiend descended the stairs and entered the lower room. Some say he dashed into the yard, glaring around vainly for some avenue of escape; but, however that may be, he was soon a few moments later moving about behind the lower windows. A dozen shots were sent through the wall in the hope of reaching him, but he escaped unscathed. Then suddenly the door on the right was flung open and he dashed out. With head lowered and rifle raised ready to fire on the instant, Charles dashed straight for the rear door of the front cottage. To reach it he had to traverse a little walk shaded by a vine-clad arbor. In the back room, with a cocked revolver in his hand, was Dr. C. A. Noiret, a young medical student, who was aiding the citizens' posse. As he sprang through the door Charles fired a shot, and the bullet whizzed past the doctor's head. Before it could be repeated Noiret's pistol cracked and the murderer reeled, turned half around and fell on his back. The doctor sent another ball into his body as he struck the floor, and half a dozen men, swarming into the room from the front, riddled the corpse with bullets.

"Private Adolph Anderson of the Connell Rifles was the first man to announce the death of the wretch. He rushed to the street door, shouted the news to the crowd, and a moment later the bleeding body was dragged to the pavement and made the target of a score of pistols. It was shot, kicked and beaten almost out of semblance to humanity.

"The limp dead body was dropped at the edge of the sidewalk and from there dragged to the muddy roadway by half a hundred hands. There in the road more shots were fired into the body. Corporal Trenchard, a brother-in-law of Porteus, led the shooting into the inanimate clay. With each shot there was a cheer for the work that had been done and curses and imprecations on the inanimate mass of riddled flesh that was once Robert Charles.

"Cries of 'Burn him! Burn him!' were heard from Clio street all the way to Erato street, and it was with difficulty that the crowd was restrained from totally destroying the wretched dead body. Some of those who agitated burning even secured a large vessel of kerosene, which had previously been brought to the scene for the purpose of firing Charles' refuge, and for a time it looked as though this vengeance might be wreaked on the body. The officers, however, restrained this move, although they were powerless to prevent the stamping and kicking of the body by the enraged crowd.

"After the infuriated citizens had vented their spleen on the body of the dead Negro it was loaded into the patrol wagon. The police raised the body of the heavy black from the ground and literally chucked it into the space on the floor of the wagon between the seats. They threw it with a curse hissed more than uttered and born of the bitterness which was rankling in their breasts at the thought of Charles having taken so wantonly the lives of four of the best of their fellow-officers.

"When the murderer's body landed in the wagon it fell in such a position that the hideously mutilated head, kicked, stamped and crushed, hung over the end.

"As the wagon moved off, the followers, who were protesting against its being carried off, declaring that it should be burned, poked and struck it with sticks, beating it into such a condition that it was utterly impossible to tell what the man ever looked like.

"As the patrol wagon rushed through the rough street, jerking and swaying from one side of the thoroughfare to the other, the gory, mud-smeared head swayed and swung and jerked about in a sickening manner, the dark blood dripping on the steps and spattering the body of the wagon and the trousers of the policemen standing on the step.["]

MOB BRUTALITY

The brutality of the mob was further shown by the unspeakable cruelty with which it beat, shot and stabbed to death an unoffending colored man, name unknown, who happened to be walking on the street with no thought that he would be set upon and killed simply because he was a colored man. The Times-Democrat's description of the outrage is as follows:

"While the fight between the Negro desperado and the citizens was in progress yesterday afternoon at Clio and Saratoga streets another tragedy was being enacted downtown in the French qurter, but it was a very one-sided affair. The object of the white man's wrath was, of course, a Negro, but, unlike Charles, he showed no fight, but tried to escape from the furious mob which was pursuing him, and which finally put an end to his existence in a most cruel manner.

"The Negro, whom no one seemed to know—at any rate no one could be found in the vicinity of the killing who could tell who he was—was walking along the levee, as near as could be learned, when he was attacked by a number of white longshoremen or screwmen. For what reason, if there was any reason other than the fact that he was a Negro, could not be learned, and immediately they pounced upon him he broke ground and started on a desperate run for his life.

"The hunted Negro started off the levee toward the French Vegetable Market, changed his course out the sidewalk toward Gallatin street. The angry, yelling mob was close at his heels, and increasing steadily as each block was traversed. At Gallatin street he turned up that thoroughfare, doubled back into North Peters street and ran into the rear of No. 1216 of that street, which is occupied by Chris Reuter as a commission store and residence.

"He rushed frantically through the place and out on to the gallery on the Gallatin street side. From this gallery he jumped to the street and fell flat on his back on the sidewalk. Springing to his feet as soon as possible, with a leaden hail fired by the angry mob whistling about him, he turned to his merciless pursuers in an appealing way, and, throwing up one hand, told them not to shoot any more, that they could take him as he was.

"But the hail of lead continued, and the unfortunate Negro finally dropped to the sidewalk, mortally wounded. The mob then rushed upon him, still continuing the fusillade, and upon reaching his body a number of Italians, who had joined the howling mob, reached down and stabbed him in the back and buttock with big knives. Others fired shots into his head until his teeth were shot out, three shots having been fired into his mouth. There were bullet wounds all over his body.

"Others who witnessed the affair declared that the man was fired at as he was running up the stairs leading to the living apartments above the store, and that after jumping to the sidewalk and being knocked down by a bullet he jumped up and ran across the street, then ran back and tried to get back into the commission store. The Italians, it is said, were all drunk, and had been shooting firecrackers. Tiring of this, they began shooting at Negroes, and when the unfortunate man who was killed ran by they joined in the chase.

"No one was arrested for the shooting, the neighborhood having been deserted by the police, who were sent up to the place where Charles was fighting so desperately. No one could or would give the names of any of those who had participated in the chase and the killing, nor could any one be found who knew who the Negro was. The patrol wagon was called and the terribly mutilated body sent to the morgue and the coroner notified.

"The murdered Negro was copper colored, about 5 feet 11 inches in height, about 35 years of age, and was dressed in blue overalls and a brown slouch hat. At 10:30 o'clock the vicinity of the French Market was very quiet. Squads of special officers were patrolling the neighborhood, and there did not seem to be any prospects of disorder."

During the entire time the mob held the city in its hands and went about holding up street cars and searching them, taking from them colored men to assault, shoot and kill, chasing colored men upon the public square, through alleys and into houses of anybody who would take them in, breaking into the homes of defenseless colored men and women and beating aged and decrepit men and women to death, the police and the legally-constituted authorities showed plainly where their sympathies were, for in no case reported through the daily papers does there appear the arrest, trial and conviction of one of the mob for any of the brutalities which occurred. The ringleaders of the mob were at no time disguised. Men were chased, beaten and killed by white brutes, who boasted of their crimes, and the murderers still walk the streets of New Orleans, well known and absolutely exempt from prosecution. Not only were they exempt from prosecution by the police while the town was in the hands of the mob, but even now that law and order is supposed to resume control, these men, well known, are not now, nor ever will be, called to account for the unspeakable brutalities of that terrible week. On the other hand, the colored men who were beaten by the police and dragged into the station for purposes of intimidation, were quickly called up before the courts and fined or sent to jail upon the statement of the police. Instances of Louisiana justice as it is dispensed in New Orleans are here quoted from the Times-Democrat of July 26th:

**"Justice Dealt Out to Folks
Who Talked Too Much**

"All the Negroes and whites who were arrested in the vicinity of Tuesday's tragedy had a hard time before Recorder Hughes yesterday. Lee Jackson was the first prisoner, and the evidence established that he made his way to the vicinity of the crime and told his Negro friends that he thought a good many more policemen ought to be killed. Jackson said he was drunk when he made the remark. He was fined $25 or thirty days.

"John Kennedy was found wandering about the street Tuesday night with an open razor in his hand, and he was given $25 or thirty days.

"Edward McCarthy, a white man, who arrived only four days since from New York, went to the scene of the excitement at the corner of Third and Rampart streets, and told the Negroes that they were as good as any white man. This remark was made by McCarthy, as another white man said the Negroes should be lynched. McCarthy told the recorder that he considered a Negro as good as a white in body and soul. He was fined $25 or thirty days.

"James Martin, Simon Montegut, Eddie McCall, Alex Washington and Henry Turner were up for failing to move on. Martin proved that he was at the scene to assist the police and was discharged. Montegut, being a cripple, was also released, but the others were fined $25 or thirty days each.

"Eddie Williams for refusing to move on was given $25 or thirty days.

"Matilda Gamble was arrested by the police for saying that two officers were killed and it was a pity more were not shot. She was given $25 or thirty days.

INSOLENT BLACKS

"Recorder Hughes received Negroes in the first recorder's office yesterday morning in a way that they will remember for a long time, and all of them were before the magistrate for having caused trouble through incendiary remarks concerning the death of Captain Day and Patrolman Lamb."

"Lee Jackson was before the recorder and was fined $25 or thirty days. He was lippy around where the trouble happened Tuesday morning, and some white men punched him good and hard and the police took him. Then the recorder gave him a dose, and now he is in the parish prison."

"John Kennedy was another black who got into trouble. He said that the shooting of the police by Charles was a good thing, and for this he was pounded. Patrolman Lorenzo got him and saved him from being lynched, for the black had an open razor. He was fined $25 or thirty days."

"Edward McCarthy, a white man, mixed up with the crowd, and an expression of sympathy nearly cost him his head, for some whites about started for him, administering licks and blows with fists and umbrellas. The recorder fined him $25 or thirty days. He is from New York."

"Then James Martin, a white man, and Simon Montegut, Eddie Call, Henry Turner and Alex. Washington were before the magistrate for having failed to move on when the police ordered them from the square where the bluecoats were Tuesday, waiting in the hope of catching Charles. All save Martin and Montegut were fined."

"Eddie Williams, a little Negro who was extremely fresh with the police, was fined $10 or ten days."

SHOCKING BRUTALITY

The whole city was at the mercy of the mob and the display of brutality was a disgrace to civilization. One instance is described in the Picayune as follows:

"A smaller party detached itself from the mob at Washington and Rampart streets, and started down the latter thoroughfare. One of the foremost spied a Negro, and immediately there was a rush for the unfortunate black man. With the sticks they had torn from fences on the line of march the young outlaws attacked the black and clubbed him unmercifully, acting more like demons than human beings. After being severely beaten over the head, the Negro started to run with the whole gang at his heels. Several revolvers were brought into play and pumped their lead at the refugee. The Negro made rapid progress and took refuge behind the blinds of a little cottage in Rampart street, but he had been seen, and the mob hauled him from his hiding place and again commenced beating him. There were more this time, some twenty or thirty, all armed with sticks and heavy clubs, and under their incessant blows the Negro could not last long. He begged for mercy, and his cries were most pitiful, but a mob has no heart, and his cries were only answered with more blows.

" 'For God's sake, boss, I ain't done nothin'. Don't kill me. I swear I ain't done nothin'.'

"The white brutes turned
"A DEAF EAR TO THE PITYING CRIES
of the black wretch and the drubbing continued. The cries subsided into moans, and soon the black swooned away into unconsciousness. Still not content with their heartless work, they pulled the Negro out and kicked him into the gutter. For the time those who had beaten the black seemed satisfied and left him groaning in the gutter, but others came up, and, regretting that they had not had a hand in the affair, they determined to evidence their bravery to their fellows and beat the man while he was in the gutter, hurling rocks and stones at his black form. One thoughtless white brute, worse even than the black slayer of the police officers, thought to make himself a hero in the eyes of his fellows and fired his revolver repeatedly into the helpless wretch. It was dark and the fellow probably aimed carelessly. After firing three

or four shots he also left without knowing what extent of injury he inflicted on the black wretch who was left lying in the gutter."

MURDER ON THE LEVEE

One part of the crown made a raid on the tenderloin district, hoping to find there some belated Negro for a sacrifice. They were urged on by the white prostitutes, who applauded their murderous mission. Says an account:

"The red light district was all excitement. Women—that is, the white women—were out on their stoops and peeping over their galleries and through their windows and doors, shouting to the crowd to go on with their work, and kill Negroes for them.

" 'Our best wishes, boys,' they encouraged; and the mob answered with shouts, and whenever a Negro house was sighted a bombardment was started on the doors and windows."

No colored men were found on the streets until the mob reached Custom House place and Villiers streets. Here a victim was found and brutally put to death. The Picayune description is as follows:

"Some stragglers had run a Negro into a car at the corner of Bienville and Villere streets. He was seeking refuge in the conveyance, and he believed that the car would not be stopped and could speed along. But the mob determined to stop the car, and ordered the motorman to halt. He put on his brake. Some white men were in the car.

" 'Get out, fellows,' shouted several of the mob.

" 'All whites fall out,' was the second cry, and the poor Negro understood that it was meant that he should stay in the car.

"He wanted to save his life. The poor fellow crawled under the seats. But some one in the crowd saw him and yelled that he was hiding. Two or three men climbed through the windows with their pistols; others jumped over the motorman's board, and dozens tumbled into the rear of the car. Big, strong hands got the Negro by the shirt. He was dragged out of the conveyance, and was pushed to the street. Some fellow ran up and struck him with a club. The blow was heavy, but it did not fell him, and the Negro ran toward Canal street, stealing along the wall of the Tulane Medical Building. Fifty men ran after him, caught the poor fellow and hurried him back into the crowd. Fists were aimed at him, then clubs went upon his shoulders, and finally the black plunged into the gutter.

"A gun was fired, and the Negro, who had just gotten to his feet, dropped again. He tried to get up, but a volley was sent after him, and in a little while he was dead.

"The crowd looked on at the terrible work. Then the lights in the houses of ill-fame began to light up again, and women peeped out of the blinds. The motorman was given the order to go on. The gong clanged and the conveyance sped out of the way. For half an hour the crowd held their place at the corner, then the patrol wagon came and the body was picked up and hurried to the morgue.

"Coroner Richard held an autopsy on the body of the Negro who was forced out of car 98 of the Villere line and shot down. It was found that he was wounded four times, the most serious wound being that which struck him in the right side, passing through the lungs, and causing hemorrhages, which brought about death.

"Nobody tried to identify the poor fellow and his name is unknown."

A VICTIM IN THE MARKET

Soon after the murder of the man on the street car many of the same mob marched down to the market place. There they found a colored market man named Louis Taylor, who had gone to begin his early morning's work. He was at once set upon by the mob and killed. The Picayune account says:

"Between 1 and 2 o'clock this morning a mob of several hundred men and boys, made up of participants in many of the earlier affairs, marched on the French Market. Louis Taylor, a Negro vegetable carrier, who is about 30 years of age, was sitting at the soda water stand. As soon as the mob saw him fire was opened and the Negro took to his heels. He ran directly into another section of the mob and any number of shots were fired at him. He fell, face down, on the floor of the market.

"The police in the neighborhood rallied hurriedly and found the victim of mob violence seemingly lifeless. Before they arrived the Negro had been beaten severely about the head and body. The ambulance was summoned and Taylor was carried to the charity hospital, where it was found that he had been shot through the abdomen and arm. The examination was a hurried one, but it sufficed to show that Taylor was mortally wounded.

"After shooting Taylor the members of the mob were pluming themselves on their exploit. 'The Nigger was at the soda water stand and we commenced shooting him,' said one of the rioters. 'He put his hands up and ran, and we shot until he fell. I understand that he is still alive. If he is, he is a wonder. He was certainly shot enough to be killed.'

"The members of the mob readily admitted that they had taken part in the assaults which marked the earlier part of the evening.

" 'We were up on Jackson avenue and killed a Nigger on Villere street. We came down here, saw a nigger and killed him, too.' This was the way they told the story.

" 'Boys, we are out of ammunition,' said some one.

" 'Well, we will keep on like we are, and if we can't get some before morning, we will take it. We have got to keep this thing up, now we have started.'

"This declaration was greeted by a chorus of applauding yells, and the crowd started up the levee. Half of the men in the crowd, and they were all of them young, were drunk.

"Taylor, when seen at the charity hospital, was suffering greatly, and presented a pitiable spectacle. His clothing was covered with blood, and his face was beaten almost into a pulp. He said that he had gone to the market to work and was quietly sitting down when the mob came and began to fire on him. He was not aware at first that the crowd was after him. When he saw its purpose he tried to run, but fell. He didn't know any of the men in the crowd. There is hardly a chance that Taylor will recover.

"The police told the crowd to move on, but no attempt was made to arrest any one."

A GRAY-HAIRED VICTIM

The bloodthirsty barbarians, having tasted blood, continued their hunt and soon ran across an old man of 75 years. His life had been spent in hard work about the French market, and he was well known as an unoffending, peaceable and industrious old man.

But that made no difference to the mob. He was a Negro, and with a fiendishness that was worse than that of cannibals they beat his life out. The report says:

"There was another gang of men parading the streets in the lower part of the city, looking for any stray Negro who might be on the streets. As they neared the corner of Dauphine and Kerlerec, a square below Esplanade avenue, they came upon Baptiste Thilo, an aged Negro, who works in the French Market.

"Thilo for years has been employed by the butchers and fish merchants to carry baskets from the stalls to the wagons, and unload the wagons as they arrive in the morning. He was on his way to the market, when the mob came upon him. One of the gang struck the old Negro, and as he fell, another in the crowd, supposed to be a young fellow, fired a shot. The bullet entered the body just below the right nipple.

"As the Negro fell the crowd looked into his face and they discovered then that the victim was very old. The young man who did the shooting said: 'Oh, he is an old Negro. I'm sorry that I shot him.'

"This is all the old Negro received in the way of consolation.

"He was left where he fell, but later staggered to his feet and made his way to the third precinct station. There the police summoned the ambulance and the students pronounced the wound very dangerous. He was carried to the hospital as rapidly as possible.

"There was no arrest."

Just before daybreak the mob found another victim. He, too, was on his way to market, driving a meat wagon. But little is told of his treatment, nothing more than the following brief statement:

"At nearly 3 o'clock this morning a report was sent to the Third Precinct station that a Negro was lying on the sidewalk at the corner of Decatur and St. Philip. The man had been pulled off of a meat wagon and riddled with bullets.

"When the police arrived he was insensible and apparently dying. The ambulance students attended the Negro and pronounced the wounds fatal.

"There was nothing found which would lead to the discovery of his identity."

FUN IN GRETNA

If there are any persons so deluded as to think that human life in the South is valued any more than the life of a brute, he will be speedily undeceived by reading the accounts of unspeakable barbarism committed by the mob in and around New Orleans. In no other civilized country in the world, nay, more, in no land of barbarians would it be possible to duplicate the scenes of brutality that are reported from New Orleans. In the heat of blind fury one might conceive how a mad mob might beat and kill a man taken red-handed in a brutal murder. But it is almost past belief to read that civilized white people, men who boast of their chivalry and blue blood, actually had fun in beating, chasing and shooting men who had no possible connection with any crime.

But this actually happened in Gretna, a few miles from New Orleans. In its description of the scenes of Tuesday night, the Picayune mentions the brutal chase of several colored men whom the mob sought to kill. In the instances mentioned, the paper said:

"Gretna had its full share of excitement between 8 and 11 o'clock last night, in connection with a report that spread through the town that a Negro resembling the slayer of Police Captain Day, of New Orleans, had been seen on the outskirts of the place.

"It is true that a suspicious-looking Negro was observed by the residents of Madison and Amelia streets lurking about the fences of that neighborhood just after dark, and shortly before 8 o'clock John Fist, a young white man, saw the Negro on Fourth street. He followed the darkey a short distance, and, coming upon Robert Moore, who is known about town as the 'black detective,' Fist pointed the Negro out and Moore at once made a move toward the stranger. The latter observed Moore making in his direction, and, without a word, he sped in the direction of the Brooklyn pasture, Moore following and firing several shots at him. In a few minutes a half hundred white men, including Chief of Police Miller, Constable Dannenhauer, Patrolman Keegan and several special officers, all well-armed, joined in the chase, but in the darkness the negro escaped.

"Just as the pursuing party reached town again, two of the residents of Lafayette avenue, Peter Leson and Robert Henning, reported that they had just chased and shot at a Negro, who had been seen in the yard of the former's house. They were positive the Negro had not escaped from the square. Their report was enough to set the appetite of the crowd on edge, and the square was quickly surrounded, while several dozens of men, armed with lanterns and revolvers, made a search of every yard and under every house in the square. No Negro was found.

"The crowd of armed men was constantly swelling, and at 10 o'clock it had reached the proportions of a small army. At 10:30 o'clock an outbound freight train is due to pass through Gretna on the Texas and Pacific Road, and the crowd, believing that Captain Day's slayer might be aboard one of the cars attempting to leave the scene of his crime, resolved to inspect the train. As the train stopped at the Madison street crossing the engineer was requested to pull very slowly through the town, in order that the trucks of the cars might be examined. There was a string of armed men on each side of the rail-road track and in a few moments a Negro was espied riding between two cars. A half dozen weapons were pointed at him and he was ordered to come out. He sprang out with alacrity and was pounced upon almost before he reached the ground. Robert Moore grabbed him and pushed an ugly looking Derringer under his nose and the Negro threw up both hands. Constable Dannenhauer and Patrolman Keegan took charge of him and hustled him off to jail, where he was locked up. The Negro does not at all resemble Robert Charles, but it was best for his sake that he was placed under lock and key. The crowd was not in a humor to let any Negro pass muster last night. The prisoner gave his name as Luke Wallace.

"But now came the real excitement. The train had slowed down almost to a standstill, in the very heart of town. Somebody shouted: 'There he goes, on top of the train!' And sure enough, somebody was going. It was a Negro, too, and he was making a bee-line for the front end of the train. A veritable shower of bullets, shot and rifle balls greeted the flying form, but on it sped. The locomotive had stopped in the middle of the square between Lavoisier and Newton streets, and the Negro, flying with the speed of the wind along the top of the cars, reached the first car of the train and jumped to the tender and then into the cab. As he did several white men standing at the locomotive made a rush into the cab. The Negro sprang swiftly out of the other side, on to the sidewalk. But there were several more men, and as he realized that he was rushing right into their arms he made a spring to leap over the fence of Mrs. Linden's home, on the wood side of the track. Before the Negro got to the top one white man had hold of his legs, while another rushed up, pistol in hand. The man who was hold-ing the darkey's legs was jostled out of the way and the man with the pistol, standing directly beneath the Negro, sent two bullets at him.

"There was a wild scramble, and the vision of a fleeing form in the Linden yard, but that was the last seen of the black man. The yard was entered and searched, and neighboring yards were also searched, but not even the trace of blood was found. It is almost impossible to believe that the Negro was not wounded, for the man who fired at him held the pistol almost against the Negro's body.

"The shots brought out almost everybody—white—in town, and though there was nothing to show for the exciting work, except the arrest of the Negro, who doesn't answer the description of the man wanted, Gretna's male population had its little fun and felt amply repaid for all the trouble it was put to, and all the ammunition it wasted."

BRUTALITY IN NEW ORLEANS

Mob rule reigned supreme Wednesday, and the scenes that were enacted challenge belief. How many colored men and women were abused and injured is not known, for those who escaped were glad to make a place of refuge and took no time to publish their troubles. The mob made no attempt to find Charles; its only purpose was to pursue, beat and kill any colored man or woman who happened to come in sight. Speaking editorially, the Picayune of Thursday, the 26th of July, said:

Escaped with Their Lives

At the Charity Hospital Wednesday night more than a score of people were treated for wounds received at the hands of the mob. Some were able to tell of their mistreatment, and their recitals are briefly given in the Picayune as follows:

"Alex. Ruffin, who is quite seriously injured, is a Pullman car porter, a native of Chicago. He reached New Orleans at 9:20 o'clock last night, and after finishing his work, boarded a Henry Clay avenue car to go to Delachaise street, where he has a sick son.

" 'I hadn't ridden any way,' said he, 'when I saw a lot of white folks. They were shouting to 'Get the Niggers.' I didn't know they were after every colored man they saw, and sat still. Two or three men jumped on the car and started at me. One of them hit me over the head with a slungshot, and they started to shooting at me. I jumped out of the car and ran, although I had done nothing. They shot me in the arm and in the leg. I would certainly have been killed had not some gentleman taken my part. If I had known New Orleans was so excited I would never have left my car.'

"George Morris is the name of a Negro who was badly injured by a mob which went through the Poydras Market. Morris is employed as watchman there. He heard the noise of the passing crowd and looked out to see what the matter was. As soon as the mob saw him its members started after him.

" 'One man hit me over the head with a club,' said George, after his wounds had been dressed, 'and somebody cut me in the back. I didn't hardly think what was the matter at first, but when I saw they were after me I ran for my life. I ran to the coffee stand, where I work, for protection, but they were right after me, and somebody shot me in the back. At last the police got me away from the crowd. Just before I was hit a friend of mine, who was in the crowd, said, 'You had better go home, Nigger; they're after your kind.' I didn't know then what he meant. I found out pretty quick.'

"Morris is at the hospital. He is a perfect wreck, and while he will probably get well, he will have had a close call.

"Esther Fields is a Negro washerwoman who lives at South Claiborne and Toledano streets. She was at home when she heard a big noise and went out to investigate. She ran into the arms of the mob, and was beaten into insensibility in less time than it takes to tell it. Esther is being treated at the charity hospital, and should be able to get about in a few days. The majority of her bruises are about the head.

"T. P. Sanders fell at the hands of the Jackson avenue mob. He lives at 1927 Jackson avenue, and was sitting in front of his home when he saw the crowd marching out the street. He stayed to see what the excitement was all about, and was shot in the knee and thorax and horribly beaten about the head before the mob came to the conclusion that he had been done for, and passed on. The ambulance was called and he was picked up and carried to the charity hospital, where his wounds were dressed and pronounced serious.

"Oswald McMahon is nothing more than a boy. He was shot in the leg and afterward carried to the hospital. His injuries are very slight.

"Dan White is another charity hospital patient. He is a Negro roustabout and was sitting in the bar room at Poydras and Franklin streets when a mob passed along and espied him. He was shot in the hand, and would have been roughly dealt with had some policeman not been luckily near and rescued him.

"In addition to the Negroes who suffered from the violence of the mob there were several patients treated at the hospital during the night who had been with the rioters and had been struck by stray bullets or injured in scuffles. None of this class were hurt to any extent. They got their wounds dressed and went out again."

WAS CHARLES A DESPERADO?

The press of the country has united in declaring that Robert Charles was a desperado. As usual, when dealing with a negro, he is assumed to be guilty because he is charged. Even the most conservative of journals refuse to ask evidence to prove that the dead man was a criminal, and that his life had been given over to law-breaking. The minute that the news was flashed across the country that he had shot a white man it was at once declared that he was a fiend incarnate, and that when he was killed the community would be ridden of a black-hearted desperado.

The reporters of the New Orleans papers, who were in the best position to trace the record of this man's life, made every possible effort to find evidence to prove that he was a villain unhung. With all the resources at their command, and inspired by intense interest to paint him as black a villain as possible, these reporters signally failed to disclose a single indictment which charged Robert Charles with a crime. Because they failed to find any legal evidence that Charles was a lawbreaker and desperado his accusers gave full license to their imagination and distorted the facts that they had obtained, in every way possible, to prove a course of criminality, which the records absolutely refuse to show.

Charles had his first encounter with the police Monday night, in which he was shot in the street duel which was begun by the police after Officer Mora had beaten Charles three or four times over the head with his billy in an attempt to make an illegal arrest. In defending himself against the combined attack of two officers with a billy and their guns upon him, Charles shot Officer Mora and escaped.

Early Tuesday morning Charles was traced to Dryades street by officers who were instructed to kill him on sight. There, again defending himself, he shot and killed two officers. This, of course, in the eyes of the American press, made him a desperado. The New Orleans press, in substantiating the charges that he was a desperado, make statements which will be interesting to examine.

In the first place the New Orleans Times-Democrat, of July 25th, calls Charles a "ravisher and a daredevil." It says that from all sources that could be searched "the testimony was cumulative that the character of the murderer, Robert Charles, is that of a daredevil and a fiend in human form." Then in the same article it says:

"The belongings of Robert Charles which were found in his room were a complete index to the character of the man. Although the room and its contents were in a state of chaos on account of the frenzied search for clews by officers and citizens, an examination of his personal effects revealed the mental state of the murderer and the rancor in his heart toward the Caucasian race. Never was the adage, 'A little learning is a dangerous thing,' better exemplified than in the case of the negro who shot to death the two officers."

His room was searched, and the evidence upon which the charge that he was a desperado consisted of pamphlets in support of Negro emigration to Liberia. On his mantel-piece there was found a bullet mold and an outfit for reloading cartridges. There were also two pistol scabbards and a bottle of cocaine. The other evidences that Charles was a desperado the writer described as follows:

"In his room were found negro periodicals and other 'race' propaganda, most of which was in the interest of the negro's emigration to Liberia. There were Police Gazettes strewn about his room and other papers of a similar character. Well-worn text-books, bearing his name written in his own scrawling handwriting, and well-filled copybooks found in his trunk showed that he had burnt the midnight oil, and was desirous of improving himself intellectually in order that he might conquer the hated white race. Much of the literature found among his chattels was of a superlatively vituperative character, and attacked the white race in unstinted language and asserted the equal rights of the Negro.

"Charles was evidently the local agent of the 'Voice of Missions,' a 'religious' paper, published at Atlanta, as great bundles of that sheet were found. It is edited by one Bishop Turner, and seems to be the official organ of all haters of the white race. Its editorials are anarchistic in the extreme, and urge upon the negro that the sooner he realizes that he is as good as the white man the better it will be for him. The following verses were clipped from the journal; they were marked 'till forbidden,' and appeared in several successive numbers:

"OUR SENTIMENTS.
"H. M. T.

"My country, 'tis of thee,
Dear land of Africa,
   Of thee we sing.
Land where our fathers died,
Land of the Negro's pride,
   God's truth shall ring.

"My native country, thee,
Land of the black and free,
   Thy name I love;
To see thy rocks and rills,
Thy woods and matchless hills,
   Like that above.

> "When all thy slanderous ghouls,
> In the bosom of sheol,[3]
> Forgotten lie,
> Thy monumental name shall live,
> And suns thy royal brow shall gild,
> Upheaved to heaven high,
> O'ertopping thrones."

"There were no valuables in his room, and if he was a professional thief he had his headquarters for storing his plunder at some other place than his room on Fourth street. Nothing was found in his room that could lead to the belief that he was a thief, except fifty or more small bits of soap. The inference was that every place he visited he took all of the soap lying around, as all of the bits were well worn and had seen long service on the washstand.

"His wearing apparel was little more than rags, and financially he was evidently not in a flourishing condition. He was in no sense a skilled workman, and his room showed, in fact, that he was nothing more than a laborer.

"The 'philosopher in the garret' was a dirty wretch, and his room, his bedding and his clothing were nasty and filthy beyond belief. His object in life seemed to have been the discomfiture of the white race, and to this purpose he devoted himself with zeal. He declared himself to be a 'patriot,' and wished to be the Moses of his race."

Under the title of "The Making of a Monster," the reporter attempts to give "something of the personality of the arch-fiend, Charles." Giving his imagination full vent, the writer says:

"It is only natural that the deepest interest should attach to the personality of Robert Charles. What manner of man was this fiend incarnate? What conditions developed him? Who were his preceptors? From what ancestral strain, if any, did he derive his ferocious hatred of the whites, his cunning, his brute courage, the apostolic zeal which he displayed in spreading the propaganda of African equality? These are questions involving one of the most remarkable psychological problems of modern times."

In answer to the questions which he propounds, the reporter proceeds to admit that he did not learn anything of a very desperate nature connected with Charles. He says:

---

[3]Sheol: the abode of the dead in early Hebrew thought.

"Although Charles was a familiar figure to scores of Negroes in New Orleans, and they had been more or less intimately acquainted with him for over two years, curiously little can be learned of his habits or mode of life. Since the perpetration of his terrible series of crimes it goes without saying that his former friends are inclined to be reticent, but it is reasonably certain that they have very little to tell. In regard to himself, Charles was singularly reticent for a Negro. He did not even indulge in the usual lying about his prowess and his adventures. This was possibly due to the knowledge that he was wanted for a couple of murders. The man had sense enough to know that it would be highly unwise to excite any curiosity about his past.

"When Charles first came to New Orleans he worked here and there as a day laborer. He was employed at different times in a sawmill, on the street gangs, as a roustabout on the levee, as a helper at the sugar works and as a coal shoveler in the engine room of the St. Charles Hotel. At each of the places where he worked he was known as a quiet, rather surly fellow, who had little to say to anybody, and generally performed his tasks in morose silence. He managed to convey the impression, however, of being a man of more than ordinary intelligence.

"A Negro named William Butts, who drives a team on the levee and lives on Washington street, near Baronne, told a Times-Democrat reporter yesterday that Charles got a job about a year ago as agent for a Liberian Immigration Society, which has headquarters at Birmingham, and was much elated at the prospect of making a living without hard labor."

According to the further investigations of this reporter, Charles was also agent for Bishop Turner's "Voice of Missions," the colored missionary organ of the African Methodist Church, edited by H. M. Turner, of Atlanta, Georgia. Concerning his service as agent for the "Voice of Missions," the reporter says:

"He secured a number of subscribers and visited them once a month to collect the installments. In order to insure regular payments it was necessary to keep up enthusiasm, which was prone to wane, and Charles consequently became an active and continual preacher of the propaganda of hatred. Whatever may have been his private sentiments at the outset, this constant harping on one string must eventually have had a powerful effect upon his own mind.

"Exactly how he received his remuneration is uncertain, but he told several of his friends that he got a 'big commission.' Incidentally he solicited subscribers for a Negro paper called the Voice of the Missions, and when he struck a negro who did not want to go to Africa himself, he begged contributions for the 'good of the cause.'

"In the course of time Charles developed into a fanatic on the subject of the Negro oppression and neglected business to indulge in wild tirades whenever he could find a listener. He became more anxious to make converts than to obtain subscribers, and the more conservative darkies began to get afraid of him. Meanwhile he got into touch with certain agitators in the North and made himself a distributing agent for their literature, a great deal of which he gave away. Making money was a secondary consideration to 'the cause.'

"One of the most enthusiastic advocates of the Liberian scheme is the colored Bishop H. M. Turner, of Atlanta. Turner is a man of unusual ability, has been over to Africa personally several times, and has made himself conspicuous by denouncing laws which he claimed discriminated against the blacks. Charles was one of the bishop's disciples and evidence has been found that seems to indicate they were in correspondence."

This was all that the Times-Democrat's reporters could find after the most diligent search to prove that Charles was the fiend incarnate which the press of New Orleans and elsewhere declared him to be.

The reporters of the New Orleans Picayune were no more successful than their brethren of the Times-Democrat. They, too, were compelled to substitute fiction for facts in their attempt to prove Charles a desperado. In the issue of the 26th of July it was said that Charles was well-known in Vicksburg, and was there a consort of thieves. They mentioned that a man named Benson Blake was killed in 1894 or 1895, and that four Negroes were captured, and two escaped. Of the two escaped they claim that Charles was one. The four negroes who were captured were put in jail, and as usual, in the high state of civilization which characterizes Mississippi, the right of the person accused of crime to an indictment by legal process and a legal trial by jury was considered an useless formality if the accused happened to be black. A mob went to the jail that night, the four colored men were delivered to the mob, and all four were hanged in the court-house yard. The reporters evidently assumed that Charles was guilty, if, in fact, he was ever there, because the other four men were lynched. They did not consider it was a fact of any importance that Charles was never indicted. They called him a murderer on general principles.

DIED IN SELF-DEFENSE

The life, character and deathm of Robert Charles challenges the thoughtful consideration of all fair-minded people. In the frenzy of the moment, when nearly a dozen men lay dead, the victims of his unerring and death-dealing aim, it was natural for a prejudiced press and for citizens in private life to denounce him as a desperado and a murderer. But sea depths are not measured when the ocean rages, nor can absolute justice be determined while public opinion is lashed into fury. There must be calmness to insure correctness of judgment. The fury of the hour must abate before we can deal justly with any man or any cause.

That Charles was not a desperado is amply shown by the discussion in the preceding chapter. The darkest pictures which the reporters could paint of Charles were quoted freely, so that the public might find upon what grounds the press declared him to be a lawbreaker. Unquestionably the grounds are wholly insufficient. Not a line of evidence has been presented to prove that Charles was the fiend which the first reports of the New Orleans charge him to be.

Nothing more should be required to establish his good reputation, for the rule is universal that a reputation must be assumed to be good until it is proved bad. But that rule does not apply to the Negro, for as soon as he is suspected the public judgment immediately determines that he is guilty of whatever crime he stands charged. For this reason, as a matter of duty to the race, and the simple justice to the memory of Charles, an investigation has been made of the life and character of Charles before the fatal affray which led to his death.

Robert Charles was not an educated man. He was a student who faithfully investigated all the phases of oppression from which his race has suffered. That he was a student is amply shown by the Times-Democrat [r]eport of the 25th, which says:

"Well-worn text-books, bearing his name written in his own scrawling handwriting, and well-filled copy-books found in his trunk, showed that he had burned the midnight oil, and desired to improve himself intellectually in order that he might conquer the hated white race." From this quotation it will be seen that he spent the hours after days of hard toil in trying to improve himself, both in the study of text-books and in writing.

He knew that he was a student of a problem which required all the intelligence that a man could command, and he was burning his midnight oil gathering knowledge that he might better be able to come to an intelligent solution. To his aid in the study of this problem he sought the aid of a Christian newspaper, The Voice of Missions, the organ of the African Methodist Episcopal Church. He was in communication with its editor, who is a bishop, and is known all over this country as a man of learning, a lover of justice and the defender of law and order. Charles could receive from Bishop Turner not a word of encouragement to be other than an earnest, tireless and God-fearing student of the complex problems which affected the race.

For further help and assistance in his studies, Charles turned to an organization which has existed and flourished for many years, at all times managed by men of high Christian standing and absolute integrity. These men believe and preach a doctrine that the best interests of the Negro will be subserved by an emigration from America back to the Fatherland, and they do all they can to spread the doctrine of emigration and to give material assistance to those who desire to leave America and make their future homes in Africa. This organization is known as "The International Migration Society." It has its headquarters in Birmingham, Alabama. From this place it issues pamphlets, some of which were found in the home of Robert Charles, and which pamphlets the reporters of the New Orleans papers declare to be incendiary and dangerous in their doctrine and teaching.

Nothing could be further from the truth. Copies of any and all of them may be secured by writing to D. J. Flummer, who is President and in charge of the home office in Birmingham, Alabama. Three of the pamphlets found in Charles' room are named respectively:

First, "Prospectus of the Liberian Colonization Society;" which pamphlet in a few brief pages tells of the work of the society, plans, prices and terms of transportation of colored people who choose to go to Africa. These pages are followed by a short, conservative discussion of the Negro question, and close with an argument that Africa furnishes the best asylum for the oppressed Negroes in this country.

The second pamphlet is entitled "Christian Civilization of Africa." This is a brief statement of the advantages of the Republic of Liberia, and an argument in support of the superior conditions which colored people may attain to by leaving the South and settling in Liberia.

The third pamphlet is entitled "The Negro and Liberia." This is a larger document than the other two, and treats more exhaustively the question of emigration, but from the first page to the last there is not an incendiary line or sentence. There is not even a suggestion of violence in all of its thirty-two pages, and not a word which could not be preached from every pulpit in the land.

If it is true that the workman is known by his tools, certainly no harm could ever come from the doctrines which were preached by Charles or the papers and pamphlets distributed by him. Nothing ever written in the "Voice of Missions," and nothing ever published in the pamphlets above alluded to in the remotest way suggest that a peaceable man should turn lawbreaker, or that any man should dye his hands in his brother's blood.

In order to secure as far as possible positive information about the life and character of Robert Charles, it was plain that the best course to pursue was to communicate with those with whom he had sustained business relations. Accordingly a letter was forwarded to Mr. D. J. Flummer, who is president of the colonization society, in which letter he was asked to state in reply what information he had of the life and character of Robert Charles. The result was a very prompt letter in response, the text of which is as follows:

Birmingham, Ala., Aug. 21, 1900.

Mrs. Ida B. Wells Barnett, Chicago, Ill.:

Dear Madam—Replying to your favor of recent date requesting me to write you giving such information as I may have concerning the life, habits and character of Robert Charles, who recently shot and killed police officers in New Orleans, I wish to say that my knowledge of him is only such as I have gained from his business connection with the International Migration Society during the past five or six years, during which time I was president of the society.

He having learned that the purpose of this society was to colonize the colored people in Liberia, West Africa, and thereby lessen or destroy the friction and prejudice existing in this country between the two races, set about earnestly and faithfully distributing the literature that we issued from time to time. He always appeared to be mild but earnest in his advocacy of emigration, and never to my knowledge used any method or means that would in the least appear unreasonable, and had always kept within the bounds of law and order in advocating emigration.

The work he performed for this society was all gratuitous, and apparently prompted from his love of humanity, and desires to be instrumental in building up a Negro Nationality in Africa.

If he ever violated a law before the killing of the policemen, I do not know of it. Yours very truly,

D. J. Flummer.

Besides this statement, Mr. Flummer enclosed a letter received by the Society two days before the tragedy at New Orleans. This letter was written by Robert Charles, and it attests his devotion to the cause of emigration which he had espoused. Memoranda on the margin of the letter show that the order was filled by mailing the pamphlets. It is very probable that these were the identical pamphlets which were found by the mob which broke into the room of Robert Charles and seized upon these harmless documents and declared they were sufficient evidence to prove Charles a desperado. In the light of subsequent events the letter of Charles, which follows, sounds like a voice from the tomb:

New Orleans, July 30, 1900.

Mr. D. J. Flummer:

Dear Sir—I received your last pamphlets and they are all given out. I want you to send me some more, and I enclose you the stamps. I think I will go over in Greenville, Miss., and give my people some pamphlets over there. Yours truly,

Robert Charles.

The latest word of information comes from New Orleans from a man who knew Charles intimately for six years. For obvious reasons, his name is withheld. In answer to a letter sent him he answers as follows:

New Orleans, Aug. 23, 1900.

Mrs. Ida B. Wells Barnett:

Dear Madam—It affords me great pleasure to inform you as far as I know of Robert Charles. I have been acquainted with him about six years in this city. He never has, as I know, given any trouble to anyone. He was quiet and a peaceful man and was very frank in speaking. He was too much of a hero to die; few can be found to equal him. I am very sorry to say that I do not know anything of his birthplace, nor his parents, but enclosed find letter from his uncle, from which you may find more information. You will also find one of the circulars in which Charles was in possession of which was styled as a crazy document. Let me say, until our preachers preach this document we will always be slaves. If you can help circulate this "crazy" doctrine I would be glad to have you do so, for I shall never rest until I get to that heaven on earth; that is, the west coast of Africa, in Liberia.

With best wishes to you I still remain, as always, for the good of the race,

By only those whose anger and vindictiveness warp their judgment is Robert Charles a desperado. Their word is not supported by the statement of a single fact which justifies their judgment, and no criminal record shows that he was ever indicted for any offense, much less convicted of crime. On the contrary, his work for many years had been with Christian people, circulating emigration pamphlets and active as agent for a mission publication. Men who knew him say that he was a lawabiding, quiet, industrious, peaceable man. So he lived.

So he lived and so he would have died had not he raised his hand to resent unprovoked assault and unlawful arrest that fateful Monday night. That made him an outlaw, and being a man of courage he decided to die with his face to the foe. The white people of this country may charge that he was a desperado, but to the people of his own race Robert Charles will always be regarded as the hero of New Orleans.

BURNING HUMAN BEINGS ALIVE

Not only has life been taken by mobs in the past twenty years, but the ordinary procedure of hanging and shooting have been improved upon during the past ten years. Fifteen human beings have been burned to death in the different parts of the country by mobs. Men, women and children have gone to see the sight, and all have approved the barbarous deeds done in the high light of the civilization and Christianity of this country.

In 1891 Ed Coy was burned to death in Texarkana, Ark. He was charged with assaulting a white woman, and after the mob had securely tied him to a tree, the men and boys amused themselves for some time sticking knives into Coy's body and slicing off pieces of flesh. When they had amused themselves sufficiently, they poured coal oil over him and the women in the case set fire to him. It is said that fifteen thousand people stood by and saw him burned. This was on a Sunday night, and press reports told how the people looked on while the Negro burned to death.

Feb. 1st, 1893, Henry Smith was burned to death in Paris, Texas. The entire county joined in that exhibition. The district attorney himself went for the prisoner and turned him over to the mob. He was placed upon a float and drawn by four white horses through the principal streets of the city. Men, women and children stood at their doors and waved their handkerchiefs and cheered the echoes. They knew that the man was to be burned to death because the newspaper had declared for three days previous that this would be so. Excursions were run by all the railroads, and the mayor of the town gave the children a holiday so that they might see the sight.

Henry Smith was charged with having assaulted and murdered a little white girl. He was an imbecile, and while he had killed the child, there was no proof that he had criminally assaulted her. He was tied to a stake on a platform which had been built ten feet high, so that everybody might see the sight. The father and brother and uncle of the little white girl that had been murdered was upon that platform about fifty minutes entertaining the crowd of ten thousand persons by burning the victim's flesh with red-hot irons. Their own newspapers told how they burned his eyes out and ran the red-hot iron down his throat, cooking his tongue, and how the crowd cheered with delight. At last, having declared themselves satisfied, coal oil was poured over him and he was burned to death, and the mob fought over the ashes for bones and pieces of his clothes.

July 7th, 1893, in Bardwell, Ky., C. J. Miller was burned to ashes. Since his death this man has been found to be absolutely innocent of the murder of the two white girls with which he was charged. But the mob would wait for no justification. They insisted that, as they were not sure he was the right man, they would compromise the matter by hanging him instead of burning. Not to be outdone, they took the body down and made a huge bonfire out of it.

July 22d, 1893, at Memphis, Tenn., the body of Lee Walker was dragged through the street and burned before the court house. Walker had frightened some girls in a wagon along a country road by asking them to let him ride in their wagon. They cried out; some men working in a field near by said it was at attempt of assault, and of course began to look for their prey. There was never any charge of rape; the women only declared that he attempted an assault. After he was apprehended and put in jail and perfectly helpless, the mob dragged him out, shot him, cut him, beat him with sticks, built a fire and burned the legs off, then took the trunk of the body down and dragged further up the street, and at last burned it before the court house.

Sept. 20th, 1893, at Roanoke, Va., the body of a Negro who had quarreled with a white woman was burned in the presence of several thousand persons. These people also wreaked their vengeance upon this helpless victim of the mob's wrath by sticking knives into him, kicking him and beating him with stones and otherwise mutilating him before life was extinct.

June 10th, 1898, at Knoxville, Ark., James Perry was shut up in a cabin because he had smallpox and burned to death. He had been quarantined in this cabin when it was declared that he had this disease and the doctor sent for. When the physician arrived he found only a few smoldering embers. Upon inquiry some railroad hands who were working near by revealed the fact that they had fastened the door of the cabin and set fire to the cabin and burned man and hut together.

Feb. 22d, 1898, at Lake City, S.C., Postmaster Baker and his infant child were burned to death by a mob that had set fire to his house. Mr. Baker's crime was that he had refused to give up the postoffice, to which he had been appointed by the National Government. The mob had tried to drive him away by persecution and intimidation. Finding that all else had failed, they went to his home in the dead of night and set fire to his house, and as the family rushed forth they were greeted by a volley of bullets. The father and his baby were shot through the open door and wounded so badly that they fell back in the fire and were burned to death. The remainder of the family, consisting of the wife and five children, escaped with their lives from the burning house, but all of them were shot, one of the number made a cripple for life.

Jan. 7th, 1898, two Indians were tied to a tree at Maud Postoffice, Indian Territory, and burned to death by a white mob. They were charged with murdering a white woman. There was no proof of their guilt except the unsupported word of the mob. Yet they were tied to a tree and slowly roasted to death. Their names were Lewis McGeesy and Hond Martin. Since that time these boys have been found to be absolutely innocent of the charge. Of course that discovery is too late to be of any benefit to them, but because they were Indians the Indian Commissioner demanded and received from the United States Government an indemnity of $13,000.

April 23d, 1899, at Palmetto, Ga., Sam Hose was burned alive in the presence of a throng, on Sunday afternoon. He was charged with killing a man named Cranford, his employer, which he admitted he did because his employer was about to shoot him. To the fact of killing the employer was added the absolutely false charge that Hose assaulted the wife. Hose was arrested and no trial was given him. According to the code of reasoning of the mob, none was needed.

A white man had been killed and a white woman was said to have been assaulted. That was enough. When Hose was found he had to die.

The Atlanta Constitution, in speaking of the murder of Cranford, said that the Negro who was suspected would be burned alive. Not only this, but it offered $500 reward for his capture. After he had been apprehended, it was publicly announced that he would be burned alive. Excursion trains were run and bulletins were put up in the small towns. The Governor of Georgia was in Atlanta while excursion trains were being made up to take visitors to the burning. Many fair ladies drove out in their carriages on Sunday afternoon to witness the torture and burning of a human being. Hose's ears were cut off, then his toes and fingers, and passed round to the crowd. His eyes were put out, his tongue torn out and flesh cut in strips by knives. Finally they poured coal oil on him and burned him to death. They dragged his half-consumed trunk out of the flames, cut it open, extracted his heart and liver, and sold slices for ten cents each for souvenirs, all of which was published most promptly in the daily papers of Georgia and boasted over by the people of that section.

Oct. 19th, 1889, at Canton, Miss., Joseph Leflore was burned to death. A house had been entered and its occupants murdered during the absence of the husband and father. When the discovery was made, it was immediately supposed that the crime was the work of a Negro, and the motive that of assaulting white women.

Bloodhounds were procured and they made a round of the village and discovered only one colored man absent from his home. This was taken to be proof sufficient that he was the perpetrator of the deed. When he returned home he was apprehended, taken into the yard of the house that had been burned down, tied to a stake, and was slowly roasted to death.

Dec. 6th, 1899, at Maysville, Ky., Wm. Coleman also was burned to death. He was slowly roasted, first one foot and then the other, and dragged out of the fire so that the torture might be prolonged. All of this without a shadow of proof or scintilla of evidence that the man had committed the crime.

Thus have the mobs of this country taken the lives of their victims within the past ten years. In every single instance except one these burnings were witnessed by from two thousand to fifteen thousand people, and no one person in all these crowds throughout the country had the courage to raise his voice and speak out against the awful barbarism of burning human beings to death.

Men and women of America, are you proud of this record which the Anglo-Saxon race has made for itself? Your silence seems to say that you are. Your silence encourages a continuance of this sort of horror. Only by earnest, active, united endeavor to arouse public sentiment can we hope to put a stop to these demonstrations of American barbarism.

LYNCHING RECORD

The following table of lynchings has been kept year by year by the Chicago Tribune, beginning with 1882, and shows the list of Negroes that have been lynched during that time:

1882, Negroes murdered by mobs	52
1883, Negroes murdered by mobs	39
1884, Negroes murdered by mobs	53
1885, Negroes murdered by mobs	164
1886, Negroes murdered by mobs	136
1887, Negroes murdered by mobs	128
1888, Negroes murdered by mobs	143
1889, Negroes murdered by mobs	127
1890, Negroes murdered by mobs	176
1891, Negroes murdered by mobs	192
1892, Negroes murdered by mobs	241
1893, Negroes murdered by mobs	200
1894, Negroes murdered by mobs	190
1895, Negroes murdered by mobs	171
1896, Negroes murdered by mobs	131
1897, Negroes murdered by mobs	156
1898, Negroes murdered by mobs	127
1899, Negroes murdered by mobs	107

Of these thousands of men and women who have been put to death without judge or jury, less than one-third of them have been even accused of criminal assault. The world at large has accepted unquestionably the statement that Negroes are lynched only for assaults upon white women. Of those who were lynched from 1882 to 1891, the first ten years of the tabulated lynching record, the charges are as follows:

Two hundred and sixty-nine were charged with rape; 253 with murder; 44 with robbery; 37 with incendiarism; 4 with burglary; 27 with race prejudice; 13 quarreled with white men; 10 with making threats; 7

with rioting; 5 with miscegenation; in 32 cases no reasons were given, the victims were lynched on general principles.

During the past five years the record is as follows: Of the 171 persons lynched in 1895 only 34 were charged with this crime. In 1896, out of 131 persons who were lynched, only 34 were said to have assaulted women. Of the 156 in 1897, only 32. In 1898, out of 127 persons lynched, 24 were charged with the alleged "usual crime." In 1899, of the 107 lynchings, 16 were said to be for crimes against women. These figures, of course, speak for themselves, and to the unprejudiced, fair-minded person it is only necessary to read and study them in order to show that the charge that the Negro is a moral outlaw is a false one, made for the purpose of injuring the Negro's good name and to create public sentiment against him.

If public sentiment were alive, as it should be upon the subject, it would refuse to be longer hoodwinked, and the voice of conscience would refuse to be stilled by these false statements. If the laws of the country were obeyed and respected by the white men of the country who charge that the Negro has no respect for law, these things could not be, for every individual, no matter what the charge, would have a fair trial and an opportunity to prove his guilt or innocence before a tribunal of law.

That is all the Negro asks—that is all the friends of law and order need to ask, for once the law of the land is supreme, no individual who commits crime will escape punishment.

Individual Negroes commit crimes the same as do white men, but that the Negro race is peculiarly given to assault upon women, is a falsehood of the deepest dye. The tables given above show that the Negro who is saucy to white men is lynched as well as the Negro who is charged with assault upon women. Less than one-sixth of the lynchings last year, 1899, were charged with rape.

The Negro points to his record during the war in rebuttal of this false slander. When the white women and children of the South had no protector save only these Negroes, not one instance is known where the trust was betrayed. It is remarkably strange that the Negro had more respect for womanhood with the white men of the South hundreds of miles away, than they have to-day, when surrounded by those who take their lives with impunity and burn and torture, even worse than the "unspeakable Turk."

Again, the white women of the North came South years ago, threaded the forests, visited the cabins, taught the schools and associated only with the Negroes whom they came to teach, and had no protectors near at hand. They had no charge or complaint to make of the danger to themselves after association with this class of human beings. Not once has the country been shocked by such recitals from them as come from the women who are surrounded by their husbands, brothers, lovers and friends. If the Negro's nature is bestial, it certainly should have proved itself in one of these two instances. The Negro asks only justice and an impartial consideration of these facts.

A Wells Chronology
(1862–1931)

1862: Ida Bell Wells is born in Holly Springs, Mississippi, on July 16, 1862, to James Wells (a carpenter) and Elizabeth Warrenton Wells (a cook). Wells is the eldest of eight children, four females and four males, two of whom die in early childhood.

Mary Jane Patterson becomes the first African American woman to receive a bachelor of arts degree from an established American college, Oberlin College in Ohio.

1863: President Abraham Lincoln signs the Proclamation of Amnesty and Reconstruction and the Emancipation Proclamation.

The Port Royal Commission establishes the first "official" school for freed slaves in the South on St. Helena Island off the coast of South Carolina.

1864: Rebecca Lee graduates from the New England Female Medical College and becomes the first African American woman physician in the United States.

1865: The Civil War ends.

President Lincoln is assassinated, and Andrew Johnson becomes the seventeenth U.S. president.

Congress establishes the Bureau of Refugees, Freedmen, and Abandoned Lands.

Congress ratifies the Thirteenth Amendment.

The southern states begin adopting Black Codes.

Vassar College, among the oldest women's colleges in the United States, is founded.

1866: The Ku Klux Klan is organized in Pulaski, Tennessee.

Fisk and Atlanta Universities are founded.

The Equal Rights Association, an organization dedicated to advancing the civil rights of African Americans and women, is established, with Elizabeth Cady Stanton as president, Frederick Douglass as vice president, and Susan B. Anthony as secretary.

1867:   Congress passes the Reconstruction Acts, and military oversight in the southern states begins.

1868:   Congress ratifies the Fourteenth Amendment.

1870:   Congress ratifies the Fifteenth Amendment.

The first African Americans elected to the Senate (Hiram R. Revels from Mississippi) and the House of Representatives (Joseph H. Rainey from South Carolina) begin their terms.

All southern states have been readmitted to the Union.

Southern states begin establishing state-supported public education.

1872:   Charlotte E. Ray, an African American, is awarded a law degree from Howard University and becomes one of the first women of any race to be admitted to the bar in Washington, D.C.

1874:   The Women's Christian Temperance Union (WCTU) is founded.

1877:   Control of legislatures in all southern states by Democrats is reestablished.

President Rutherford B. Hayes removes the last military troops from the South.

Radical Reconstruction ends.

1878:   Ida B. Wells becomes the family provider after both of her parents and a younger brother die in a yellow fever epidemic. She leaves Rust College and begins a teaching career.

1880:   Wells is invited by her aunt to move to Memphis, Tennessee, where she secures a better teaching position. She participates in social and political activities.

1881:   The Atlanta Baptist Female Seminary (later Spelman College), the oldest college for women of African descent, is founded.

1884:   Wells sues the Chesapeake, Ohio, and Southwestern Railroad and wins, but the suit is overturned by the Tennessee Supreme Court.

Wells writes her first article for the *Living Way* about her railroad lawsuit.

1889:   Wells becomes co-owner, with Rev. Taylor Nightingale and J. L. Fleming, of the *Free Speech and Headlight.*

1890:   The National American Woman Suffrage Association unifies the National Woman Suffrage Association and the American Woman Suffrage Association.

1891:   Wells writes an editorial against the all-white Memphis Board of Education, loses her teaching job, and becomes a full-time journalist.

1892:   Thomas Moss, Calvin McDowell, and Wil Stewart are lynched on March 9, 1892. Wells publishes her "Eight Men Lynched" editorial in the *Free Speech* on May 21, 1892. Forced into exile from the South by terrorist threats, Wells accepts a position as reporter for the *New York Age.*

This year marks the first peak of mob violence against African Americans.

At the invitation of clubwomen from New York and Brooklyn, Wells begins a career as a public speaker. She addresses 250 African American women from three states on October 5, 1892, at Lyric Hall in New York City at a testimonial dinner given in her honor.

Wells publishes *Southern Horrors: Lynch Law in All Its Phases* as a pamphlet with five hundred dollars raised for her at the testimonial dinner.

Anna Julia Cooper, educator and community activist, appeals for the rights, interests, and recognition of African American women in the essay collection *A Voice from the South.*

1893:   Wells makes her first speaking tour of England, Scotland, and Wales.

With Frederick Douglass, Ferdinand L. Barnett, and I. Garland Penn, Wells publishes an eighty-one-page pamphlet, *The Reason Why the Colored American Is Not in the World's Columbian Exposition.*

1894:   Wells makes her second speaking tour of England, Scotland, and Wales, sending home articles that are published in the Chicago *Inter Ocean* as "Ida B. Wells Abroad."

1895:   Wells publishes *A Red Record,* her second pamphlet.

Wells marries Ferdinand L. Barnett and begins raising a family.

Frederick Douglass dies on February 20, 1895.

1896:   The National Association of Colored Women (NACW) is founded; Mary Church Terrell is named its first president.

1900:   Wells publishes *Mob Rule in New Orleans,* her third pamphlet.

1902:   Gertrude Bustill Mossell, journalist and activist, publishes the essay collection *Afro-American Women and Work.*

1909:   The National Association for the Advancement of Colored People (NAACP) is founded as an interracial organization dedicated to social and legal reform.

1919:   This year is the second peak of mob violence against African Americans.

1920:   An interracial network of moderate southern leaders organize the Commission on Interracial Cooperation, which grows in the mid-1920s to become the major interracial reform organization in the South.

1922:   Mary Burnett Talbert, NACW president from 1916 to 1920, organizes at the request of the NAACP the Anti-Lynching Crusaders, a group that draws from a broadly based network of African American women community activists.

1930:   This year is the third peak of mob violence against African Americans.

Jessie Ames Daniels organizes the Association of Southern Women for the Prevention of Lynching, the first organization of white women against lynching.

1931: Wells dies on March 25, 1931. Lynchings of African Americans continue to be reported each year after her death until 1953, when there are none reported for the first time since 1882. After 1953 lynchings continue to be reported.

Between 1882 and 1931, according to figures collected by the NAACP, 3,318 African American men, women, and children were lynched "at the hands of parties unknown."

Questions for Consideration

1. As a "public woman," Ida B. Wells can be viewed as unusual among nineteenth-century women. What makes her so?
2. The title of Wells's autobiography is *Crusade for Justice*. Given the pamphlets in this collection, how would you characterize Wells as a "crusader"?
3. Wells is sometimes placed within the "muckraking" tradition of journalism, a type of reporting noted for exposing real or apparent misconduct on the part of prominent individuals. What aspects of Wells's work might place her in this category? What connections can you draw between this type of reporting and what we today call "investigative" journalism?
4. Wells made a point of using data from white newspapers to support her claims about mob violence. What was the advantage in her use of this strategy?
5. Consider Wells's British campaign. Why was it important to position lynching as an international concern? What did Wells expect to gain?
6. As historical documents, what do the pamphlets in this collection suggest about the conditions and challenges that confronted African Americans? Women? African American women? Identify and discuss issues related to race, gender, and class.
7. What connections did Wells make between ending mob violence against African Americans and improving the lives of African American women?
8. Discuss the following themes in Wells's pamphlets: woman's place, justice, equality, political and economic power, law and order.
9. What evidence of cooperation and division between African American women and white women seems apparent during this era?
10. What do you consider to be the most distinctive features of the pamphlets? What stands out most when you study these pamphlets as "public" documents designed to enlighten and persuade?

11. Why did the accusation of "rape" make an effective excuse for mob violence? On what grounds did Wells claim these acts of violence to be unlawful?

12. What solutions did Wells offer to the problem of mob violence? Can these solutions be seen as having led to the decline of mob violence in the twentieth century? If so, how?

Selected Bibliography

BY AND ABOUT IDA B. WELLS

DeCosta-Willis, Miriam. *Ida B. Wells: The Memphis Diaries*. Boston: Beacon Press, 1994.

Duster, Alfreda M. *Crusade for Justice: The Autobiography of Ida B. Wells*. Chicago: University of Chicago Press, 1970.

Greaves, William, producer. *Ida B. Wells: A Passion for Justice*. Installment of the PBS series *The American Experience*. New York: Video Dub, 1990.

Humrich, Shauna Lea. "Ida B. Wells-Barnett: The Making of a Reputation." Master's thesis, University of Colorado, 1989.

Hutton, Mary M. B. "The Rhetoric of Ida B. Wells: The Genesis of the Anti-Lynch Movement." Ph.D. diss., University of Indiana, 1975.

Royster, Jacqueline Jones. "'To Call a Thing by Its True Name': The Rhetoric of Ida B. Wells." In *Reclaiming Rhetorica,* edited by Andrea Lunsford, 167–84. Pittsburgh: University of Pittsburgh Press, 1995.

Thompson, Mildred I. *Ida B. Wells-Barnett: An Exploratory Study of an American Black Woman, 1893–1930*. Black Women in United States History, vol. 15. Brooklyn: Carlson Publishing, 1990.

Tucker, David M. "Miss Ida B. Wells and Memphis Lynching." In *Black Women in American History: From Colonial Times through the Nineteenth Century,* edited by Darlene Clark Hine, 1085–95. Black Women in United States History, vol. 4. Brooklyn: Carlson Publishing, 1990.

LYNCHING

Banta, Martha. "The Razor, the Pistol, and the Ideology of Race Etiquette." Paper presented at the Ohio State University, Columbus, April 20, 1994.

Brundage, W. Fitzhugh. *Lynching in the New South: Georgia and Virginia, 1880–1930*. Urbana: University of Illinois Press, 1993.

Cameron, James. *A Time of Terror: A Survivor's Story*. Baltimore: Black Classic Press, 1994.

Carby, Hazel V. " 'On the Threshold of Woman's Era': Lynching, Empire, and Sexuality in Black Feminist Theory." *Critical Inquiry* 12 (Autumn 1985): 262–77.

Du Bois, Ellen Carol, and Linda Gordon. "Seeking Ecstasy on the Battlefield: Danger and Pleasure in Nineteenth-Century Feminist Sexual Thought." In *Pleasure and Danger: Exploring Female Sexuality,* edited by Carol S. Vance, 31–49. Boston: Routledge & Kegan Paul, 1984.

Giddings, Paula. "The Last Taboo." *Race-ing Justice, En-gendering Power,* edited by Toni Morrison, 441–65. New York: Pantheon Books, 1992.

Ginzburg, Ralph. *100 Years of Lynching.* Baltimore: Black Classic Press, 1988.

Grant, Donald L. *The Anti-Lynching Movement: 1883–1932.* San Francisco: R & E Research Associates, 1975.

Hall, Jacqueline Dowd. *Revolt against Chivalry.* New York: Columbia University Press, 1993.

Harris, Trudier. *Exorcising Blackness: Historical and Literary Lynching and Burning Rituals.* Bloomington: Indiana University Press, 1984.

"Lynching." *The Oxford English Dictionary.* Compact edition. 1971.

"Lynch Law." *The Oxford English Dictionary.* Compact edition. 1971.

Raper, Arthur F. *The Tragedy of Lynching.* Chapel Hill: University of North Carolina Press, 1933.

Zangrando, Robert L. *The NAACP Crusade against Lynching, 1909–1950.* Philadelphia: Temple University Press, 1980.

POST–CIVIL WAR HISTORY

Bullock, Penelope. *The Afro-American Periodical Press, 1838–1909.* Baton Rouge: Louisiana State University Press, 1981.

Cox, LaWanda, and John H. Cox, eds. *Reconstruction, the Negro, and the New South.* Columbia: University of South Carolina Press, 1973.

Du Bois, William E. B. *Black Reconstruction.* New York: Harcourt, Brace & Co., 1935.

Franklin, John Hope. *Reconstruction: After the Civil War.* 2nd ed. Chicago: University of Chicago Press, 1994.

Franklin, John Hope, and Alfred A. Moss, Jr. *From Slavery to Freedom: A History of Negro Americans.* 6th ed. New York: McGraw-Hill, 1988.

Greene, Theodore P., ed. *American Imperialism in 1898.* Boston: D. C. Heath, 1955.

May, Ernest R. *American Imperialism: A Speculative Essay.* New York: Atheneum, 1968.

McWhiney, Grady, ed. *Reconstruction and the Freedmen.* Chicago: Rand McNally, 1963.

Myrdal, Gunnar. *An American Dilemma.* New York: Harper & Brothers, 1944.

Perlo, Victor. *American Imperialism.* New York: International Publishers, 1951.

Rozwenc, Edwin C., and Thomas Lyons. *Reconstruction and the Race Problem.* Boston: D. C. Heath, 1968.

Said, Edward. *Culture and Imperialism.* New York: Alfred A. Knopf, 1993.

Woodward, C. Vann. *Origins of the New South, 1877–1913.* Baton Rouge: Louisiana State University Press, 1951.

———. *The Strange Career of Jim Crow.* 3rd ed. New York: Oxford University Press, 1974.

WOMEN'S HISTORY

Alexander, Adele Logan. "How I Discovered My Grandmother." In *Black Women in American History: From Colonial Times through the Nineteenth Century,* edited by Darlene Clark Hine, 15–23. Black Women in United States History, vol. 1. Brooklyn: Carlson Publishing, 1990.

Aptheker, Bettina. *Woman's Legacy: Essays on Race, Sex, and Class in American History.* Amherst: University of Massachusetts Press, 1982.

Berkeley, Kathleen C. " 'Colored Ladies Also Contributed': Black Women's Activities from Benevolence to Social Welfare, 1866–1896." In *Black Women in American History: From Colonial Times through the Nineteenth Century,* edited by Darlene Clark Hine, 61–83. Black Women in United States History, vol. 1. Brooklyn: Carlson Publishing, 1990.

Carby, Hazel V. *Reconstructing Womanhood: The Emergence of the Afro-American Woman Novelist.* New York: Oxford University Press, 1987.

Cooper, Anna Julia. *A Voice from the South.* Schomburg Library of Nineteenth-Century Black Women Writers. New York: Oxford University Press, 1988.

Dickson, Lynda F. "Toward a Broader Angle of Vision in Uncovering Women's History: Black Women's Clubs Revisited." In *Black Women's History: Theory and Practice,* edited by Darlene Clark Hine, 103–19. Black Women in United States History, vol. 9. Brooklyn: Carlson Publishing, 1990.

Helly, Dorothy O., and Susan M. Reverby, eds. *Gendered Domains: Rethinking Public and Private in Women's History.* Ithaca: Cornell University Press, 1992.

Hine, Darlene Clark, ed. *Black Women in America: An Historical Encyclopedia.* 2 vols. Brooklyn: Carlson Publishing, 1993.

Jones, Beverly Washington. *Quest for Equality: The Life and Writings of Mary Eliza Church Terrell, 1863–1954.* Black Women in United States History, vol. 13. Brooklyn: Carlson Publishing, 1990.

Jones, Jacqueline. *Labor of Love, Labor of Sorrow.* New York: Vintage Books, 1985.

Lengermann, Patricia Madoo, and Ruth A. Wallace. *Gender in America: Social Control and Social Change.* Englewood Cliffs, N.J.: Prentice-Hall, 1985.

Lerner, Gerda. *The Creation of Feminist Consciousness: From the Middle Ages to 1870.* New York: Oxford University Press, 1993.

Lubiano, Wahneema. "Black Ladies, Welfare Queens, and State Minstrels: Ideological War by Narrative Means." In *Race-ing Justice, En-gendering Power,* edited by Toni Morrison, 323–63. New York: Pantheon Books, 1992.

Matthews, Glenna. *The Rise of Public Woman.* New York: Oxford University Press, 1992.

Morrison, Toni, ed. *Race-ing Justice, En-gendering Power.* New York: Pantheon Books, 1992.

Mossell, Mrs. N. F. *The Work of the African American Woman.* Schomburg Library of Nineteenth-Century Black Women Writers. New York: Oxford University Press, 1988.

Neverdon-Morton, Cynthia. *Afro-American Women of the South and the Advancement of the Race, 1895–1925.* Knoxville: University of Tennessee Press, 1989.

Perkins, Linda. "Black Women and Racial 'Uplift' Prior to Emancipation." In *Black Women in American History: From Colonial Times through the Nineteenth Century,* edited by Darlene Clark Hine, 1077–94. Black Women in United States History, vol. 3. Brooklyn: Carlson Publishing, 1990.

Porter, Dorothy. "The Organized Educational Activities of Negro Literary Societies, 1828–1846." *Journal of Negro Education,* 5 (October 1936): 555–74.

Salem, Dorothy. *To Better Our World: Black Women in Organized Reform, 1890–1920.* Black Women in United States History, vol. 14. Brooklyn: Carlson Publishing, 1990.

Terrell, Mary Church. "The Duty of the NACW to the Race." In *Quest for Equality.* Edited by Beverly Washington Jones, 139–50. Black Women in United States History, vol. 13. Brooklyn: Carlson Publishing, 1990.

Vance, Carole S. *Pleasure and Danger: Exploring Female Sexuality.* Boston: Routledge & Kegan Paul, 1984.

Wesley, Charles Harris. *The History of the National Association of Colored Women's Clubs: A Legacy of Service.* Washington, D.C.: National Association of Colored Women's Clubs, 1984.

EDUCATION

Anderson, James D. *The Education of Blacks in the South, 1860–1935.* Chapel Hill: University of North Carolina Press, 1988.

Chamberlain, Mariam K., ed. *Women in Academe: Progress and Prospects.* New York: Russell Sage Foundation, 1988.

Gordon, Lynn D. *Gender and Higher Education in the Progressive Era.* New Haven: Yale University Press, 1990.

Jones, Jacqueline. *Soldiers of Light, Soldiers of Love: Northern Teachers and Georgia Blacks, 1865–1873.* Chapel Hill: University of North Carolina Press, 1980.

Lawson, Ellen N., and Marlene Merrill. "Antebellum Black Coeds at Oberlin College." In *Black Women in American History: From Colonial Times through the Nineteenth Century,* edited by Darlene Clark Hine, 827–35. Black Women in United States History, vol. 3. Brooklyn: Carlson Publishing, 1990.

Moss, Alfred A., Jr. *The American Negro Academy: Voice of the Talented Tenth.* Baton Rouge: Louisiana State University Press, 1981.

Noble, Jeanne L. *The Negro Woman's College Education.* New York: Columbia University Press, 1956.

Pearson, Carol S., Donna L. Shavlik, and Judith G. Touchton, eds. *Educating the Majority: Women Challenge Tradition in Higher Education.* New York: American Council on Education, 1989.

Sage: A Scholarly Journal on Black Women 1, no. 1 (Spring 1984). Black Women's Education.

Index

Abolitionist movement, 19, 25, 35
Afric-American Female Intelligence
    Society, 25
African American community
    Black Codes and, 6–8, 11–12
    establishment of anti-lynching
        organizations by, 13–14
    Harper's Weekly spread on violence
        against, 42–43 (illus.)
    Jim Crow laws and, 12
    mass meetings and political
        conventions organized by, 12–13,
        69–70
    post-Reconstruction era and, 4–8, 21
    professional women's organizations in,
        21–22
    response to mob violence and
        lynchings by, 11–14, 35
    secret terrorist organizations and
        violence against, 8, 60
    Southern Horrors call for self-help in,
        68–72
    voting rights for, 5, 7–8
    Wells on impact of lynchings on, 3–4
    Wells's early years in, 14, 15–16
African American men
    number of lynchings of, 10
    race and gender stereotypes in
        lynching and, 30–31
    rape charges against. *See* Rape
        charges against African American
        men
African American women
    anti-lynching movement and, 26, 37, 40
    clubs and, 23–26, 37, 40
    higher education opportunities for, 21
    movement for social equality and legal
        reform and, 22
    post-Reconstruction period and, 25, 31
    professional organizations for, 21–22

race and gender stereotypes in
    lynching and, 30–31
rape charges against white men by,
    31
Wells's prominence among, 22–23
See also Women
African Methodist Episcopal (AME)
    Church, 12, 13, 199
    Daughters of Allen of, 25
    Wells's activities in, 16, 18
Afro-American Council, 39
Afro-American League, 13, 14
Alexander, Sadie T. M., 21
Anti-Lynching Bureau, 39
Anti-Lynching Committee, 36, 38
Anti-Lynching Crusaders, 26
Anti-lynching movement
    African American anti-lynching
        organizations and, 13–14
    African American women's clubs and,
        26, 37
    British influence on, 35–36, 131,
        136–38, 156
    Free Speech editorial by Wells and,
        1–2, 4, 18
    mass meetings and political
        conventions organized against,
        12–13
    Wells's arguments in, 29–33
    Wells's contributions to, 2, 18, 26,
        39–40, 41
    white southern liberal organizations in,
        40–41
    Woman's Era magazine and, 24,
        25
    women's movement for social equality
        and legal reform and, 22
Anti-Lynching Society of England,
    37
Apprentice laws, 7

221